BASKETBALL COACH'S SURVIVAL GUIDE

Practical Techniques and Materials for Building an Effective Program and a Winning Team

William E. Warren, Ed.D.

Griffin, Georgia

Larry F. Chapman

Head Men's Basketball Coach
Auburn University at Montgomery
Montgomery, Alabama

PARKER PUBLISHING COMPANY
West Nyack, New York 10995

Library of Congress Cataloging-in-Publication Data

Warren, William E., 1941–
    Basketball coach's survival guide / William E. Warren and Larry F. Chapman.
        p.   cm.
        ISBN 0-13-094384-3 : Spiral   ISBN 0-13-543381-9 : Paper
        1. Basketball—Coaching.   I. Chapman, Larry F.   II. Title.
        GV885.3.W37   1992   92-5549
        796.323'2—dc20   CIP

Printed in the United States of America

10 9 8 7 6 5 4 (S)   10 9 8 7 6 5 4 3 (P)

ISBN 0-13-094384-3   ISBN 0-13-543381-9 (P)

PARKER PUBLISHING COMPANY
West Nyack, NY 10994

A Simon & Schuster Company

On the World Wide Web at http://www.phdirect.com

Prentice-Hall International (UK) Limited, *London*
Prentice-Hall of Australia Pty. Limited, *Sydney*
Prentice-Hall Canada Inc., *Toronto*
Prentice-Hall Hispanoamericana, S.A., *Mexico*
Prentice-Hall of India Private Limited, *New Delhi*
Prentice-Hall of Japan, Inc., *Tokyo*
Simon & Schuster Asia Pte. Ltd., *Singapore*
Editora Prentice-Hall do Brasil, Ltda., *Rio de Janeiro*

About the Authors

WILLIAM E. WARREN, ED.D., has nearly twenty years of experience as a coach at the junior high, high school and college levels and a lifetime basketball coaching record of 290 wins and 88 losses. In two years of coaching girls' track at Toombs Central High School, his teams won the Georgia State Class A Championship once and finished second once. He received two state Coach of the Year awards in girls' track during those years.

Dr. Warren has taught and coached at all levels and has written or coauthored eight other coaching books, including *Coaching and Motivation* (Prentice Hall, 1983) and *Coaching and Winning* (Prentice Hall, 1988). His articles have appeared in *Scholastic Coach, Athletic Journal, The Coaching Clinic*, and *Coach and Athlete*.

LARRY F. CHAPMAN, head basketball coach at Auburn University at Montgomery, has been coaching basketball for twenty-six years at the high school and college levels. In his thirteen years at AUM, the Senators have had nine twenty-win seasons, including seven of the last nine, averaging 20.8 wins per season.

In 1987–88, Coach Chapman's AUM Senators had a 32–3 season record and won their second consecutive district title, thus earning a berth in the national championship. Although they lost in overtime, Coach Chapman was selected the NAIA's National Coach of the Year, and the star of the 1987–88 team, Orlando Graham, was named Player of the Year.

for Louise Warren and Sandra Chapman
and for
Clint, Larry Jr., Christa, and Luke

Foreword

by Bobby Cremins
Head Basketball Coach
Georgia Institute of Technology

I've known Larry Chapman for many years. His reputation as an outstanding basketball coach is richly deserved, as anyone who has played for him, coached against him, or watched his teams play will tell you. More importantly, though, Coach Chapman is a fine person, the sort of person you'd want your son or daughter to play for. AUM is lucky to have him; he's a proven winner who has his priorities in order. He's built a solid tradition of excellence at AUM—and he's done so in a manner that reflects his Christian background.

I don't know Bill Warren as well as I know Coach Chapman, but what I know *of* him is impressive. Hey, anyone who has written coaching textbooks with Bob Cousy and Jerry Tarkanian obviously knows the game of basketball, and Warren's coaching books on motivation and winning show that he knows a great deal more about the game than just Os and Xs.

Whether you've been a basketball coach for as long as I have or you're just entering the profession, I think you're in for a treat in reading the *Basketball Coach's Survival Guide*. It covers the entire range of basketball coaching survival skills you'll need from your first day of coaching to your last—and it does so in a way that is entertaining and easy to read. They've even taken a dull subject like basketball coaching philosophy and made it interesting and entertaining—and you'll never look at officials the same way after reading the section on "Referees from A to Zebra."

There are other topics that you don't normally find in basketball coaching textbooks, such as the importance of communication, building a family atmosphere on your team, and the world beyond coaching. The sections on finding the best offensive and defensive styles for your team offer new approaches to old subjects, and the sections on practice planning, scouting, and game plans are equally valuable to new coaches and veterans alike.

As anyone who has seen me pacing and prowling the sidelines during Georgia Tech basketball games already knows, I'm a worrier. I worry about anything and everything that could cause us to lose games. But one thing I *don't* have to worry about is standing behind my belief that you'll like the *Basketball Coach's Survival Guide.* I think you'll enjoy and learn from it regardless of whether you read it from cover to cover or merely use the forms and borrow from the hundreds of coaching tips and techniques you'll find in it.

There's something for every basketball coach in this book, regardless of whether you're trying to teach sixth-grade girls how to play the game or going after an NCAA berth in the Final Four. What you *won't* get is John Salley, Mark Price, Dennis Scott, Duane Ferrell, Brian Oliver, Bruce Dalrymple, Jon Barry, or any of the other fine players I've had the privilege of coaching here at Georgia Tech. You'll have to recruit or develop those kinds of players yourself.

Bobby Cremins
Atlanta, Georgia
April 1992

About This Survival Guide

If you've been a basketball coach for longer than the last fifteen minutes, you're already aware that *coaching basketball is a difficult job*. Whether you're pursuing championships every year or building your program toward that worthy goal, coaching basketball is never easy. The problems basketball coaches face may be as subtle as a wink or as obvious as a nuclear explosion, but they're always there—countless responsibilities, pressures, and demands on your time and patience that can drive you up the wall and out of coaching if you let them get the best of you.

The secret to surviving in such a demanding profession is to *find ways to make your job easier*, which is precisely what the *Basketball Coach's Survival Guide* is all about. Survival in basketball coaching requires commitment, dedication, and a deep and abiding love for the game—but without planning, preparation, and organization as well, your time and efforts are likely to be wasted through duplication or oversight, both of which are eminently avoidable.

Based on the authors' combined forty-seven years of basketball coaching experience on all levels, from junior high girls' teams through university men's level, this book provides broad perspectives, in-depth analyses, and timely advice and coaching tips for neophytes and veteran coaches alike regarding ways you can organize yourself for effective coaching and broaden your understanding of the game and the coaching process as well.

Specifically, we've attempted to address the following questions, problems, and concerns:

- What does it take to be a successful basketball coach?
- Can coaching burnout be avoided, or is it a natural result of coaching too long or too intensely? How do you know if you're taking your coaching too seriously?
- How do you know if you're overworked, underpaid, and under appreciated—and more important, what can you do about it?
- How do you go about setting goals and priorities in your life and your coaching?
- How important is nonverbal communication as a coaching tool and motivational technique?

- What are the keys to effective communication? Should you relate to your players personally as well as professionally? If so, where do you draw the line?

- Is it possible to build a closely knit, highly motivated, and totally dedicated basketball team with players of average skills or below? Or does it take special players to create such an atmosphere on your team?

- Why is it important to understand your personal coaching philosophy? If, as you say, everyone has one, why should you take the time to study yours? How will it make you a better coach?

- Which is more important, emphasizing your team's strengths or hiding your team's weaknesses? Negating an opponent's strengths, or attacking his weaknesses?

- Which should you build your offense around, (1) your shooters, (2) your speed, (3) your height, (4) your defense, or (5) none of the above? (Hint: (1) is correct. See Section 5 for explanation and analysis.)

- What factors should be considered in determining which defense is best for your team? Are aggressive defenses better than passive defenses?

- Given today's tight athletic budgets, how can you cut corners financially without sacrificing quality in your basketball program? Can fund raising play a large part in this process?

- Can paperwork be organized for more effective coaching?

- How long should team tryouts be conducted? What should you expect to have accomplished as a team by the end of preseason practice?

- How much preparation should go into practice planning? How important are time allotments for drills in daily practices? How do you decide which aspects of the game to cover in a given practice?

- What are breakdown drills, and how can they help you install or practice your offenses and defenses?

- Is scouting really necessary? How do you go about scouting a team and preparing a scouting report? Is it necessary to prepare a different game plan for every game?

- How much (and when) should you deviate from your original game plan, strategy, and tactics in games? How do game situations and time remaining affect strategy?

- What are the differences between road games and home games in terms of preparation, coaching, and playing?

- Should you run up scores against weaker teams?

- How can you keep scores respectable against weaker (and stronger) opponents?

- How should you handle blowouts against you?

- What does a coach need to know about referees? What, if anything, can be done about poor officiating? How can you use referees to your team's advantage?

- What chores and responsibilities does a coach face in postseason, and the summertime? What aspects of player development should you work on during those periods?

- Is there life after coaching? What adjustments and options does a coach face after hanging up his or her whistle and retiring the clipboard?

Because basketball coaching is such a broad and complex activity, its very nature requires a great deal of paperwork. In various places within the text we have included samples of completed forms that may prove useful in showing you how to organize your paperwork into simpler, more easily managed segments.

We have also provided an appendix that contains over two dozen forms and checklists, which are ready for duplication and use.

No one has all the answers where basketball coaching is concerned—except, of course, the fans in the stands, whose ideas and opinions are, let us say, sometimes less than well informed. Still, with nearly half a century of basketball coaching experience and more than 850 wins between us, including making enough mistakes along the way to qualify us as five-star generals in Sadaam Hussein's Iraqi army, in our vainer moments we like to think that we've learned a thing or two along the way. In passing along the rudiments of that experience to you, the reader, we also offer our heartfelt wish that

When that One Great Scorer comes to mark against your name,
He'll marvel at your coaching skills that never lost a game.

Larry Chapman

William Warren

Contents

Section 10   SCOUTING 147

Section 11   GAME PLANS 183

Coaching Tasks and Preparation—Preseason
Managers' Game Duties Checklist
Player Evaluation Form—Preseason Tryouts

Forms for Section 9
Daily Practice Schedule
Weekly Practice Schedule

Forms for Section 10
Pregame Scouting Form
Scouting Checklist—Individual Skills
Scouting Checklist—Team Defense
Scouting Checklist—Team Offense
Scouting Form
Scouting Report
Scouting Schedule
Shot Chart

Forms for Section 11
Game Plan
Game Plan Evaluation

Forms for Section 12
Defensive Stat Sheet
Game Pattern Chart
Lineup Efficiency Chart
Offensive Stat Sheet
Stat Summary Sheet

SECTION 1

Surviving (and Thriving) in Basketball Coaching

All coaches are thinkers, or else they wouldn't survive.

—*Joe Paterno*

SURVIVAL PRINCIPLES

Surviving professionally means different things to different people. For some, it means having a long and successful coaching career; for others, it means getting through another day of "double, double, toil and trouble," as the witches in *Macbeth* put it. In either case, certain principles will enhance a coach's chances of surviving professionally for another decade or another day. Some of them are do's, some of them are don'ts—and all of them are important.

1. Don't expect to be an overnight success in coaching. Winning consistently is not a matter of luck, nor is staying in coaching for a decade or more. Both require commitment and hard work. As television's Monty Hall ("Let's Make a Deal") put it, "Actually, I'm an overnight success. But it took twenty years."

2. Don't take it too seriously. It's true; it *is* just a game. Talking about baseball, Hall of Famer Tom Seaver said, "The good players feel the kind of love for the game that they did when they were Little Leaguers." And although as coaches we want to do our best, many of us are guilty of taking our

1

work too seriously—of putting in too many hours on the job, of worrying and fretting over an endless stream of player problems and coaching decisions, and of developing ulcers and high blood pressure from trying to cope with external or self-imposed pressures to win.

3. *Don't promise more than you can deliver.* The quickest and surest way out of town is to tell everyone within earshot that you're going to win it all this year, and every game along the way. Championships and undefeated seasons are more easily talked about than achieved; all the talk in the world won't help you on those nights when the team's shooting goes stone cold. The time to talk about winning it all is when the final buzzer of the season goes off and you've won it all.

Of course, optimistic predictions can be a motivating force for your team—but they can also serve to motivate your opponents as well.[1] That's why most coaches never predict anything about an upcoming game, except that they'll show up if the bus doesn't break down on the way. They seldom discuss upcoming games in terms of winning, whether with the media, their boosters, or their own players. In the poet Robert Frost's words, we may have "promises to keep," but we also have "miles to go before (we) sleep." And depending upon how much we promised, sometimes those miles can be very long indeed.

4. *Don't try to do all of the work yourself.* Of all the survival principles we'll discuss, violating this one probably has the greatest potential to drive you out of coaching prematurely. Prolonged overwork can create a state of mental, physical, and emotional fatigue that saps your energy and drags you down like a case of walking pneumonia.

You don't mind the work so much if you're young and a workaholic, because your hard work denies your players the handy complaint that *they're* the ones who are doing all the work. Still, you should be aware that, if you're a young coach who wants to become an old coach (rather than a young ex-coach who burned out too soon), you need to take advantage of all the short-cuts you can find.

The shortest cut of all is to find dependable people to do part of your work for you.

A veteran coach told us that in his first year of coaching high school basketball he served as varsity head coach (with no assistants and little assistance); B-team coach; unpaid athletic director; referee for the other coach's B-team games; athletic bus driver; scout (an hour and a half per game, not including travel, and then two more hours at home writing up scouting reports); fund raiser (there was no booster club, and only a handful

---

[1]There's an old Jamaican saying that applies here: "No call alligator long mouth until you pass him."

of fans who attended home games); launderer; athletic trainer; teams tactician (twelve hours per week preparing daily practice schedules and game plans for varsity *and* B-team games); full-time teacher (with six fifty-minute classes a day and no planning period); Beta Club sponsor (unpaid); school newspaper advisor (also unpaid); and gym custodian who not only varnished the gym floor twice a year but also climbed up into the rafters to work on the electric motors that raised and lowered the goals because the only extension ladder in the school system was on permanent loan elsewhere—and he kept the antiquated plumbing system afloat by unclogging the commodes at least twice a week.

"But I was young then," the coach said, "and I was glad to accept those challenges for the opportunity to coach varsity basketball." If he had it all to do over again, he added, he'd send out applications to every high school in the nation, if necessary, to find a place where his workaholic tendencies could be satisfied by coaching basketball while someone else played Tarzan thirty feet above the gym floor.

If you're a young coach with a similar horror story to tell, you already know the truth: It ain't worth it. And it won't get any better until you find yourself another zip code where you don't have to be responsible for keeping the toilets running properly.

"God grant me the courage to change those things which can be changed, the serenity to accept those things which cannot be changed, and the wisdom to know the difference." You've probably heard those words, written by theologian Reinhold Niebuhr (1892–1971), a thousand times before. They are, as Jack Nicholson put it in *The Shining*, "Words to live by, Lloyd, my man. Words to live by." If you apply them to your present coaching situation—and your personal life as well—you should be able to avoid the kind of migraines that come from trying to batter down brick walls head first. A warning, though: Accepting with serenity what you cannot change does not mean spending two decades coaching with a basketball in one hand and a plumber's helper in the other. It's always good to undergo a certain amount of hardship early in your career, whether to test your resolve and dedication, to teach you humility, or to teach you how to extract gallons of achievement from pint jars of talent—but it's never wise to dedicate your whole career to that pursuit. Wisdom lies in knowing when to admit to yourself that you cannot fulfill your coaching potential in your present situation.

5. *Try to space out your work.* Even in the best of situations, the demands of coaching basketball will consume most of your time from mid-October through March. If you work at it, you may be able to ease your preseason and in-season burden somewhat by working on various aspects of your program during the off-season.

For example, if you have already developed program continuity, you probably have a good idea who's coming back next season, which not only gives you a leg up in preparing next year's eligibility sheets, and the like, but also hints at what offenses and defenses you're likely to use. That in turn may allow you to revise your daily practice schedules in advance—assuming, of course, that you saved them as you should have done. And if you evaluated and made notations on your practice schedules regarding the success or failure of the drills that you used last season, you can use the off-season to find new and better drills to replace the ones that didn't achieve the desired results.

6. Be organized. One way to be organized is to file everything. If you're familiar with Murphy's Law, you know that two days after you throw something away, you need it again. The solution is, of course, not to throw it away in the first place. File it. And so you can find it in your files, use key words in your headings. Don't file everything under *B* for "basketball" just because you're a basketball coach.

Another aspect of organization is to approach your coaching—and your busywork as well—in terms of priorities. What sort of priorities? Well, a clogged drain in the dressing room is one kind of priority. Dealing with players' problems is another—and usually a *high* priority, too, except during practice and games, in which case dealing with problem players may be a higher priority.

Priorities refer to what you need to do with your time, as opposed to what you might want to do. For example, if (as is the case with some basketball coaches we've known) you absolutely *must* get in thirty-six holes of golf every Saturday and Sunday, in season and out, you're allotting more than six hours of your valuable time every week to what is essentially a leisure-time activity. If your opponents spend that same six hours looking for ways to beat you while you're trying to decide whether to let it all hang out on your next drive or lay up short of the water—well, we believe that in the long run those figures will catch up with you. Other coaches aren't going to stop working just because you decide to take a six-hour breather for rest and relaxation every weekend. And if you're a young coach who thinks that basketball coaches aren't really so intense that they eat, sleep, and live the game twenty-four hours a day, you're as wrong as you can be. Ask any experienced coaches you know: They'll tell you that they often wake up at night thinking about game strategy or what they might try at practice tomorrow. And if you give them an edge, they'll use it against you with the coldblooded ruthlessness of a serial killer.

Organizing your time in terms of priorities ensures that your most pressing problems receive proper attention. For you to keep up with everything, several firms offer excellent time-management and planning systems, with notebooks ranging in price from $20 to $125 or more. Investing $40 in one of these handy organizers is not only a wise decision professionally; it's also tax deductible as a business expense.[2]

---

[2]The shoes, shorts, sweatsuits, socks, and other clothing that you wear in your work are also tax-deductible—but only if *you* paid for them, not the school.

7. Evaluate everything—and use your evaluations. Coaches are ultimately responsible for the success or failure of their basketball programs. If you as a coach hope to achieve your potential in a given situation, you should strive to monitor the progress of every phase of your program. This means taking time out after daily practices to sit down and evaluate your drills, time allotments, and so on—and recording those evaluations in writing so you won't forget them. In like manner, after games you should evaluate the effectiveness of your game plans and scouting reports, noting problem areas and jotting down ideas that might work next time you play that opponent. You should also periodically evaluate yourself, your assistant(s), your team, the referees, your program, and your goals (and progress toward them). Why? Because evaluation is the key to improvement. Ongoing evaluation of every aspect of your program can help to ensure that you have your priorities in order; it can also point out the need to find more effective ways to deal with problems.

8. Teach basketball's fundamental skills. This may seem to be a silly thing to say, but it's not. Nowadays, young people from peewee leagues through the pros are so deficient in basic skills that many of them couldn't guard a preschool toddler without hand-checking him—and when's the last time you saw a player shoot from a jump stop rather than a stride stop? Or block a shot without swatting the ball into the stands?

The fundamentals situation in basketball is this bad: Your team will look well coached if you can teach your players *one skill*, namely, assuming and maintaining an effective defensive stance (feet spread, knees bent, tail down, back straight, head and shoulders up), while moving or stationary. They won't want to do it, of course, because it's easier to play defense the way the pros do, by standing up, leaning forward from the waist, and hand-checking. But that low, balanced stance will make them very effective defenders and will make you look like a very good coach in anybody's league.

Offensively, today's players on all levels look as if they learned their individual fundamentals on the playground and their team patterns from their coaches. Athletic ability—quickness and vertical jumping ability—have all but replaced technique where offensive fundamentals are concerned. (The major exception to this rule is in girls' and women's basketball, since most girls still learn to play the game through team experiences rather than by visiting parks and playgrounds. In that respect, at least, it's much easier to teach offensive fundamentals to girls than boys, because they have fewer bad habits to correct.)

At any rate, while teaching fundamental skills is difficult and time consuming, it's never wasted time because *all* basketball eventually reduces to the offensive and defensive fundamentals inherent in the basic one-on-one confrontation. You have to understand the fundamentals to teach them, of course—but even if have you never played the game there are countless books, instructional videos, and the like, available on the subject. Coaching basketball without teaching its fundamental skills is like coaching a football team without teaching the players how to block and tackle.

9. Learn to communicate effectively. While we'll have more to say about this critical aspect of coaching in Section 2, we'll point out now that you already communicate effectively in the sense that your every word, gesture, and facial expression communicates. But do those words, gestures, and facial expressions send messages that will help your team and your program, or hinder their progress?

Teaching is communication; so is motivation. You cannot teach *or* motivate effectively unless you develop an approach to communication that is as precise and internally consistent as your game plans and practice schedules.

Make no mistake of it, the ability to communicate effectively is the single most important coaching skill you can possess. And because it is a *learned* skill, you can master the art of communicating—and teaching and motivating as well—by laying the groundwork that will ensure its effectiveness in any coaching situation.

In Section 2, you'll find out exactly how it's done.

SECTION 2

The Art of Communication

You don't have to be a disciplinarian. . . . You can have control without being a guy with a lot of rules and a lot of mouth. You gain control, sometimes with sarcasm, sometimes with humor. If I was coaching today, I don't have to prove I'm the boss every day. Some coaches do. They say "I'm the boss. *You* do this. *You* do this. *You* do this. *Every single day.*" Learn to keep your mouth shut. And stay away from the players sometimes.[1]

—Arnold "Red" Auerbach

We begin communicating even before we're born, as any expectant mother who has delighted to her unborn child's calisthenic exercises will tell you. At birth, we cry loudly with practically our first inhalation of oxygen—and for the rest of our lives thereafter we express our pleasure or displeasure with the world around us through a broad array of verbal communicative techniques. In a sense, even death itself is a form of communication: It's a basketball coach's ultimate way of telling his detractors that they can all go to where he's gone.

---

[1]Quoted by Ailene Voisin, "Daly Holds Edge to Be U.S. Coach," *Atlanta Journal* (Dec. 31, 1990), p. D11.

——————— NONVERBAL COMMUNICATION ———————

While as coaches we generally think of communication in oral terms—the spoken word—the fact is, everything we do communicates. Facial expressions portray happiness, sadness, anger, fear, and every other feeling in the broad and complex range of human emotions. Our standing, sitting, and walking posture can be almost equally revealing. Likewise the gestures we use, whether consciously or unconsciously. They are all part of the total package of *ourselves* that we display *for others to see*—our body language.[2] And because, like us, our players have spent their entire lives learning not only how to communicate but also how to interpret others' communications, it is important that we understand the ways that our actions influence and affect our players. It is also important to understand that, because much of our body language is either unconscious, physiological, or reflexive (e.g., nail biting as a sign of tension or nervousness, increased cardiorespiratory activity in response to stress, and pupil dilation during times of great excitement), it does no good to try to present a false face to the world, especially our players. We can only be ourselves, for better or worse.

Kids nowadays are smarter than we sometimes give them credit for—just as *we* were smarter than our parents thought we were. To paraphrase Abraham Lincoln, we may fool some of our players some of the time, and others all of the time, but there's no way in Hades that we're going to fool all of them all of the time. We can tell them anything and hope they'll believe it—but they *won't* believe it if our actions don't bear out the truth of our words.

Still, thus far we've been discussing generalities. Let's consider two traits that all of us want our players to have, *enthusiasm* and *willingness to work hard*. If we expect our team to adopt those qualities as a way of life, we had better have them in abundance ourselves. To the extent that our daily practices are uninspired and ill prepared because *we* are uninspired and ill prepared, our teams will suffer similarly in practice *and* in games.

Enthusiasm and willingness to work hard are more than topics for posters in the dressing room; they are qualities that we either carry within us on a continuing basis or we don't. And if we don't, the best we can realistically hope for is that our players will emulate us in trying to fake them, because it all starts at the top. Enthusiasm is contagious; unfortunately, so is apathy. So are hard work and laziness. All of them are habit forming, and if we pay lip service to the virtues of enthusiasm and hard work without adopting them ourselves, our players will see through us like an X-ray.

That's what we mean by nonverbal communication.

---

[2]If you're unfamiliar with the subject and want to find out more about how you unconsciously express your true nature through body language, you might want to read Julius Fast's *Body Language* (New York: Pocket Books, 1970).

---------------------------------- **THE FIVE SENSES** ----------------------------------

We perceive the world around us through our five senses: taste, touch, hearing, sight, and smell. Of those, two—taste and smell—have little to do with coaching (although we once knew a basketball coach who had his players eat garlic before games, presumably to disrupt opponents' concentration at close quarters).

Sight

First impressions are often inaccurate—but they are important because they are often difficult to change.

In most cases, the first impression we make on our players is *visual.* They see us even before they hear us. Thus, if we hope to convey positive images of ourselves we must endeavor to assure that what they see is in fact what they are getting. We don't have to wear coats and ties to daily practices to validate our status as professionals, of course—but a sloppy or slovenly appearance may carry the message that we will accept sloppy or slovenly play.

The same applies to the players' dressing rooms, the coaches' offices, and the gym itself: All convey visual images that can either help us or hinder us, depending on the extent of our efforts to make them habitable. Dirty, unpainted walls; littered floors; and perpetually unclean dressing rooms—any or all of these form a gloomy backdrop for convincing players that "We've got *pride* on our *side.*"

Neat, attractive facilities, on the other hand, provide positive visual images that reinforce the values we transmit to our players; so do the motivational slogans, posters, and signs that we put up in the gym and dressing rooms. Likewise the traveling outfits or dress codes for road games that many teams adopt: They instantly identify the team as an entity that is radically different from (and, by inference, better than) its surroundings.

Special attire for road games can serve as an important extension of the uniforms that players don for games, namely, uniting them for a common purpose. In the same sense that the act of putting on the kelly green Boston Celtic uniforms carries the unstated message "You're special; you have something to live up to," traveling outfits can by their uniqueness create that same sort of feeling on *your* team, even if your winning tradition is not nearly so great as that of the Celtics. After all, every winning tradition has to start somewhere.

If you're interested in finding shortcuts to success—and who isn't?—one way to build pride in a hurry is to have your team select a traveling outfit (not their warmups, incidentally) that the players will be proud to wear, win or lose. You can pay for them by having fund raisers such as car washes; however you do it, you'll be glad you did. Just as you want your players to wear their uniforms with pride, they *will* wear their traveling outfits proudly in victory or defeat; it's simply a matter of exchanging one uniform for another before and after games.

In all our combined years of coaching, we've never known a single instance in which a team that dressed proudly failed to play proudly, win or lose.

Finally, there are two other fringe benefits to be derived from adopting travel outfits or dress codes: First, the players' pregame concentration tends to be greater than if they were dressed haphazardly or casually (e.g., in overalls, jeans, or camouflage pants), since they are already "in uniform," so to speak; and second, losing games will not impair their pride beyond recovery because they will still feel a sense of pride in the way they look, both individually and as a team, regardless of how they played. The traveling outfit serves as a reminder that, win or lose, they are still a team and not just a collection of individuals.

We also believe that, in selecting new game uniforms, players will be prouder of the uniforms if they are allowed to choose them themselves (within reason, of course). It may not matter who selects the uniforms if our team has won 136 straight games—but then again, it might. The selection process itself binds players more closely together (and, incidentally, offers clues regarding who the team's leaders really are). And if the players are proud of their uniforms, they will wear them proudly and play hard to justify their pride.

What does all this have to do with communication? It simply means that every step we take in improving our basketball program, whether verbal or nonverbal, communicates. It isn't necessary to describe our long-range goals to our players every day, although occasional reminders are not only worthwhile but necessary. And because words sometimes lose their effectiveness when we rely on them too heavily—as Keith Jackson once told Howard Cosell, "It's all right to hold a conversation, but you should let go of it now and then"—we as coaches should always be on the lookout for ways to communicate our values and philosophy nonverbally, too.

Touch

Of the five senses, touch is the most direct and intimate. It is the most powerful form of communication that we have at our disposal. It is also the most critical in terms of human development: A laboratory monkey that is separated from its mother at birth will cling to a warm cloth figure shaped vaguely like itself—and if it is isolated from all forms of companionship, the newborn will quickly show signs of severe behavior disorder. Once placed with others of its kind, it will be unable to function in ways that are socially acceptable.

The entire range of human emotions can be expressed through physical contact: a gently reassuring touch; an angry shove; a firm, confident handshake; a consoling touch in times of grief; an encouraging pat on the back. Physical contact brings people together, however fleetingly; and while the resultant bond may not always be friendly, it *is* powerful. That's why we see basketball players huddling before free throws with their arms draped casually around each other's shoulders: What they are saying doesn't matter, but what they are *doing* matters greatly—they are reaffirming their commitment to each other.

The Coach and Contact. Coaches—especially males who are coaching girls or women—are rightfully wary of using contact as a coaching tool. And coaches have been fired for displays of anger that involved physical abuse of players, other coaches, referees, or fans. In these days of easy litigation, in which parental spanking constitutes child abuse, the coach who allows his or her anger to extend to physical contact is living on legally borrowed time. Yet the fact remains: Touch *is* a powerful motivator; it can be a valuable coaching tool when used judiciously. Many of today's youngsters receive so little parental attention at home that they respond positively to *any* attention they receive from their coach, whether it be a casual conversation, a smile, or a pat on the back every now and then.

Children—and adults as well, for that matter—never outgrow their need for love and affection. At the same time, ours is an age of noncommitment and self-involvement, and the result is that many children receive little or no daily reassurance that they are loved. The familiar bumper sticker Have You Hugged Your Child Today? may seem trite, but in fact many parents *don't* take the time to hug their children and tell them that they love them every day—or every month, for that matter. Is it any wonder that youngsters so often turn to sex or drugs to find meaning in their lives?

Coaches can use touch as a coaching tool or motivational device in various ways:

- If you want to ensure that a player listens to you, during a timeout huddle, touch him and look him in the eye as you address him by name. Also demand that the player look *you* in the eye!

- If you want to achieve the same effect with all of your players, have them stand in a circle with all hands (including yours) joined in the middle.

- To acknowledge a player's efforts when he leaves the game to sit on the bench, you might stand up, applaud, and touch hands with him or pat him as he passes you—and to broaden the effect you can have everyone on the bench do likewise whenever a teammate leaves the game.

- To develop unity in a situation in which a team is fragmented into small cliques—or to make new players on the squad feel as if they're part of the family from the very beginning—you might try requiring your players to touch hands with their teammates every time they meet in the halls or elsewhere, except during games and practice.

In installing such a rule, you should explain the importance of every player's accepting his teammates and treating them with respect, regardless of whether he likes them or not. The touching is a symbol of that acceptance, not only for the players involved but for everyone else who sees them doing so. (Of course, the rule should include the team managers and student trainers, too—and possibly the coaches and their spouses as well.)

If all of this seems silly, it's not—at least, it's no sillier than seeing 280-pound pro football linemen holding hands in a huddle. There's a method to the madness here: We've used touch rules with our teams over the years with startling results—startling, because we never expected anything so simple as touching hands to break down barriers that kept players apart in the first place. It's based on the notion that you have to reach out to touch someone— and the other person has to reach out, too, for contact to occur. The mutual aspect of reaching out is, or can be, the beginning of a sense of team belonging. The bonds it creates are powerful and long lasting.

Look at it this way: If even *one* of your players' lives is made better as a result of his teammates' acceptance of him, everyone on the team benefits. If *all* of the players know that you and their teammates accept them, respect them, and support them, there is virtually no limit to how far above their actual ability they will play to keep from letting their teammates down.

And it all starts with a simple touch.

VERBAL COMMUNICATION: THE ART OF RELATING TO YOUR PLAYERS

1. Spend time with your players away from practice. As coaches we generally wear our "game faces" in daily practice and at games, when we are professionals working at our chosen calling. In terms of the team's function as a second family, however, it is important for the players to get to know us away from the basketball court—and for us to get to know our players as well.

We aren't just talking about discussing players' personal problems with them, either, although that aspect of our relationship with them is certainly important. We've held cookouts—with and without parents being invited— and hosted pajama parties and trips to the beach or wherever else the players wanted to go; we've had ice-cream socials and popcorn parties at which the players watched videotapes of our recent games; and we've made utter fools of ourselves by letting our players try to teach us the latest dance steps—all for the sake of *getting to know each other better.*

In socializing with our players, it is important that we do so within the context of the player–coach relationship, which is essentially a player–*parent* relationship. It's one thing to use a social setting to make yourself accessible and approachable to your players; it's something else entirely to have a few drinks or share a joint or two with the boys, or to even hint at a sexual interest in a player.

Like it or not, we are role models of acceptable adult behavior for our players. Many of our players will model their own behavior after things they see us do or hear us say. If we want our players to respect us, it must be on *our* terms, not theirs. We can and should have fun with our players in the social settings that we devise—but never at the expense of our status as ethical, responsible adults.

In social situations, the rule of thumb for relating to students is: *Treat your players the way you'd want a coach to treat them if they were your kids.*

That's not a bad way to relate to them in practice and in games, either.

2. If you want your players to respect you, treat them with respect. And require them to treat each other with respect. Although desirable, it isn't absolutely necessary for your players to like you or each other in the beginning. What *is* important is that they respect you as head coach and each other as members of the team. The simplest way to approach the problem is to confront it head-on during preseason tryouts by explaining your expectations.

Every year, we give the same little speech after announcing who has made the squad:

> We'll be spending a lot of time together during the next four months or more. If you don't think you can get along with the coaches and your teammates, you shouldn't be here. You're wasting your time and ours.
>
> If there's even one person here whom you can't treat with respect as a valuable member of this team, you should get up and leave right now, because everyone here is special to us. Every member of the team will need your support, not just right now but throughout the days to come.
>
> We may or may not win every game this season, but we'll all be winners if we stick together and think of the *team* rather than ourselves.

Beyond that, treating players with respect means treating them as if they are important to the team and you—as they should be, or else you should not have put them on the team in the first place. We've seen coaches make fun of their players and belittle them to their faces, or talk disparagingly about them behind their backs, and we've wondered *Why?* What possible good could it do the team or a player to make him a laughingstock or the object of ridicule?

3. Be fair. Some people will tell you that you're supposed to treat every player alike, but it just isn't true. (It's also impossible.) Some players respond better to gentle prodding or encouragement, while others need challenges or criticism. Some need a pat on the back or a helping hand, others prefer a boot to the butt—figuratively, of course. So you can't treat them all alike, and you shouldn't even try.

But you *can* be fair with all of your players.

Your players don't really expect much of you. They don't expect you to solve all of their problems. They don't care whether you're a Methodist, or overweight, or black, or physically attractive, or intelligent. They generally will accept you whether your basic coaching style is laid back or loud and frenzied, as long as you're consistent with them. They don't even know or care whether you're a brilliant coach; all they care about is how you treat them. And if you treat them fairly, they will respect you for it.

Treating players fairly means applying the same set of rules to everyone, superstars as well as third-stringers: the player averaging 34 ppg. who cuts practice should be subject to exactly the same penalty as the benchwarmer who couldn't score if the opponents remained in their huddle after a timeout. Selective enforcement of team rules breeds resentment and disharmony, which is exactly the opposite of what the team concept is all about.

A commonly encountered problem regarding fairness is that of playing-time allotment. In our experience, at least, the criticisms we've received regarding playing-time allotment have come from disgruntled parents who are irked that their son is spending "pine time" on the bench while another, obviously inferior, player is playing ahead of him. It doesn't matter that Johnny runs so slowly that he looks as if he's wading waist-deep in the surf, or that he couldn't guard a potted plant; all that's important to the angry parents is that "Johnny deserves to play more than the other players because he's my kid, and that makes him special!"

We've never had that problem with our players, though—possibly because we like to tell them that, unlike most coaches, we *do* play favorites: Our favorites are the kids who bust their buns hustling throughout every second of daily practice. They're the players who work so hard that we couldn't keep them on the bench in games if we wanted to.

"If you want more playing time, *earn it!*" we challenge them. "Do a better job than the people who are playing ahead of you, and we'll have you out on the court so fast you won't have time to get your warmups off. Give us the kind of results that we need from you, and you'll get more playing time than Hammer's latest rap video."

Along with that, we're firm believers in defining players' roles in games as precisely as possible, which helps considerably in determining whether a player is accomplishing everything that he's supposed to. We believe that a youngster is most likely to play up to his potential when he knows exactly what is expected of him—and with lesser-skilled players, those expectations sometimes reduce to two phases of the game: playing tough defense (a universal requirement for continued or increased playing time), and, say, rebounding.

Before sending the sub into the game we'll remind him of his priorities: "You don't have to beat the press or run the offense or score points; that's not your responsibility. All we need for you to do is front the posts, block out on the boards, and *get rebounds*." Admittedly, it's asking a lot to expect a player to front the post and still rebound effectively; yet it must be done, because that's the way we play that defense. We've tried to simplify the player's responsibilities as much as possible to keep him focused on what he's supposed to be doing—and after the game all we need to do is check the stat sheets to see if he did a good job in those areas. If he did, his p.t. increases; if not—well, he has little room for complaint when the stats show that other players are doing a better job of what he is supposed to be doing.

"The Team above all": Our players probably hear that phrase hundreds of times during their playing days with us. They understand that, like them, *we* have responsibilities to the team, one of which is to allot playing time on the basis of who can get the job done. So it's nothing personal, but merely a case of doing what's best for the team.

It's natural for substitutes to want more playing time—but not for them to resent us for not playing them more when their practice and game performances haven't earned additional playing time. Resentment is selfish, and selfishness is not a desirable trait for team-sport players. Basketball requires self-sacrifice on the part of everyone for the good of the team. If a player wants to be treated as an individual first and as a team member second, he should consider switching to an individual sport such as golf or wrestling.

4. Be honest with your players. Horror novelist Stephen King is right: Kids *do* have built-in b.s. detectors. We had them, too, when we were kids. But as we got older we found out that *everybody lies to everybody else about everything*. Our whole adult society is based on lies, from politicians' promises to our smiling warmly and exchanging friendly handshakes with people we utterly despise.[3] We even teach young people to lie in school. (Remember the teacher asking the class, "Who talked while I was out of the room?" when you were in elementary school?) It's hardly surprising, then, that young people find it difficult to trust adults.

If you want to bridge the generation gap, be honest with your players. That doesn't mean telling them that they're ugly or smell bad, or that you don't like them, of course—but it *does* mean being the person you say you are. If you preach to your players about the evils of alcohol and drugs, you'd better not keep a pint of vodka hidden in the back of your filing cabinet. If you promise a player increased playing time next game, you can bet that he'll hold it against you if you don't follow through on your promise. If you really care about your players as you say you do, you'll monitor their grades and

---

[3]"My doctor told me I had six months to live. When I couldn't pay the bill, he gave me another six months."—Henny Youngman

classwork and encourage them to come to you with their personal problems. And when they talk over their problems with you, you'll keep what they tell you strictly confidential.

Honesty *is* the best policy. Being honest with your players will give you virtually unlimited access to them. If they believe you, they will believe in you and trust you. That in itself is both a great honor and a great responsibility, because there just aren't that many adults that any young person trusts.

If your players trust you, your coaching will be personal as well as team oriented, and you can mold them into whatever kind of players you want them to be—a process that Bear Bryant referred to as "holding them in your hand."

5. Let your players know what you stand for—and what you won't stand for. Teach them what is right. What we're talking about here is values. Honesty is a value. So are commitment, dedication, cooperation, loyalty, sacrifice, and other qualities necessary for success in team sports.

Each of us has his or her own set of values. Because over a period of time we tend to attract players into our program who will at least accept if not adopt our values, it is necessary for us to transmit to our players our personal beliefs regarding proper and improper behavior and attitudes. It is a mistake to expect players to do the right thing if we have not taken time to tell them what proper behavior consists of.

An example: players and fighting. We're aware that this is only a personal preference, but we've always believed that few, if any, circumstances justify our players' fighting their teammates, opponents, or anyone else. Our teams play a hard-nosed, physical brand of basketball, but we neither encourage nor condone fighting as a way of solving problems. Fighting is an individual activity and thus does not satisfy team needs. In fighting, a player loses control of himself, and we never want our players out of control.

When teammates fight, they sow seeds of disharmony that can tear down the unity that we've worked so hard to build, and one or another of them may suffer injury that will further weaken the team. When players fight opponents, they run the risk of incurring injury and suspension from the game and possibly from future games as well. And when players fight, say, students from the general school population, they face possible injury and suspension from school—and they become no better than the students they fight.

"There are always alternatives to fighting if you don't lose control of your emotions," we tell our players in preseason. "If your legs aren't broken, you can always walk away from a fight. But if fighting or maintaining a macho image is more important to you than being on the team, then by all means go ahead and fight because you're not the sort of player we need." And if the team is more important to them, we point out, we expect them to come to us with the problem. If we can't solve it, then the principal can. Or the police.

As we said, it's just a personal preference of ours. We happen to believe that nothing good comes from our players' fighting except ego gratification if the player happens to win the fight. And even then he (and the team) is the loser if his playing time is curtailed due to injury or suspension. But we seldom have had problems in this regard because we take time to let our players know how important we consider the problem to be.

You may not agree with our view—and that's all right too. The important thing is, you should take time to tell your players what *you* consider important. It's a matter of expectations: If you set high behavioral standards for them to live up to because you consider them to be special, and you tell them so, they will generally do their best to live up to your expectations.

Remember, *your players want your approval.* As the psychologist William James wrote, "The deepest principle of human nature is the craving to be appreciated." If you let your players know that you appreciate them when their behavior reflects the values you consider important, you enhance the likelihood of their adopting other values that are important to you.

Fighting, taunting beaten opponents, intentionally trying to injure opponents, reacting to the taunts of opposing fans in the stands, arguing with coaches—all are examples of behavior that should be beneath the dignity of a proud team. Can you picture a Dean Smith–coached team engaged in a wild, full-scale melee on the court? Or a Tarheel player standing nose-to-nose at courtside with Coach Smith or one of his assistants, shouting obscenities at them? We can't, because Coach Smith is a class act, always has been and always will be. He wouldn't stand for such behavior. He wouldn't retire their jerseys, he'd burn them. And his players know it.

6. Let your players know that what is important to them is important to you. This doesn't mean that you should carry a jam box loaded with rap tapes on your shoulder, or try to keep up with current teenage jargon so you can converse with your players on their level. But it *does* mean caring about them and their problems and concerns off the court as well as on. It means letting them know that they are important to you personally as well as professionally—as well they should be, since their personal problems affect their on-court performances. It means getting to know your players' parents and girl- or boyfriends, and finding time to help players come to grips with their problems.

Being a teenager is one of the most difficult experiences imaginable. Past childhood but still learning how to cope with adult problems and responsibilities, teenagers are often confused about their identity and unsure about their future. Team membership can be an enormously positive, stabilizing force in their lives at a time when they desperately need stability, acceptance, and guidance. Knowing that their coach is genuinely concerned about their well-being and welfare is a vital link in the chain that binds your team together.

7. Let your players know that you care about them. Support the good things that they do. As we've pointed out repeatedly, it all starts at the top, with the head coach. If you expect your players to accept each other, the first step is to let them know that you accept them wholeheartedly and without reservation. If from the very start you express confidence in them, their self-confidence will grow. If by your words and deeds you show that you honestly care about them, you won't have to worry about dreaming up clever motivational halftime talks to raise the level of their intensity.

What we're really talking about here is *reducing your coaching to a personal level*—not just working on individual fundamentals, but establishing yourself in your players' eyes as a coach who cares about them. And not just by being nice to them, either, since games aren't won with niceness. Parents aren't always nice to their children, no matter how much they love them. But in loving families the parents respect each child's individuality and offer attention and affection as well as discipline in "train(ing) up a child in the way he should grow," as the biblical king David put it. It's all part of being what is known as a *players' coach.*

Jerry Tarkanian is a players' coach; so are such disparate personalities as Bob Knight, Pat Summit, John Chaney, Mike Kryczewski, John Thompson, and Lou Carnesecca. The list could go on to infinity, because every successful basketball coach is a players' coach. You can be as abrasive and demanding as Vince Lombardi or as mellow as an old housecat, and the results will be the same if your players know that you're behind them 100 percent of the time. They will play as hard for you as if their lives were at stake, if they know that you love them and want what's best for them and the team.

That's why we consider it imperative for us to be honest with our players: If we say that we love them but our actions never show it, they won't believe it.

It's all right to "use" players to further team goals, because that's the only way those goals will be achieved. Anyway, all of us "use" each other: Principals use teachers to further educational goals; players use the team to fulfill personal needs such as acceptance, recognition, or getting college scholarships. Coaches use players to win games. (We certainly don't select players on the basis that they will help us to *lose* games.) But there's a price tag that comes with the willingness to let oneself be used—and in our players' case that price tag is acceptance, affection, respect, support, and honesty. They are the same qualities that form the basis for a loving family. We ignore them at the risk of having our teams fragmented by division, mistrust, and jealousy.

Put it this way: How hard would *you* work for a coach who treated you like a member of his family? Or for teammates who love you as they love their own brothers and sisters?

For many of us, coaching is basically negative in nature; that is, we try to identify problems and correct them while they are still minor flaws in our players' performances. Still, this corrective aspect of coaching can lead to overlooking or taking for granted the good things that the players do. Fortunately, this potential defect can be overcome with minimal effort on our part simply by taking time occasionally to single out players for recognition when they do things right. Whether the recognition is public (i.e., expressed to members of the media), semiprivate (made at team meetings or at the end of daily practice, to end those sessions on a positive note), or in private informal conversations with the players in question doesn't matter. What matters is just doing it. Every player, whether Michael Jordan or a nervous eighth-grade benchwarmer, needs to be singled out for praise by his coach at least occasionally—and some players need it more often than others.

The art of coaching is to know who needs it *now*.

We also believe that it's good coaching to recognize and support our players' accomplishments off-court as well as on. One way to challenge players academically is to present recognition awards or trophies to each of our players at the basketball banquet who excel in the classroom—say, by maintaining a B average or better for the entire school year; another is to present a trophy to whichever player has raised his grade-point average the most during the present year. Players should also be recognized by the coach for holding offices or receiving awards in school clubs, or for participating in worthwhile activities such as drama or debate. Some coaches want their players to be one-dimensional in the sense of dedicating their lives to basketball; we don't happen to think that way. We want them to be students first and basketball players second—but we also want them to pursue other positive avenues if they are so inclined, not at the expense of improving their basketball skills but in addition to it. If they choose to participate in school clubs, we're all for it as long as it does not lessen their desire to play basketball. We want them to be their teammates' best friends, too—but not their *only* friends.

8. Successful coaching is not a matter of knowing how to relate to whites, blacks, males, or females; it's knowing how to relate to people. If you're a white coach whose team is composed mainly of blacks—or if you're a male who is coaching girls or women—you should not be apprehensive about whatever cultural, socioeconomic, or sexual differences you will encounter. If treated with respect, blacks and women will accept a white coach or a male as easily as if no differences existed at all. In fact, because they understand racial or sexual bias to a far greater extent than a white male ever will, blacks and women are far more likely to accept him than white male players who don't really need basketball to enhance the quality of their lives.

Start with the notion that your players aren't black, white, Hispanic, Oriental, male, or female: They're *athletes*. Treat them as athletes, and you won't have any trouble relating to them in a positive manner. Dismiss the cruel (and totally inaccurate) stereotypes of blacks as lazy, dimwitted, and impervious to pain, or girls and women as dainty, emotionally unstable creatures who get their way by crying, and what you're left with is basketball players who, regardless of their race or sex, want to be accepted by their coach and teammates.

Laziness comes in all colors—but so do commitment, dedication, and loyalty. Racism and sexism are unnatural, *learned* traits. We may never completely overcome them in our society, but a white male coach can overcome them on his teams by respecting every player's right to fair and equal treatment from the coach and his or her teammates.

For black players, finding an adult white male who considers them a part of his family is likely to be a novelty at first—after all, black players have racial biases based on their own experiences too—but as they discover that his feelings for them are genuine, they eventually will lower their own barriers and accept him as completely as they would accept a black coach. As one of Jerry Tarkanian's black players put it, "He ain't white, man; he's *Armenian.*"

The same holds true for men coaching girls and women. The so-called Battle of the Sexes has gone on unabated ever since Adam asked Eve why she took a bite out of that apple—and doubtless it will continue for as long as the human species exists. Men don't understand women, never have and never will. But male coaches can understand the girls and women they coach by ignoring their sex and regarding them as athletes. Only when a male coach brings sex into the picture, whether by making sexual advances toward a player or expecting less from girls and women than he would expect if he were coaching boys or men, does gender become a real problem in his coaching.

9. Try to deal with small problems before they become big problems. Whether we're talking about players' problems or problem players, the secret is, as Barney Fife put it, to "*nip it* in the *bud!*"—that is, to deal with problems quickly, directly, and as forcefully as necessary to keep them from getting any worse.

The easiest problems to resolve are those involving disputes or misunderstandings among players on the team, or between one or more players and you or an assistant coach. They may not be *fun* to work with—problems seldom are fun—but they are easily resolved because the same four words apply universally to any such problems: *The Team Above All.*

If team membership is to be truly special, ego and personal needs must always give in to the needs of the team. No one, not even us as coaches, can be allowed to disrupt the unity and harmony that make the team a second family.

When misunderstandings arise, they should be discussed openly in the coach's presence, and resolved there as well. We've apologized to players, many times, both privately and in front of their teammates, when we've been wrong—and we've had players do the same thing when they have been wrong.

Our guidelines for players' problems with teammates or coaches are few—but they are largely inflexible:

- *Don't even* think *about telling outsiders about your problems with teammates.* What goes on in the gym, stays in the gym. No exceptions to this rule are permitted. Violators will be shot at sunrise. (Not really, but you get the picture.)
- *Confront your teammate about your problems with him.* (Talking about it to his face is better than talking behind his back.) If you can't bring yourself to confront your teammate, tell us about it and we'll talk it out together in the privacy of the coach's office. But don't try to ignore problems, or let them fester like infected sores. And don't expect them to go away if you don't tell us about them. That only makes them worse.
- *Problems between players and/or coaches* will *be resolved to everyone's satisfaction at a single conference held in the coach's office.* If you leave before the problem is talked out and resolved—or if you are unwilling to accept the coach's decision as final and in the best interests of the team—don't forget to stop by the locker room to pick up your belongings. If you can't say "I'm sorry" to your teammates when the occasion requires that sentiment, then you *aren't* sorry, you don't need the team anymore, and it certainly doesn't need you.

If you as coach really want to make a lasting impact on quarreling players at such a conference, end it by having them hug and make up. (It's a dandy addition to the "touch rule" we discussed earlier in this section.) If you do, you won't have any further quarreling from those two players, at least: They'll do *anything* to avoid having to hug and make up again in the future.

Regarding problem players, we recommend two books that offer valuable insights toward handling problem athletes: *Coaching and Motivation,* by William E. Warren (Prentice Hall, 1983), and *Psychology of Coaching,* by Thomas Tutko and Jack Richards (Allyn and Bacon, 1971). For this book's purposes, however, we'll merely point out that because you haven't been associated with your players since birth, you aren't responsible for their psychological or behavioral problems; and because you are neither a professional psychologist nor a psychiatrist, you aren't responsible for resolving those problems. You'll try, of course, for the sake of the individual and the team, but you should also be willing to *stop* trying when or if it becomes clear that the problem player's negative behavior or attitude cannot be changed and is affecting the team adversely.

10. Try to deal with problems in a positive manner whenever possible. Team membership should always be viewed by players and coaches in a positive manner. But when tempers flare, as they do occasionally, affected parties may overreact verbally or physically. Players should be encouraged not to say or do things in the heat of anger that will affect their future status on the team.

When players lose control, they should be instantly separated from the causes of their anger and given time to cool off emotionally. Later, when they are better able to confront the problem rationally, they can talk out the problem at length as described in item 9 on the previous page. In that discussion, the coach can lay a positive groundwork by enumerating the players' good points at the very beginning. (It's hard to stay mad when someone is telling you how good you are.) She should also point out that their problem is only a temporary misunderstanding and thus can be easily resolved because team membership requires that everyone accept everyone else, including their good and bad points. Such a statement implies that the misunderstanding had better be minor, or else one or both of them will suffer the consequences.

We've asked players point-blank, "Do you like So-and-so?" They always respond yes, of course, since the player is standing right there—and besides, they think that they're required to like their teammates, although we never tell them so. (We tell them that they must get along with their teammates, be supportive of them, and treat them with respect.)

Having gotten them to admit to liking each other, we can usually resolve their differences by talking them out and finding points of compromise that they can live with.

If the problem happens to involve a member of the opposite sex whose attention both players covet—a common problem—we may point out the extreme unlikelihood that the third party will wind up marrying either of them, given the fickle nature of teenagers. And we *will* suggest that, while girl–boy relationships are as changeable as the weather, friendships such as those among teammates will last for a lifetime.

Family Matters

The bond of brotherhood makes all men one.

—Thomas Carlyle

THE FAMILY PLAN

Although deplorable, the fact that for many youngsters home is a place where, as one wit put it, "If you go there, they have to take you in," works in our favor. Players who do not receive adequate love, affection, or attention at home are likely to adopt our Team as their second family—if, that is, a family atmosphere exists on our Team.

In a very real sense, a Team should be a family rather than a collection of individuals. That's why we're capitalizing the word *Team* throughout this section: to underscore the special nature of Teams as they ought to be. Family members do not always agree, of course; but if they are truly a family, their differences and occasional disagreements will not sever the bonds of respect, affection, and acceptance that hold them together. The Team that plays together, stays together.

A high school coach told us that the proudest moment in his coaching career came, not when his Team won its first state championship or when he was named state Coach of the Year, but earlier that season when the players gave him, his assistant coach, and their wives T-shirts for Christmas presents. On back of the shirts were the names *Daddy, Mama, Uncle Stan,* and *Aunt Jane.*

It may not seem like much to you and me—but because the sentiment was real it meant the world to the coaches, their wives, and the players.

———————— **CREATING THAT "SPECIAL" FEELING** ————————

For a collection of individuals to be a Team, it must function differently from other collections of individuals; that is, it must function as a cohesive unit in which each individual feels a sense of responsibility and obligation to his teammates for his actions on and off the court. The deeper that sense of individual responsibility and obligation to the group is felt by its members, the more the group will achieve.

Thus, we should try very hard to teach our players that, as members of our Team, they are *special*. We should take pains to create a positive atmosphere in which our players feel that being on our Team is a special privilege that not everyone can attain. We should want them to feel that they are important to us, and to their teammates as well. But because they are special, they have special responsibilities to their teammates and coaches. They must be different from other people who are neither athletes nor members of the Team.

Without straining ourselves, we could probably name fifty ways in which athletes in team sports are different from nonathletes. The problem goes deeper than that, however, because we want our players to be not merely different from, but *better than*, the general school population—in behavioral terms as well as in basketball skills. Behaviorally, we should expect our players to be better than other people because they represent not just themselves but the Team as well. When outsiders see our players cutting classes, cheating on tests, getting into fights, or being sent to detention hall for misbehavior, it makes everyone on the Team look bad.

The process begins by telling the players that they're special and requiring them to operate within the framework that we create for proper treatment of and by their teammates and us—acceptance, respect, and support. That's the only special treatment they can expect to receive—but it's a *lot*. In return for that total acceptance, respect, and support, they are expected to commit themselves just as completely to fulfilling the goals that we set for the Team.

For unto whom much is given, of him shall much be required: and to whom men have committed much, of him they will ask the more.

—*Luke 12:48*

The "GOTCHA!" Principle. Once a player has committed himself to our Team concept, we've got him. When he agrees to accept, respect, and support his teammates wholeheartedly regardless of whatever differences may exist, the inevitable outcome can only be a closely knit Team. We cannot realistically expect our Team to win every game—or perhaps even *half* of our games, depending on the players' skills—but we have the right not to only expect but to *demand* that every player accepts, respects, and supports his teammates and us. And in doing so, we are force-feeding them heavy doses of the very same qualities that generate deep and lasting friendships.

In case you're reading this late at night and missed the point, here it is: If our players are united by a sense of obligation to each other, there is virtually no limit to how hard they will work to keep from letting down their teammates. Their work ethic and receptivity to coaching will be constantly high, because their basic motivation comes from within themselves rather than from a coach standing over them with a whip in one hand and a chair in the other.

We must all hang together, or assuredly we shall surely hang separately.

—*Benjamin Franklin at the signing of the Declaration of Independence, July 4, 1776*

BUILD AN "US-AGAINST-THE-WORLD" MENTALITY ON YOUR TEAM

Every successful athlete and coach is paranoid to a certain extent. After all, even as our players are running through their daily practice drills and patterns, scattered groups of people who don't like us or our Team very much are plotting, scheming, and rehearsing ways to beat us. These groups are our upcoming opponents. Upsets occur when players forget that fact.

There's a personal aspect to this "you-and-me-against-the-world" way of thinking, however, that hits even closer to home: If our players enjoy a special relationship with each other, there are going to be people in our school who, because they do not play on our Team and therefore cannot share in that special relationship, are going to be resentful or jealous of our players.

The fact that we expect our players to be different from the nonathletic students in our school can be another source of resentment; so can the fact that most nonathletes do not understand the depths of commitment and sacrifice that are necessary for a person to become a superior basketball player. The underachievers in our school are likely to resent *anyone* who is trying to accomplish more than they are.

Rather than allowing negativity to affect our Team adversely, we can use that negativity to strengthen the Team, by pointing out the necessity of hanging together, as Ben Franklin put it.

Despite whatever paranoid connotations it may have, an "us-against-the-world" approach is an excellent way to keep our players focused on Team goals. It is easily understood and accepted by the players if the Team bonds are strong, because there just aren't many people in anyone's life that he can rely on absolutely for acceptance, respect, and support, without any strings attached. That's why Team membership is so special: One's teammates are likely to be the largest collection of dependable, supportive friends that he will have in his entire lifetime.

While it binds players together, the "us-against-the-world" approach also provides an excellent alternative to the "us-against-each-other" attitude that coaches sometimes encounter when their teams lose games frequently. Teams with strong emotional ties among the players and coaches can weather the storms of occasional or even frequent losses without resorting to blaming each other (or the coach) for those losses.

——————————— FOCUSING ON SUCCESS ———————————

One of every team's goals is to win as many games as possible. Winning consistently builds pride and confidence and serves to focus a team's efforts to a far greater extent than losing does. There may be many worthwhile lessons to be learned from losing, but only winning can teach you how to win.

Still, let's be realistic: Not every team wins consistently. For every team that wins a game, another team loses. Some teams lose games more often than they win. Some teams win only rarely. With such teams, a coach's greatest challenge is likely to be finding ways to maintain a positive Team attitude in the face of consistently negative results on the scoreboard. If you watch a magician closely, you'll notice that his hands are constantly in motion as she's performing. There's a reason for it, of course: In moving her hands, she divides our attention between them and her face as she talks. And as one of her hands gestures dramatically to underscore something that she's saying, you can bet that her other hand is loading up with the gimmicks that produce her magic. It's called *sleight of hand,* and the principle underlying its use should be familiar to any coach who has ever survived a prolonged losing streak.

There is nothing fun about losing games, whether occasionally or frequently.[1] Losing is inherently negative: The short end of the score spells out F-A-I-L-U-R-E in terms that are instantly recognizable. Losing consistently tends to lower team morale, individual and team expectations, and individual

---

[1]When Georgetown's John Thompson was asked by a reporter if his team had learned anything from a recent loss, he grumbled, "We prefer to learn from winning."

tolerance for continued hard work. Yet as pressure to win mounts with each loss, our natural tendency as coaches is to work the players and ourselves longer and harder to overcome the flaws in our performances that have caused us to lose. However, our efforts are doomed to failure in a losing situation unless, like the magician, we direct our players' attention away from what we don't want them to see and toward the things that we want them to focus on.

The best way to achieve this, of course, is to maintain a positive attitude ourselves. If we refuse to allow ourselves or our players to treat losses as anything but necessary steps in building a winning basketball program, we will have taken a huge step forward in overcoming negativity in a negative situation. And if, instead of increasing the pressure on ourselves and our players by driving the Team with relentless and unabated fury, we take time out at least occasionally to do different, silly, or "fun" things at our daily practices—as we might do if we were seeking to relieve the pressure of an undefeated season—we're likely to find that the players will stay focused on the important things that we're trying to accomplish.

Sure, we want them to work hard at practice, win *or* lose—but what incentive do they have if the enjoyment of winning has escaped them and daily practices are little more than two and a half grueling hours of physically abusing each other? If in our frenzied efforts to overcome losses by sheer weight of physical effort we manage to take all of the anticipation and enjoyment out of our daily practices, we'll lose players who might have stayed with the Team under less rigorous conditions. Especially on losing Teams, players need to be reminded constantly that basketball, and being on our Teams, can be fun as well as productive.

What sort of activities are we talking about? Well, we can have one-on-one contests, or scrimmages against the coaches and managers, or weak-hand shooting contests, or "out-of-position" scrimmages in which the big men play outside and the guards play the posts, or free-throw competitions for prizes or penalties, or ball-handling contests (e.g., seeing who can spin the ball on his finger the longest), or whatever else occurs to us to take the players' minds off losing and negativity. We don't have to devote all, or even much, of our daily practices to this sort of thing: All that's necessary is one or two of them slipped into a two-and-a-half-hour practice session to break the monotony and routine of drills and patterns and hard work that have thus far proved ineffective in building a winning record.

At no time in coaching is it more important for us to reinforce our personal bonds with our players than when the Team is losing consistently. By our actions we teach our players how to handle losing (and winning) without going off the deep end—but when we are losing, our players also watch us for signs of rejecting them or blaming them for losses. They blame themselves of course—at least, some of them do—and such thinking is as misguided and unproductive as crediting themselves for the Team's wins. Our task as coaches is to convince each player that neither winning nor losing affects our basic feelings for him any more than his parents' love for him is based on the quality of his grades in school. He should know that, as long as he remains committed to his teammates and us, we will continue to support him and believe in him. And he *will* know those things if we take the time to tell him.

"Coaches don't win games; they just lose them." You've probably heard that phrase a thousand times before. It's wrong, of course: Winning programs are always the result of someone's good coaching somewhere along the way over an extended period of time. But coaches should always take the blame for losses, first, because it's the classy thing to do, and second, because we want to avoid having players accept or assess the blame for defeats on themselves or their teammates.

THE TEAM AND WINNING

Although better left unstated by us, our primary goal as basketball coaches is to win games—not just today or tomorrow but hopefully for years to come. An effective feeder program is the key to success on a long-term basis; winning *now* means finding the best athletes in our school and convincing them that playing basketball for us is a good investment of their time.

To help our players play better, we teach them basketball skills and drill them in various techniques. To ensure that they play hard, we create a familylike Team atmosphere in which they feel obligated to their teammates and us to give their best effort at all times, in practice and in games. Lack of skills may limit the Team's winning ability initially—but emotional ties will keep them together during hard times as skills develop. And when players whose emotional ties are already strong begin to win consistently, the result is a snowballing effect in which good things happen with such rapidity and regularity that their momentum seems to overcome all obstacles in the Team's path to success.

While it's always fun to be associated with winning, the effect is magnified a hundredfold when players are so closely united as to simply refuse to accept defeat or anything less than their best efforts on the court, whether individually or as a Team. In such a setting, the coach is replaced in his role as Team motivator by the players themselves—and let us tell you from personal experience, coaches, if you ever have such a team you'll understand why we've spent considerable space in this section writing about the need for closely knit teams—and you'll want every other team you ever coach to strive for the same kind of closeness.

We've mentioned elsewhere that every coach should undergo a losing streak early in his career; well, every coach should also undergo the exhilarating experience of coaching a Team whose athletes are completely loyal to him, dedicated to their teammates, and totally committed to the goals he has set for the Team. In such an atmosphere, impossible dreams no longer seem impossible. Miracles *can* happen when players believe—and we're paraphrasing the apostle Paul here—that "I can do all things through *the Team*, which gives me strength."

Can we create such an unconquerable attitude on our Teams? Sure we can. Thousands of coaches do it every year, even with teams whose physical skills are highly conquerable. It's just a matter of finding kids who want to be part of something bigger and better than themselves—our Team—and teaching them how to behave and think as well as how to play the game of basketball.

You and Your Basketball Coaching Philosophy

Coaching is what I do best. I enjoy the intensity, the
nightly competition that accompanies the games. I don't
know what else I could do that would give me that
satisfaction.

—Pat Riley

A wide receiver whose NFL team failed to make the playoffs in 1990 suggested that his team ought to switch to the run-and-shoot offense. His coach responded quickly and negatively, saying that such a move was out of the question because he (the coach) knew absolutely nothing about the run-and-shoot. "And that's the best reason for not using it," the coach concluded.

Well—no it's not, coach. The best reason for not using a particular offense or defense is that it's not right for your team and personnel. If your players are so quick that they can dodge raindrops in a cloudburst, you don't need a playing style that slows them down and reduces their quickness advantage; and if your team is slower than the U.S. Mail you shouldn't plan on overwhelming your opponents with full-court pressure defense or fast-breaking. But ignorance is not an acceptable reason for adopting or dismissing any pattern or playing style.

Once you decide that there's nothing more you need to know about basketball, you'll never learn anything else about the game.

—— A QUIZ TO DETERMINE YOUR BASKETBALL PHILOSOPHY ——

We'll begin by taking a test.

Don't worry, it's just a little test—a pre-test, actually, consisting of five questions. You won't have to study for it, and you won't fail it because there are no *right* or *wrong* answers, just options for you to choose between. It's not a final exam, either: As that learned professor of football coaching, the late Paul "Bear" Bryant, liked to point out, coaches' final exams are witnessed by critical fans and screaming crowds in the gyms and stadiums where we play our games. Those are the tests that *really* count.

So let's take the test and see what happens. If the questions seem perplexing or somewhat restricted in some cases, it's because basketball is basically a very simple game that can be very difficult to coach. And if your answers are not always cut-and-dried, simple affairs, it's because we're not just asking questions about basketball; what we're really doing is asking questions about *you*.

Afterward, we'll analyze the problems posed by each question to see how they interact to form your basketball coaching philosophy—and in Sections 5 and 6 and we'll see how your answers to those questions can help you determine which offensive and defensive styles are best for your team.

THE HIGH-FIVE, IN-YOUR-FACE BASKETBALL COACHING PHILOSOPHY TEST

☐ ☐   1. Which do you consider to be more likely to happen: (a) players
A B   making good plays to win games, or (b) players making mistakes to lose games?

☐ ☐   2. Which is more important: (a) finding a style of play to fit your
A B   players, or (b) teaching your players a system that reflects your concept of how the game should be played?

☐ ☐   3. Which do you prefer: (a) a diverse offensive and defensive attack
A B   in which you change looks constantly to create confusion and keep opponents off-balance, or (b) would you rather do just two or three things and count on perfect execution to make them work?

☐ ☐   4. Assuming that you're going to win a game by 20 points anyway,
A B   which would you prefer: (a) scoring 100 points or more, or (b) holding your opponents to 36 points?

☐ ☐   5. Which do you prefer: (a) a loosely structured offense that offers
A B   players considerable freedom to use their creativity and individual initiative in setting up scoring opportunities, or (b) a patterned offense that generally limits and defines players' movements and shot selection?

Scoring: Give yourself one point for each **A** response and two points for each **B** response you checked.

If your score was 9–10 points: You function most comfortably (and probably most effectively as well) when you are controlling as many variables as possible. Your approach to coaching is basically conservative; that is, you take chances only when the odds are clearly in your favor, or when no better alternative is available. You prefer zone defense to man-to-man in most situations, and your teams are always solid defensively because you devote so much of your practice time to individual and team defense. You aren't really comfortable coaching superstars who require special treatment, and you don't encourage your players to take three-point shots. Your game plans are relatively simple; they don't change much from game to game. You probably consider yourself to be a better practice coach than a game coach due to the limited number of changes you're ready and willing to make and your steadfast belief that games are won or lost in daily practice. You do an outstanding job of building closely knit teams and getting the most out of players of average ability or below. You're probably also an excellent motivator.

If your score was 7–8 points: The key words that describe you are *adaptable* and *selective.* You likely have a broad understanding of the game and a practical approach to systems and styles of play. Given experienced players, your system tends to be complex: Offensively, you're likely to use either a freelance attack based on a simple pattern or a patterned attack with plenty of options and freelance possibilities; defensively, you tend to change looks frequently, whether to keep opponents guessing, to respond to certain offensive challenges or strategies, or to alter the mode of defensive attack. With less experienced players, you'd probably run a continuity offense and low-risk zone defense. You believe in fast-breaking, but you aren't fanatical about it: If it's three-on-three at the end of the break, you'd just as soon pull the ball out and set up in your half-court offense as force the ball inside without the advantage of numerical superiority.

If your score was 5–6 points: You're a "player's coach"; that is, your teams play a brand of offense and defense that your players like and your fans enjoy watching. You're basically a gambler who likes up-tempo basketball and doesn't mind seeing his defenders go for the steal or his shooters take the three-point shot when it's there; defensively, you prefer pressure man-to-man, run-and-jump, or at least aggressive zone defense such as trapping or help-and-recover. You're probably a very good game coach, especially when you have a point guard that you've trained to think like yourself. You're at your best coaching skilled, experienced players who function well in freelance offenses and aggressive, high-risk defenses. Your up-tempo playing style is a form of motivation in itself. You've been at your school for a number of years, or at least long enough to have developed program continuity to the point where you seldom lack effective leadership or skilled players.

You're also more likely to handle superstars or problem players effectively than coaches who are more conservative in their values and approach to coaching.

─────────────── **ANALYZING THE QUESTIONS** ───────────────

1. *Which do you consider to be more likely to happen, players making good plays to win games, or players making mistakes to lose games?*

The question we are really asking here is, "Are you basically aggressive or passive in your approach to winning games?"

As players, most of us probably favored an aggressive approach to playing the game; as coaches, our aggressive tendencies may be tempered by the fact that it's easier to lose games by making mistakes than it is to win games by making good plays or by *not* making mistakes, especially since we're counting on someone other than ourselves to make the play or avoid the mistake. Every coach ideally would prefer to win games than to back into victories by finding ways to avoid losing; still, a win is a win is a win, and most of us will take them however we can get them, short of asking the refs if they take Visa or MasterCard.

The fly in the ointment here is *pressure*: Some players respond well in pressure situations; others don't. But the problem we're exploring is, besides the clock and the crowd, whom do you prefer to apply offensive and defensive pressure to control games and their outcomes—your team or the opponents? The answer may not be quite as obvious as it appears at first glance.

If you'd rather go after opponents aggressively and relentlessly to force them into mistakes that they might not make otherwise, you're trying to win games—but you're also increasing the likelihood of mistakes by your own players that could lose games. For an aggressive strategy to succeed, you need players who are skilled enough to execute the strategy and experienced enough to handle the pressure—and you as coach need enough of the gambler's spirit to loosen the reins and let your players go for the win. It's not always an easy thing to do, especially if you believe that games are more often lost than won.

On the other hand, if you prefer to run a patient, ball-control offense, play cautious, basket-oriented defense, and wait for the opponents to make mistakes, you're trying not to lose games—but you're also giving opponents the opportunity to seize control of the game by pressuring you into mistakes.

There are, of course, combinations and variations of these approaches, depending on such factors as the score, time remaining, players in foul difficulty, relative ability of your players and the opponents to handle or apply pressure, and so on, but the basic premise still exists: With all other factors being equal, you either prefer a conservative, cautious approach that doesn't lose games, or you are willing to take chances in order to win games. In either case, your team's playing style should reflect your philosophy and preference.

2. *Which is more important, finding a style of play to fit your players, or teaching your players a system that reflects your concept of how the game should be played?*

If this were the SAT, NTE, or GRE, the correct response would be "finding a style of play to fit your players," a more educationally satisfying response than coldly fitting players into a system that does not take into account the unique nature of their needs and abilities. And if that were the case, one of the finest basketball coaches of all time, Indiana's Bob Knight, would miss the question because Coach Knight doesn't make broad changes in his basketball philosophy for anybody, not even Isiah Thomas.

Of course, there's nothing wrong with changing what you've been doing offensively or defensively, as long as the changes are made with the team's best interests in mind; still, by an overwhelming majority most coaches prefer to avoid making major changes in their playing style for any of several reasons. First, there's *compatibility*: If the coach fully understands and believes in a given style of play, he'll be more likely to make it work with his team than another playing style that he is less familiar with or has less confidence in. Second, there's *expedience*: If the players are already familiar with a playing style, it's easier and less time consuming to make adjustments in the basic pattern than to throw it all out and start over with a new and radically different set of patterns and playing style. Third, there's *consistency*: If you want your players to understand your system and your philosophy, you can't go around changing it every time you run across something new that sounds promising. And if you're using a total-program approach in which all of the schools in your feeder program are using your offenses and defenses, you have even more incentive to stay with what you're already doing for the sake of *continuity*.

3. *Which do you prefer: a diverse offensive and defensive attack in which you change looks constantly to create confusion and keep opponents off-balance, or would you rather just do two or three things and count on perfect execution to make them work?*

Our reason for including this question was to remind you that, regardless of your coaching philosophy, no offense or defense will be any more effective than the players who run it. The more experienced, highly skilled, and intelligent your players are, the more they will be able to absorb in terms of additions to their basic offenses and defenses—but the converse also applies. Your goal is to confuse the opponents, not your own players.

4. *Assuming that you're going to win a game by 20 points anyway, which*

would you prefer: scoring 100 points or more, or holding your opponents to 36 points?

No, there was no (c) "both" response to this question. Don't be greedy.

In one sense, this was a trick question—at least, tricky where sports reporters, fans, and others who don't know much about basketball coaching are concerned. We weren't asking whether you think good defense wins games; that's an indisputable fact. Both situations—scoring in triple figures and holding opponents to low scores—generally require effective defense. This question identifies the game tempo that you prefer—and the general offensive and defensive styles you'll need to achieve and maintain that tempo as well.

If you prefer an up-tempo game and scoring points by the bushel basketful, you'll want to fast-break practically every time you get your hands on the ball—and because you'll get the ball back quicker by stealing it or forcing a turnover than by waiting to rebound missed shots, you'll want to full-court press and use some kind of pressure man-to-man or aggressive half-court zone defense as well. Teams generally average scoring about one point for every shot per game; if you're intent on averaging in triple digits over an entire season, you're going to need to take about three shots a minute to do it. And because the opponents get the ball back every time you score, they'll average more ppg. than if you played at a slower tempo, regardless of how good your defense is. On the other hand, the slower and more deliberately you play offensively, the less points your opponents are likely to score. (That fact should come as no great surprise, since it's difficult for them to score when they don't have the ball.)

While trends for the present and the foreseeable future are toward up-tempo basketball, there's nothing wrong with slowing things down to a more manageable pace if that's your style—that is, as long as you've prepared your team in three respects:

- You absolutely *must* be prepared to deal with teams who play at a faster tempo, including beating their presses.
- Your players must understand your system thoroughly and be willing to play within its limitations, especially regarding freelancing and shot selection.
- Because your slower pace will tend to reduce both teams' scoring (and possibly the margin between the teams as well), your players must be prepared to handle the pressure of playing in close games: Since you won't blow out many opponents by averaging, say, 50 ppg. over an entire season, you'd better be ready to handle the nail-biters by finding ways to avoid losing games when you can't win them outright.

5. *Which do you prefer: a loosely structured offense that offers players considerable freedom to use their creativity and individual initiative in setting*

up scoring opportunities, or a patterned offense that generally limits and defines players' movements and shot selection?

Your answer to this question describes the amount of offensive control you prefer to exercise over your players; at the same time, it identifies the type of man-to-man offensive style that you'll be most comfortable with.

First, let's rule out the ridiculous: None of us wants to see our seven-feet-two-inch center putting up hook shots from the hash marks. Second, let's consider the obvious: Part of our response to this question likely will be dictated by our players' offensive talents and shooting ability. Still, we should be aware that setting (or not setting) limits on our players' shot selection and freelance offensive movement is a vital part of game preparation. To whatever extent we prefer not to control our players' offensive actions, whether individually or as a team, they will take it on themselves to explore and define their own shooting and ballhandling limitations with the eagerness of a teenager borrowing the family car for the first time. And that's why most coaches prefer to set some kind of limits, however broad, on what their players should and should not attempt to do offensively.

Shot Selection. At one end of the continuum are coaches who strictly define and delimit both where and how often their players are permitted to shoot. (The most obvious and familiar examples of this are calling a timeout to set up a last-second shot for the team's best shooter, and looking for layups in a spread-court delay offense such as the four corners.) Many coaches use spot-shooting drills in daily practices to familiarize players with the court positions where they are most likely to get shooting opportunities in games. When players spend considerable time rehearsing not just the shots they are most likely to take in specific areas of the court but also the moves and cuts that free them from defensive pressure at least momentarily, the resultant familiarity improves their concentration and confidence, which in turn increases their chances of making the shots in games.

Other benefits of restricted shot selection are likely to include improved offensive rebounding (because the player's teammates know when and from where he is most likely to shoot); improved court balance (for the same reason); and improved field-goal percentage (whether because your best shooters are taking most of the shots or your players understand the difference between low- and high-percentage shots. Knowing when *not* to shoot is just as important as knowing when to shoot).

At the other end of the shot selection continuum are coaches who, like ex-Denver Nuggets head coach Paul Westhead, prefer to give their players more or less unrestricted freedom in creating and taking shots from anywhere within the same zip code as the basket, as long as they run hard and keep the game's tempo at a triple-digit pace. Without going into the specifics of this revolutionary (and generally unpopular) concept at this point, we'll note that simply increasing the game tempo does not win games, nor does it necessarily yield triple-figure scores if you don't have the shooters to light up the scoreboard. And even in a completely unrestricted playing style, players should understand that *freedom entails responsibility.* They must be able to distinguish between good and bad shots as with any offensive style of play.

Precisely where your preferences lie along this continuum doesn't really matter, as long as you and your players are operating on the same wavelength. Regardless of your style of play, it is absolutely paramount that you teach your players to recognize low-and high-percentage scoring opportunities and to avoid them in the former case and take full advantage of them as they arise in the latter case.

Freelancing. At worst, freelancing can be a sign of lazy coaching: After all, how much coaching skill does it take to let players do whatever they want on offense, whenever they want to do it? Fortunately, such lazy coaches seldom win enough games to stay in the profession very long. (One wonders if they eventually become principals and urge their teachers to allow students to freelance in the classrooms.)

At best, freelancing—which, incidentally, refers to *unplanned offensive movements initiated spontaneously by one or more players*—creates problems for defenses that are seldom encountered in patterned offenses or set plays, due to the unpredictable nature of freelance basketball. (If that doesn't make sense, imagine yourself guarding Michael Jordan at a wing position, with the other eight players on the other side of the court.) Freelancing is almost an inevitable part of basketball offense, since practically every half-court situation eventually reduces to one-on-one confrontations between shooter and defender. Freelancing permits highly skilled players to express themselves creatively in one-on-one situations, but because it also tends to focus attention on individual achievement rather than team goals (although the two may overlap), most coaches prefer freelancing to occur within the context of a structured offense of some kind. Ultimately, the problem boils down to who will control the team's offensive flow and thrust, the coach or the players—and most coaches simply are unwilling to leave such important decisions entirely to the discretion of their players.

Patterned Offenses. If the very thought of freelancing ties your stomach in knots and leaves you drenched in cold sweat, the obvious alternative is *set plays* or a *continuity pattern.* Set plays are predetermined movement sequences designed to yield a scoring opportunity or otherwise benefit the offensive team; continuity patterns are set plays in which the movements may be repeated, first on one side of the court and then the other, without the players having to reset themselves in their original positions.

The chief advantage of using set plays or continuity offenses lies in their predictability, and thus their potential for being controlled by the coach. While freelance offenses are largely spontaneous, set plays or continuity patterns can be repeated as many times as necessary for the desired scoring situation to arise. And because predictability invites defensive overplaying to disrupt the pattern, continuity offenses feature individual options and automatics designed to attack the overplay or restore continuity to the pattern.

Set plays and continuity offenses also offer strong high-percentage shooting possibilities, and they are usually excellent choices for patient, ball-control teams and coaches who dislike taking chances. On the negative side, they are generally unsuited for up-tempo basketball because they seldom yield quick shots, and they offer far fewer opportunities to showcase the talents of superior individual players than most types of freelance or passing-game offenses.

SECTION 5

Finding the Best Offensive Style for Your Team

There's two things in coaching. One is winning, and the other is misery.

—*Chuck Knox*

PRIMARY OFFENSIVE CONSIDERATIONS

Whether constructing a house or building a basketball offense, it is important to start with a solid foundation. In basketball coaching, that foundation is your offensive philosophy, the way you think the game should be played.

As young coaches just starting out in the profession, we thought it was critical to our teams' success for us to control every possible offensive variable. In our philosophy, there was no room for mistakes because *mistakes lose games*, so we ran tightly controlled continuity patterns in which we knew exactly where every player was supposed to be throughout every second of the offense. We knew exactly what shots we wanted taken, who was to take them, and where they were to be taken from. Shot selection was a *very* high priority in our offensive philosophy, and so we agonized whenever anyone shot from farther out than fifteen feet because those were not high-percentage shots—and frankly, we didn't have a great deal of faith in our kids' ability to create their own shots.

We're older now, more experienced and hopefully wiser, and our offensive philosophy has changed considerably over the years. Kids are better prepared to do their own thing nowadays, partly because the game has changed and

41

partly because more kids are playing the game now, especially girls. And while we aren't ready to turn over the offense entirely to the players yet—we haven't loosened the reins *that* much—we now make a conscious effort to devise offensive schemes that enable our players to use their creativity and initiative to the fullest extent possible within the team context. (Twenty years ago we were teaching our players automatics designed to combat defensive overplaying and restore the continuity of our basic patterns; today we simply tell players, "Take it to the hole if you see daylight.")

Some things haven't changed, though.

- We still believe that it's important for a coach to settle on certain theories or principles to direct his thinking, lest he wander from one idea to another in a state of uncertainty.

- We still believe that a coach should select an offensive system that he has faith in and stick with it. He doesn't necessarily have to run the same patterns year after year, but the core of the offense should be retained, with variations added as necessary to deal with changing situations and different personnel. It is incredibly difficult to install a new offensive system in one year. To be frank, we doubt that most coaches could completely master a system that is entirely new to them in that short span—and their players would experience even more difficulty in making the adjustment successfully. Such dramatic changes should be undertaken only if no other course of action is likely to solve your program's offensive problems in the foreseeable future.

- We still believe that it's important for a coach to select an offensive style that complements his defensive style—that is, using an aggressive offensive style such as fast-breaking to complement an aggressive defensive style such as pressing, trapping, or pressure man-to-man; or using a passive, ball-control offensive style to complement a passive defensive style such as sagging or sinking man-to-man, or basic zone defense. For example—and this is purely an opinion—we feel that it is neither strategically wise nor entirely fair to one's players to expect them to give 110 percent in an aggressive, high-risk defensive style that is geared toward stealing the ball rather than protecting the basket, then turn around and expect them to slow their pace to a crawl in a patient, possession-oriented half-court offense. Either approach in itself is perfectly acceptable—but not when used together. They simply are not compatible.

——— BUILDING YOUR OFFENSE AROUND YOUR SCORER(S) ———

Let's start by clarifying the terms as we're using them. We define a *shooter* as a player who can make a reasonably high percentage of his open shots taken from wherever he prefers to shoot. Under that rather broad definition, except at the very lowest levels of rec basketball league play, virtually every team has at least one fairly competent shooter.

Shooting skill alone is not enough for a coach to build his offense around, however, because a capable defender can shut down a shooter who does not possess the complementary skills necessary to combat defensive pressure. Thus, we feel that offenses should be built around a team's *scorers*, not its shooters. In our scheme of things, a scorer is a player who is consistently capable of creating scoring opportunities for himself *and* his teammates.

In team terms, your scorers are the players you (and their teammates, as well) look to when crunch time arrives and you absolutely, positively, must have the points *now*, if not ten seconds ago. And because you look to those players when games are on the line because they're capable of delivering the goods under pressure, it's also natural to go to them as often as possible in your regular offense.

That's why we say that it's important to build your offense around your scorers.

What are the skills necessary for a player to become a consistently high scorer? First, of course, he must possess the shooter's touch and eye. Then, if he's a guard or a small forward, he must be able to (1) handle the ball well enough to penetrate the defense and create scoring opportunities, whether for himself or his teammates, and (2) create scoring opportunities for himself or his teammates *without* the ball, as by setting and using screens effectively.

If he's a center or a power forward, he must be able to (1) move effectively with *and* without the ball in the post area in setting up his shot or open shots for his teammates and (2) work the offensive boards for second- and third-shot opportunities.

Using Your Scorers to Best Advantage

In theory, at least, if you don't score, you won't win.[1] No matter how good your defense is, the principle is the same: You've got to find ways at least occasionally to "put the pill in the bucket," as Joe Dean referred to scoring, or you can forget about winning.

How you score the points is another thing entirely. Some teams rely heavily on outside shooting; some teams prefer an inside-oriented power game; some teams play to their transitional strengths; and some teams— those of championship caliber usually—are capable of winning games with any or all of the above. Which method you prefer depends on how many good shooters you have and the nature of their skills as well. Your job as coach is

---

[1]In fact, it usually takes a lot of scores to win. That's the difference between theory and practice.

to determine *who* your scorers are, and *where* and *how* they are most likely to score, then to devise an offensive system that creates maximum scoring opportunities for your best scorers in the areas of the court where they function most effectively.

• *No effective scorers.* If you have no consistently good shooters or scorers on your team—a not unheard of situation, especially on lower levels of play where youngsters are just starting out in basketball—your best bet is to either develop an effective transition game featuring hard-nosed defense that will yield layups and quick follow shots while you have numerical superiority at the end of fast breaks or use an inside-oriented offense to create scoring opportunities around the paint. (Regarding the latter: If your players can't make the perimeter shots they shouldn't be encouraged to take them, except possibly if you're very strong on the boards and plan to score via second and third shots. The thinking is, it's easier to make a ten-foot shot than it is to make a twenty-foot shot.)

A shuffle- or wheel-type continuity pattern offers four advantages for a weak-shooting team:

1. The shooting areas are predictable (and generally close to the basket), which enhances shot selection, offensive rebounding, and follow-up shots.

2. The constant movement and ball rotation tends to lull the defense into making halfhearted, automatic switches that can yield further short-range scoring opportunities.

3. The patterns themselves tend to slow down the game tempo—and with a weak-shooting team you *don't* want to become involved in high-scoring free-for-alls.

4. Although your players may miss most of their shots anyway—let's hope not!—you'll still benefit from increased fouls by the opponents if you go inside on them; after all, most players can easily be coached *not* to foul a shooter who is putting up bricks from three-point range if he's not going to make the shots anyway. (Your bonus here may be that, in defensing your inside-oriented game, the opponents' best big men may get in early foul trouble, which helps your team *and* hurts the opponents.)

• *One effective scorer.* Although you're better off if your team has *one* effective scorer than if it has none, you still face serious difficulties in generating any kind of consistently effective team offense. First, of course, you must devise an offensive style that gets the ball into your scorer's hands as often as possible—but you must do so in such a manner that the opponents cannot take away your offense by double- or triple-teaming him. (This was precisely the problem facing the New Orleans/Utah Jazz with Pete Maravich, and later on, the Chicago Bulls in Michael Jordan's early pro career.) Beyond that, however, you should also consider structuring your defense to keep your-scorer out of foul difficulty, whether by having him guard the opponents' weakest offensive threat or by "hiding" him in your zone defense (e.g., by putting him at the point in a 1–2–2 or 1–3–1 zone).

To protect your scorer from combination defenses or double-teaming, your offensive system must feature movement by at least four (and preferably five) players—and not just random movements such as clearouts, which would allow the defense to sag toward the scorer, but *purposeful* movements that constitute a threat to the defense, such as setting and using screens and cutting to openings or seams in the coverage.

For example, if you rely heavily on scoring from your post player, you'll probably want to restrict his movements to the area in and around the paint; if so, the other players' movements must be threatening enough to occupy their defenders' attention as mentioned previously. Without such purposeful movement by the other players in your offense, you can expect one of two things to happen: Either your "big man" will disappear from the offense for long stretches, or else his shooting will be confined largely to the perimeters of the half-court. And once the other opponents on your schedule discover that your offense can be shut down by sagging toward your scorer to double-team him whenever he gets the ball, every team you face will adopt that defensive style to shut him down.

If all of this seems to hint at the need for a continuity-type offense with constant movement and multiple shooting options—you're right, that's exactly the sort of pattern that a team with one good scorer needs. And while most continuity patterns offer shooting options for every player in turn, they can also be adapted to increase the number of options involving your shooter without having his teammates standing around idly watching the action.

A final note: If your one Great Scorer is a guard, you might want to consider using a double-stack offense such as the one used by Bob Cousy while he was coaching at Boston University (see Figure 5–1). While it normally appears as a series of set plays rather than as a repetitive continuity pattern, the double stack has three redeeming qualities that far outweigh any possible disadvantages: It guarantees one-on-one coverage of your guard, it offers penetration possibilities every time he has the ball, and it keeps at least two offensive players near the boards at all times.

Although space limitations prohibit exhaustive analysis of the double stack, all that's necessary at this point is to imagine your scoring guard with the ball in Figure 5–1. If the possibilities appear inviting, see *Basketball: Concepts and Techniques* (2nd. ed.) by the Cooz, Frank Power, and William Warren (Boston: Allyn & Bacon, 1983) for a more detailed analysis.

• *Two effective scorers.* The 1979 NCAA Championship game featured a team with one outstanding scorer—Indiana State's Larry Bird—facing a Michigan State squad with two outstanding scorers, Greg Kelser and Magic

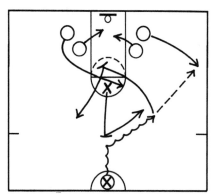

Figure 5–1 Double-Stack Offense,
Basic Movements

Johnson. And while the game was fairly close, it was hardly surprising that the Spartans won, 75–64, because it's easier to find a way to defense one high scorer than two.

Ideally, a two-scorer-oriented offense will feature the two scorers isolated with the ball and two defenders on one side of the court, with the other three players trying to look busy on weak side. (If that sounds familiar, it's because your favorite pro team, whichever one it is, uses that format almost exclusively in its half-court offense, thanks to the *illegal defense* rule that prohibits double-teaming the low post when the ball is established on one side of the court.)

Unfortunately for us as coaches, other levels of play contain no such built-in offensive advantages. If we try to emulate the pros' style, we're likely to find more manpower covering the ball side low post than we'd find guarding the crown jewels in the Tower of London. So we'll have to vary our attack somewhat—but how? The answer depends to a great extent on who our best scorers are.

With two scoring guards, your half-court offense may feature screens for the guards, splitting the post, or other movement sequences designed to maximize their scoring potential. If either or both of your scorers is a forward or center, you can use techniques such as inside screens, post interchanges, or a double-post alignment to get the ball to them near the basket.

There's one additional factor to consider in adopting or designing an offense around one or two effective scorers, namely, that your offense changes dramatically whenever one or both are on the bench. A two-scorer offense becomes a one-scorer (or no-scorer) offense, and a one-scorer offense limps along without a wing or a prayer until the other scorer's return. The way to handle the problem is to prepare for it in your daily practices by practicing *without* your scorer(s) in the lineup part of the time. You can't just pay lip service to this portion of your offensive preparation, either: Games will be won or lost by your team's ability to function at least temporarily on offense in your best player's absence, whether due to injury, fatigue, or foul difficulty.

• ***Three, four, or five effective scorers.*** You should consider yourself fortunate if you have three, four, or five players in your lineup who are consistently effective scorers; after all, most teams have only one or two players whom they look to consistently for point production.

Taking the situations in reverse order, with five scoring threats your greatest problem is likely to be keeping your individual players content with their reduced scoring production when they could be scoring more in a less talented lineup. (John Wooden has said that, with his best teams at UCLA, this was in fact the most difficult coaching problem he faced.)[2] When every player in the lineup is a scoring threat every time he touches the ball, players may become reluctant to give up the ball for fear that they won't get it back or receive their fair share of shots. Egos can become bruised, jealousies may fester and spread like untreated gangrene, and dissension and disharmony can destroy much of the team's championship potential.

The answer, of course, rests in the sort of program you've built (or are building). If from the very start you establish an atmosphere on your team in which players understand that their loyalty, support, and affection for their teammates is not just a nice-sounding phrase but an absolute requirement for making and remaining on the team, and is more important to you than winning or any individual skills the players may possess, you shouldn't have any serious problems with your five-star lineup. And if you *do* encounter irreconcilable differences of opinion along the way, you can still excel as a team with a three- or four-star lineup.

A five-star lineup will score consistently regardless of what offensive style you select. If your players are truly outstanding offensively, you could probably align them in a shotgun or punt formation without suffering any serious kind of offensive letdown.

Seriously, though, you'd want first to get your players in proper physical condition to win—Coach Wooden always wanted his teams in shape to play hard for five quarters, not four—second, teach them the movement sequences and rules governing a given passing game or freelance offense;[3] third, use drills and scrimmaging to practice the offense; and finally, sit back and watch the fireworks. Perhaps we've oversimplified the process a bit—after all, coaching basketball is never easy—but the fact remains: You won't spend many evenings burning the midnight oil trying to find an offense that will work when every player in your lineup can burn the nets with Wilson Jets.

---

[2]One year, Coach Wooden had *eight* former high school All-Americans on his UCLA team. And you thought *you* had problems?

[3]Of course, you can use any offense you like—but set plays and continuity patterns are probably too rigidly confining to use the players' talents to maximum advantage. The more highly skilled players are offensively, the more freedom they require to create scoring opportunities. Loosely structured offenses such as the passing game give them that freedom. Ask Dean Smith.

• *Four good scorers.* The same holds true for a lineup featuring four good scorers: With so many weapons in your arsenal, opponents will have great difficulty in matching up with you or hiding their weaknesses defensively, since in all likelihood their defensive strength is not as broad as your offensive strength. Your main offensive problems will be keeping your scorers happy and deciding how to use the nonshooter. For example, will you use him primarily in nonshooting roles such as setting screens and rotating the ball to weak side? Or use your regular offense without adaptations to compensate for his offensive shortcomings? Arguments can be made for and against both approaches; still, it's *your* team and your decision, and your wisest course of action is to do what you think is best for the team.

• *Three good scorers.* Under our original definition of a scorer as a player who consistently creates scoring opportunities for himself and/or his teammates, the only way a three-scorer lineup can hurt you is if all three of your scorers are big players and your guards are inexperienced or fundamentally weak. (If that's the case, your top priorities will be improving your guards' ballhandling skills and court awareness and finding ways to beat the presses and work the ball inside.) In other cases, the presence of three scorers in the lineup affords broad attacking potential throughout the half-court—provided, of course, that your patterns are designed to keep the ball in your scorers' hands as much as possible and in the areas of the court where they operate most effectively.

With a three-scorer lineup, we'd recommend using either a motion-oriented freelance offense or a continuity pattern modified to feature the three scorers—in both cases have the other players serve primarily in auxiliary roles. The surest path to winning lies in *doing things right*—not just in terms of avoiding mistakes, but also in creating problems for the defense that will cause *them* to make mistakes. Your scorers can accomplish both of those goals simultaneously—and consistently, as well—which is why your half-court offense should be built around them to the fullest extent possible.

Creating a Scoring Offense

In a broad sense, the easiest way to score consistently is to fast-break consistently. Within the narrower confines of a half-court offensive system, however, there are basically three ways of scoring: by driving, shooting over the opponents, and cutting and screening.

Driving Every team needs at least one player who is a strong threat to drive. Driving provides a sudden, direct assault on the basket *with the ball*; as a result, it places intense pressure, not just on individual defenders, but on the entire defensive team as well. Every drive undertaken by the offense requires quick, *correct* responses from the defenders or else the defensive structure will collapse.

There are several ways to create driving opportunities:

- Clearouts (i.e., players moving away from positions near the ball) create space for one-on-one confrontations along the perimeter.
- Screens on the ball may create favorable driving conditions by altering defensive matchups (e.g., a center covering a point guard) or rendering defensive players out of position to stop the penetration.
- Well-executed cuts or screens away from the ball always offer strong driving possibilities—assuming, of course, that the ball is delivered to the player at the point of attack before the defense can adjust to the movements.

Opportunities to drive should be an integral part of any offensive pattern, and players should know exactly when and where those opportunities will arise within the pattern. (They should also know where their teammates are when they're driving, since one or more defenders may converge on the ball to stop the drive.)

Shooting Over the Opponents Every offensive pattern contains shootover possibilities: Any time a defender plays off the ball far enough for a shot to be taken over him, he is essentially giving up the shot if the offensive player wants to take it. Players need to be told where their open shots are likely to occur within the pattern, they need to be drilled in spot shooting from those areas, and they need to be taught to distinguish between low- and high-percentage shots *for them*, both in the basic pattern and in freelance situations arising out of the pattern.

Cutting and Screening If there is a lost art in basketball, it has to be playing without the ball. While players generally enjoy performing ballhandling, passing, and shooting drills in daily practice, many of them are less highly motivated to work on phases of individual and team offense that involve playing without the ball, considering such time to be dead time. Certainly television deserves a share of the blame for this problem via the camera's relentless, unblinking focus on the ball; pro basketball hasn't helped the situation, either, with its no-zone defense rule virtually mandating the use of one-on-one and two-on-two ball-side confrontations while the rest of the offensive team stands idly watching and waiting for someone to shoot.[4] Whatever the causes may be, however, the net result—no pun intended—is to

---

[4]As Mr. Rogers might put it "Can you spell *b-o-r-i-n-g*?" The NBA hierarchy could solve the problem easily by allowing zone defenses and cutting back the shot clock to eighteen seconds. They won't do it, though, because the present constant parade of one-on-one and two-on-two matchups gives the superstars more scoring opportunities than they would get in a team-oriented half-court offense.

make our job more difficult. More than ever before, kids have to be motivated to move effectively without the ball in a half-court offense, whether to set up teammates' shots via clearouts or setting screens, or to create shots for themselves by cutting or using screens.

At any rate, players need to practice the various cutting and screening aspects of their team offense both in breakdown segments and within the overall pattern. The basic forms of cutting and screening are shown in Figure 5–2.

About the patterns shown in Figure 5–2:

- In the *pass-and-cut*, if 01 cuts away from the ball, 03, 04, or 05 could cut to the ball-side corner—or, 01 and 03 could simply interchange.
- The variation of the *give-and-go* shown here is Adolph Rupp's "guard around" sequence that his Kentucky Wildcats used with great success for four decades. It's basically a screen-and-roll—except that 01 creates the screen by cutting around 02.
- While 02's *clearout* move creates space for 01, 04's clearout move to the corner creates space for 05 in the lane after he screens for 03.
- A *seam* is the space between two or more defenders' zones of responsibility. Another common method of attacking the seams is for a ballhandler to dribble into the gap between two outside defenders, thus occupying both of them while he passes to an open teammate at the wing (see Figure 5–11, page 67).
- *Flashing* refers to any sudden or unexpected move into the lane or the pivot by a post man. Flashing is a simple and highly effective maneuver against either zone or man-to-man defense; practicing the movement from various ball positions should be a daily part of working with your big men and their inside moves.
- Although *splitting the post* isn't seen as much nowadays as it used to be because it brings three defenders near the ball, it still can be an effective offensive maneuver, especially when used to initiate a larger pattern such as a continuity offense.
- *Down screens* are presently in vogue in many types of offenses, especially freelancing. They can be used either to initiate an offensive sequence by creating a lead at the wing, or to get the ball to a big man near the basket. (Both techniques are shown.)
- *Post interchanges* are used to alter inside matchups against switching forms of man-to-man defense and to score easy buckets against teams that would rather fight through screens than use automatic switches.
- *Double screens* are a feature of several types of continuity offenses. (The direction of 03's cut around the double screen will depend, of course, on how his man plays him to defense his cut; in either case, he

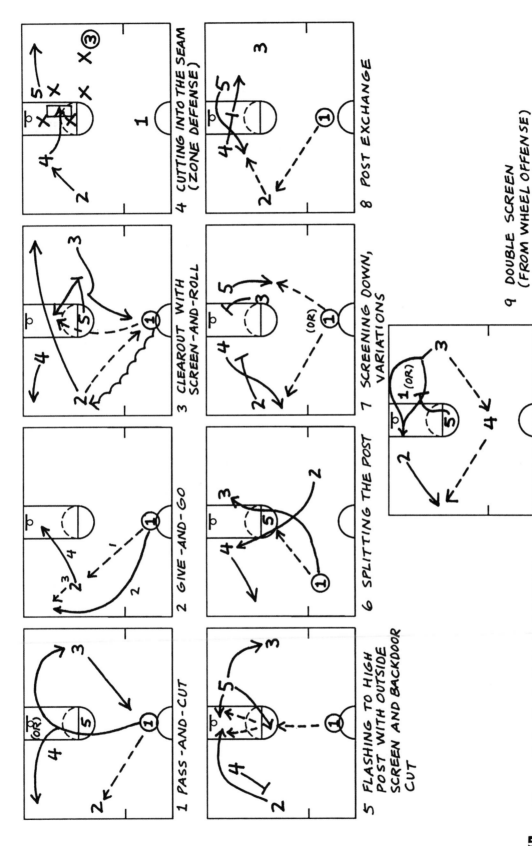

Figure 5-2 Basic Cuts and Screens

51

should drive his man into the double screen rather than simply using a "banana" route that allows his man to slide through.)

OTHER FACTORS TO BE CONSIDERED IN SELECTING AND USING AN OFFENSIVE SYSTEM

Speed

With a quick team, you should consider using an up-tempo playing style that not only enhances but magnifies the effects of your team speed. Using quickness in the form of pressing defense and fast-breaking like the James gang after a bank job can wear down opponents who are superior in other respects. Consider the following as our personal testimonial to speed:

In 1976–77, our high school girls' basketball team went 20–3 and averaged 76 ppg.—and our starting lineup measured 5'5", 5'4", 5'4", 5'3", and 5'2½". (And to compound the unbelievability of the situation, our team shooting from the field was a combined *36* percent for the season, and only *one* player on the squad was above 40 percent!) Those 76 ppg. were the result of averaging *54* steals and forced turnovers per game. When we weren't stealing the ball and making layups, we were putting up shots in our half-court offense that were as far off the mark as Iraqi SCUD missiles—but when you average a steal or forced turnover *every thirty-five-and-a-half seconds for an entire season*, you're bound to get a lot of high-percentage shots.

Oh, by the way. Those same girls won the state track title that year, including first-place finishes in the 50-, 100-, 220-, 440-, and 880-yard and mile relay running events.[5]

That's what speed can do for an otherwise mediocre team.

Thoughts concerning the proper use of team speed and quickness:

1. The greater your team speed, the more important it becomes to use it to control opponents, especially when your team height is no better than average.

2. Speed alone does not ensure effective fast-breaking. Equally important is your commitment to the idea of using fast-breaking as an integral part of your overall offensive system; without that commitment on your part (including daily in-depth instruction and drill in the various phases of the break), your players will never develop the kind of anticipation that regularly creates turnovers and fills the lanes before opponents can adjust to the transitions.

To put it more simply: *What you get out of fast-breaking will be a measure of what you put into it.* If you practice it occasionally, you should expect

---

[5]The GHSA switched to metric distances shortly thereafter.

it to work no more often than occasionally. If you practice it peripherally—that is, by using repetitive full-court fast-break drills purely for their conditioning value—fast-breaking will in all likelihood remain an unacceptably high-risk phase of your offense.

In terms of using your speed effectively on offense to dictate game tempo, it is important to fast-break every time you get the ball, because to whatever extent you fail to fast-break the tempo will be slowed accordingly.

    a. With a small, fast team look for quick shots off the break whenever you don't get the layup. Don't give the big defenders time to set up in the lane to block your shots or rebound your missed shots.

    b. If, for whatever reason, you're uncomfortable with the quick-shot strategy, at least use constant motion by all five players in your half-court offense to keep the opponents' big men busy. You *don't* want to allow them to rest in a lazy zone defense: The time to let them rest is when the game is over, after you've made them run eight or nine miles to keep up with everyone else.

When all five players move in a coordinated offensive attack, someone will be open. It then becomes a matter of *getting him the ball at the right time*. Timing is at the center of all offensive strategy.

In aligning your small, quick team, you should consider setting your center at high post, three to four feet outside the lane, to keep the middle open for driving and cutting.

3. While it's highly unlikely that a plow horse or a mule will ever win the Kentucky Derby, it *is* possible to improve players' quickness. Virtually every coach uses a variety of Pete Maravich–type ballhandling drills to improve players' manual dexterity, and reaction and anticipation drills to improve quickness. Maybe you can't make Secretariats out of slow-footed, heavy-handed plodders—but you can make them as fast, quick, and sure-handed as they can be within the limitations of their athletic potential, and if you've done that you don't have to apologize to anyone.

A lack of team speed and individual quickness can be as disastrous for a team as its presence is beneficial. Quick teams can press you and fast-break you to the brink of a nervous breakdown, and their high-speed attack can wear you down physically like a second job working in a coal mine. (If you're faster than I am, I'll have to work harder than you just to stay up with your cruising speed. And if *you* turn it up a notch and *I* turn it up a notch, *I'll* run out of notches long before *you* do—assuming, of course, that we're both in good shape.)

Thus, the moral of Aesop's fable about the tortoise and the hare: *Slow and steady wins the race.* It's the only way to deal with superior speed. Height alone won't do it, since the hares will try to keep the game in your backcourt, where your height advantage is more than offset by their speed. Shooting may not help much either, because the hares won't let you stationary shoot, and every time you put the ball on the floor they'll be after you like ants swarming over a wasp.

How, then, can a team cope with an opponent's superior speed? Here are a few suggestions:.

- Scouting can provide precise information as to how, where, and when the opponents will press you, and how they play their half-court defenses as well.
- In beating the presses—and in your half-court offense as well—keep your players spread and your dribbling to a minimum. Instead, use prearranged pass-and-cut techniques (i.e., quick passes to teammates cutting to openings or seams in the defense). Do not allow players to cross with the ball, and be very careful about passing to the corner or setting screens, either of which could set up defensive traps.
- In organizing your half-court offense, pay special attention to court balance and the utter necessity of keeping at least one—and possibly two—players in position to defense the opponents' transitions. (If one of your guards penetrates, for example, you may not be able to maintain a rebounding triangle under the boards; instead, one of your forwards may have to move outside with the other guard to offer court balance against the opponents' fast break.)

4. Finally—and most important of all—be aware at all times that *You cannot beat a superior running team at its own game.* The reason? Simply that they are more familiar with handling the pressures of high-speed basketball than your players are. You may get a few—or even a lot—of easy baskets for awhile if you adjust your tempo to theirs—but over the long haul they will make fewer mistakes and convert more fast-break opportunities than you will because the high-speed game is well within the limits of their comfort zone, both physically and mentally. And when your team reaches its own limits within that style of play and begins to backslide, your players will incorrectly assume that the solution to regaining their offensive touch lies in playing even faster, not in slowing down the tempo to a more reasonable level.

Playing out of control is like taking drugs: easy to start, incredibly difficult to stop.

Height

Although height is by no means the answer to every team's offensive prayers, it certainly helps to have an Andre the Giant or two prowling the paint at both ends of the court. Still, height must be used effectively or else it is wasted. (We once saw a high school team with a six-feet-seven-inch kid shooting fallaways from the corners and a six-feet-one-inch player in the pivot, and we thought we were seeing some kind of psychological experiment in role reversal. It's the same feeling we get whenever we see Patrick Ewing putting up outside jumpers like World B. Free: *Is that the way it's spozed to be?*)

There are only six possible height combinations a team can have on the court at one time. Since your team—and ours—falls somewhere within these borders, we'll consider the advantages, disadvantages, and offensive strategies compatible with each combination in turn.

(Note: While the word *tall* means whatever you want it to mean, we're using the term relative to your *opponents'* height, not your own team's: a 6'3" high school center might be considered tall by his teammates if everyone else on the team is 5'9" or smaller—but he's still small if most of the teams he faces have at least two players 6'5" or taller.)

• *Five small players.* We alluded to this type of lineup in the previous section dealing with speed. What we *didn't* mention in that analysis was that, if your five players are slow, too, your margin for error is as small as your lineup. With such a team, you should adopt a no-mistakes offensive style that emphasizes constant movement, patient shot selection, and precise execution in terms of passing, cutting, setting and using screens, court balance, and offensive rebounding. Even that may not be enough to pull you through, but it gives you your best chance for competing against taller, faster opponents.

Incidentally, there are two additional factors you need to consider in structuring your offensive rebounding scheme with a small, slow team: First, you may need to send just two, and not three, players to the boards when your opponents are a serious fast-breaking team; and second, teach your biggest player (or best jumper) to go weak side to rebound missed shots at your offensive end, since more errant field goal attempts are overshot than undershot.

• *Four-small, one-tall lineup.* First, try to keep the big player out of foul trouble. (On offense, teach him a variety of moves and fakes so he won't commit offensive fouls. Assign an assistant coach to work with him individually every day if he's awkward or inexperienced—or do it yourself if you don't have an assistant coach.) Second, keep him near the paint, especially if he's slow or relatively immobile. Use inside screens to alter unfavorable matchups. And third, use a motion-oriented offense featuring screens and cuts by all four of the small players; otherwise, the opponents will sag toward your big man and double-team on inside passes.

If you have one or more big players who are both aggressive and physically dominating, you should consider using an *inside power game* to take advantage of his or her skills in the pivot. While other forms of offense generally are geared toward movement and creating high-percentage shots, power game attacks are more basic: They attack the defense through the posts, where superior inside players can use their offensive skills to best advantage in one-on-one confrontations.

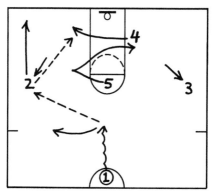

Figure 5–3   Power Game, Basic
Movements

The real beauty of a power-game attack—which, incidentally, can be run from *any* offensive alignment—is its simplicity: Instead of trying to confuse defenders with complex patterns or multiple cuts, the offensive team merely keeps its post players inside, moving around as necessary to achieve or maintain position on their defenders, while the other players move in more or less freelance fashion to improve passing angles inside and create space to eliminate double-teaming at the posts.

In the power sequence shown in Figure 5–3, all offensive movements are freelance except 2's flare to the corner after passing inside to 4 at low post. For example, 1 could have executed a pass-and-cut through the lane to weak side, with 3 filling at the point; 5 could have stayed at high post; 2 could have passed to 5 at high post; or 1 could have passed to 3 or to 5 at high post. (4's movement with either 1's or 2's pass to high post is keyed to the direction of 5's subsequent penetration.)

With the pass to 4 as shown, however, 2's flaring movement keeps his man from doubling down on 4—or sets up 2's baseline shot or drive via a return pass if his man tries to double-team 4.

On the pass to 4, 5 either stays at high post or flashes into the lane behind his man and clears to weak side if he doesn't get the pass: 5's options are keyed to what 4 does with the ball and how long it takes 4 to initiate his shot or movement into the lane.

For all their obvious strengths, power-game offenses contain one very large drawback, namely, that your big player (or players) must be aggressive and capable of taking advantage of the one-on-one confrontations that the offense creates for them near the basket, or else the offense will bog down into a series of meaningless perimeter passes and cuts that threaten nothing but the patience of the spectators in the stands.

• ***Three-small, two-tall or two-small, three-tall lineups.*** It hardly requires an understanding of Einstein's theory of relativity here to realize that these situations call for three- and two-guard lineups, respectively. Both

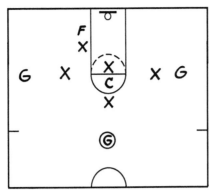

Figure 5–4 1–3–1 Offensive
Alignment

lineups offer vastly increased inside/outside versatility over teams with one tall player, or none, since it's possible with very little effort or imagination to devise an offensive scheme that keeps your big men constantly in favorable scoring and rebounding position.

A three-guard lineup is perfectly suited for fast-breaking, since it features an offensive mismatch every time that the defense fails to get three players back to stop the break. (The same is true of a two-guard lineup in which one or more of the forwards is capable of filling the third lane on the break.)

As far as half-court offense with a three-guard lineup is concerned, a 1–3–1 offensive alignment offers obvious possibilities for high–low post play (see Figure 5–4), while a 1–2–2 alignment features the big men even closer to the basket (see Figure 5–5). A 2–1–2 alignment is equally obvious as a means of initiating a two-guard offense, since it begins with the rebounding triangle already in place (see Figure 5–6). Of course, all of this changes when the ball becomes established on one side of the court and players initiate

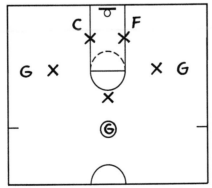

Figure 5–5 1–2–2 Offensive
Alignment

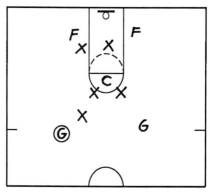

Figure 5–6   2–1–2 Offensive Alignment

their cuts, screens, and so on, but the principle remains: *Certain alignments facilitate certain moves.*[6] If you're running a passing-game offense, for example, the alignment will determine where the cuts, screens, and entry passes should occur.

Still, you may prefer a given pattern-oriented (as opposed to alignment-oriented) style such as a continuity offense, and that's all right, too. The important thing is to recognize your players' strengths—and their limitations—before you install any offensive system. Adopt a style, and adapt it as necessary to enhance your players' skills and hide their weaknesses. Using that basic principle as your guide, you won't go wrong in building your team offense.

Four-tall, one-small lineup. Assuming for the moment that your "small" player is a capable ballhandler who penetrates fairly well, and none of your "tall" players are mobile enough to function as a second guard, you might give some thought to the double-stack offense mentioned earlier in the section. (see Figure 5–1). Essentially, it's a variation of the basic 1–2–2 alignment shown in Figure 5–5, with the wings aligned at or near low post. Admittedly, the basic alignment has four defenders as well as four offensive players stationed near the basket—but if your four big men are bigger than their defenders, you'll win most of the battles under the boards.

Lest we do injustice to Coach Cousy's fine offense, we should point out that the double stack's versatility is by no means limited to the penetrating move and cuts to the wing and into the lane as shown in Figure 5–1. Indeed, the Cooz devised an elaborate system of set plays and options built around the double-stack alignment; and as Figure 5–7 shows, the basic alignment is in fact ideal for setting up a passing game offense.

---

[6]This is especially true regarding *set plays*, many of which feature screens, post interchanges, and the like, arising out of the basic alignment.

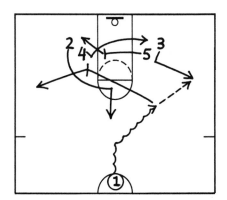

Figure 5-7   Double Stack to Passing
Game

Of course, if some of your tall players are capable of filling the shooting guard/small forward slots, your offensive capabilities expand accordingly. Add speed to that equation, and now we're talking championship potential. With tall, fast players, all that's necessary to win championships is good attitudes and work habits and the basic skills that you teach and drill your players in every day at practice.

Five tall players. The same principle applies to *all* tall, talented lineups:

> Teach 'em what they need to know,
> Then sit back and watch 'em go.

If your tall lineup is truly talented and athletic, your chief problem may be avoiding the tendency to over-coach them by using an intricately designed offensive pattern that, although it may be time-tested and highly effective in other situations, is too complex or confining to suit your players' needs and abilities. (Or if, as we are, you're a firm believer in teaching basketball's fundamentals, you may actually spend too much practice time refining the players' individual skills, when what they need is more time scrimmaging or working on aspects of their team play.)[7]

With five—or even four—tall, talented players in your lineup, teach them something simple offensively and let them use their height and athletic ability to overwhelm opponents. After all, gimmicks are necessary only when it's the *other team* who has the advantage.

On the other hand, it's hardly an exaggeration to say that most teams are not tall *and* talented throughout their lineup. Even with five seven-

---

[7]The rule here is that the more fundamentally sound a team is, the less practice time is necessary to maintain or improve those skills via individual drills.

footers in your lineup, you still have to beat the presses to score. That's why most tall teams have tall players warming the bench. If you decide to go with an all-skyscraper lineup, be sure that you're ready to deal with the presses and half-court pressure defense, because that's what opponents will use to compensate for their inability to match up with you defensively.

Court Balance

In developing any offensive system, one of the most important factors to be taken into account is court balance—the symmetrical arrangement of players within the half-court. There are three aspects of court balance to consider: horizontal balance (sideline to sideline), vertical balance (baseline to the center line), and inside–outside balance.

Horizontal balance. During a timeout, a middle-school player interrupted the coach to observe, "They've only got three players on my side of the court when I have the ball; why don't we put all five of our players on my side? That would give us more people than them, wouldn't it?" The coach patiently explained that when five offensive players are bunched together on one side of the court like baby chicks in a cardboard box they get in each other's way so much that it doesn't take all five defensive players to guard them. "Anyway," the coach concluded, "we have to consider rebounding, too: We need somebody on the other side of the basket when you shoot, to get the rebound in case you shoot too hard."

"Uh-uh," a teammate grumbled. "When *he* shoots, what we need is somebody in the *stands* to catch it!"

Vertical balance. This aspect of court balance refers to the necessity of keeping as few as one player (or possibly as many as three players) outside when shots are taken or players penetrate, to deal with the opponents' fast-break. How many players are necessary to provide vertical balance depends on the potency of the opponents' fast-break.

The only time vertical balance does not have to be taken into account is when, in the final seconds of a close game, the need for an offensive rebound and a quick score outweighs the threat of the opponents' fast-breaking. If you're going to lose anyway without the score, you might as well send all five players to the boards.

Inside–outside balance. As we just noted, the only time when all five players should go inside at the same time is when a team's chances of winning hinge on making its next attempt or putting in the follow shot. Similarly, the only time when all five players constitute an offensive threat from the perimeters of the offensive half-court is when they are using a four-corner type of slowdown or delay pattern to protect a lead. At other times such strategies are likely to be self-defeating because the tandem inside–outside scoring threat places far greater pressure on the defense than either one offers by itself.

Thus, the inside–outside principle as applied to team offense: Every scoring option within an offensive pattern should create pressure on the defense, inside and outside. How such pressure is created and applied depends on the pattern and the players involved, of course—but it must be there for that phase of the pattern to create problems for the defense.

A simple inside–outside technique that is used regularly in the pros is to clear out a side for a Dominique Wilkins–type of small forward to go one-on-one from the wing—in effect, having the player constitute *both* threats via the drive and layup or jumper.

More common, however, is the use of one or more post players as inside threats, with other players aligned in or filling perimeter openings via cuts, screens, and so on. While most coaches like to keep their big men near the basket to facilitate offensive rebounding, they also will not hesitate to post up a big guard (think: Magic Johnson) on a smaller defender if the defense does not adjust to it.

Post play. You must be able to go inside whenever it is to your advantage to do so—and even when it is *not* to your advantage you must maintain the inside threat by filling the post, or else the defense will take away your perimeter game as well.

Because the post threat is the most basic element of *any* team offense, players should be coached to feed the post at any time and from any position. The advantages of effective post play in a freelance offensive system are so obvious as to not require spelling out; in a controlled offense or continuity pattern, hitting the posts usually signals breaking the pattern to attack via freelance movements or automatics such as splitting the post or cutting back-door to the basket.

In developing inside–outside balance within a team offense, it is important to organize your rebounding so that your tall men or best jumpers are in position to go to the glass when shots are taken. It's not always easy to consider rebounding when you're devising offensive patterns, since creating high-percentage scoring opportunities is naturally a higher priority than planning ways to rebound missed shots; still, it must be done because offensive rebounding is too important to overlook. When players who are out of position try to rebound, the result is often unnecessary fouls.

The easiest solution to the problem is, of course, to keep the post man inside, combating overplaying by moving him around (e.g., flashing him to high post, using post interchanges, or setting inside screens) while the other players are occupied elsewhere with other aspects of the offense. Whatever offense is used, post play should not be overlooked, because the proximity of the posts to the basket means that an effective post man has a good chance to score any time he gets the ball, whether by high-percentage field-goal attempts or by free throws when he is fouled.

Perimeter play. In theory (but not in practice), it's easier for a player to make a ten-foot shot than it is for him to bury a twenty-footer. In fact, most players naturally prefer the longer shot, not just because it's crowd pleasing or worth three points, but also because the farther out you shoot from, the less likely you are to find a hand in your face as you go up to shoot. (And if a youngster happens to be a terrible shooter, the longer shot is less open to criticism if he misses it, since no one can be faulted for missing a three-point shot.)

Still, there's more to being a perimeter scoring threat than simply standing beyond the three-point line waiting for a teammate's pass. Players who are fortunate enough to be good perimeter shooters should be drilled constantly in ballhandling techniques that will expand their scoring opportunities. And in devising inside–outside threats within his half-court offense, a coach should be aware that any time a player cuts to the basket, the defense is necessarily compressed to some extent in covering the cut. The result of this momentary compression is an opening created *behind* the cutter. With the defense forced back, the outside shot can be taken from closer range and thus becomes a better-percentage shot than if no cut to the basket had occurred.

The same principle applies to setting and using screens: An outside shooter screening for a teammate who is cutting to the basket may find himself open if his defender has to help cover the cutter. And if the defenders switch, the shooter can roll to the basket, putting added pressure on the defender who has already switched once (X4 in Figure 5–8).

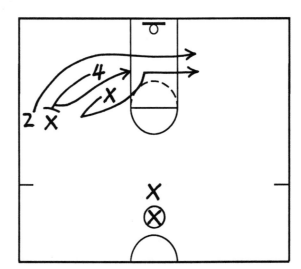

Figure 5–8 04 Rolling to the Basket
After Defensive Switch

DEVELOPING AN EFFECTIVE MAN-TO-MAN OFFENSE: FINAL THOUGHTS

In developing an all-purpose man-to-man offense, it is important to remember that different teams play their man-to-man defenses in different ways. Some teams apply pressure to the ball and primary passing lanes; others apply pressure to the ball but not elsewhere (sinking defense). Some stress sliding through screens; others use automatic switches. For your offense to function effectively against *all* of these styles, each phase or option of the pattern must be thoroughly tested and practiced against each of the defensive styles.

ATTACKING THE ZONE DEFENSES

To combat zone defenses effectively, you must first understand what teams hope to accomplish by using zone rather than man-to-man defense. After all, man-to-man is basketball's oldest and most basic form of defense—and given five skilled defenders working together it is also unquestionably the most effective defense in basketball. Such basketball coaching legends as John Wooden and Adolph Rupp absolutely refused to play half-court zone defense (although Wooden's full-court zone press was devastating, and in Rupp's later years at University of Kentucky he used what he called a "modified, stratified, parabolic man-to-man half-court defense").

The first clue as to why a team might prefer zone defense to man-to-man lies in the fact that *zone defense is basically negative*; that is, its use is dictated by the need to hide some kind of defensive problem or vulnerability that could render man-to-man defense less effective than zone defense.

A second clue regarding why teams use zone defense lies in the fact that *due to the nature of the zone concept, all zone defenses possess inherent weaknesses*. Those weaknesses may not always be readily apparent—they vary according to the style of zone defense being used—but they do exist. Such weaknesses might include lack of team speed or quickness, lack of playing experience or familiarity with the complexities of man-to-man defense, lack of height, one or more players in the lineup who are fundamentally weak defensively, or key players in foul difficulty. Whether your team is capable of exploiting such weaknesses is another story entirely; that's what the continuing search for effective zone offenses is all about.

But if zone defensive teams and the zone defenses themselves have built-in weaknesses (someone once asked in a basketball coaching class), that should make them easy to beat, right? Wrong. It's a tradeoff. Teams give up certain things in abandoning man-to-man defense—primarily, the ability to dictate ball and player movement—to gain other advantages that are more easily attained, and with less risk.

Principles and Techniques of Zone Offense

1. The best way to defeat a zone defense is to fast-break. Much of the effectiveness of any zone defense lies in the defensive players' ability to set themselves in predetermined positions to stop offensive thrusts within their zones. Fast-breaking reduces the defenders' preparedness by attacking them *before* the defense is set.

2. A zone offense must be broad enough in scope to feature different modes of attack arising from different areas of the court. This is because zone defenses can be played in several different ways. We'll have more to say about that later.

3. Neither ball movement nor player movement by itself will effectively attack a zone defense. This is because individual defenders and their zones constantly shift and change in relation to the ball. Both elements—ball *and* player movement—must occur to create any kind of meaningful threat to the defense. Holding the ball or dribbling around the perimeter while players cut requires only minor defensive adjustments to cover the ballhandler and the cutters, and passing the ball while the offensive players remain stationary permits defenders to shift quickly without confusing their responsibilities.

4. Zone offensive patterns should provide simultaneous inside–outside threats to the defense. Except for trapping defenses, *all* zone defenses are both ball oriented and basket oriented;[8] that is, while defenders are constantly adjusting their positions relative to the ball, their primary concern is defending the posts, lane, and basket. The result is defensive compression toward the basket area and lane. Spreading offensive players along the perimeters serves as a counterbalance to that compression by enlarging the individual defenders' areas of responsibility, sometimes to the extent of overextending the limits of their effective coverage.[9]

Spreading an offense can be achieved in either of two ways, by aligning the players along the perimeters or using cutters to create an overload on one side of the court. Both methods are shown in Figure 5–9.

There are countless ways to create an overload; how the movements are structured depends on (1) how many players will be involved in the overload, (2) which players you want to occupy the various positions in the overload, and (3) how many defenders shift to ball side with the wing pass. In the example shown in Figure 5–9, 05's cut to the ball-side high post or corner is usually predetermined by the particular pattern being used, but it can also be freelance in the sense of his cutting to high post *instead* of the corner if high post happens to be open. In either case, his movement and the pass to 02 establish a three-man overload on ball side, which will in turn require at

---

[8]Trapping defenses are ball oriented.

[9]Spreading the defense is also an effective way to combat trapping.

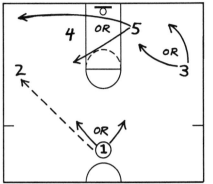

Figure 5–9 Simple Movement to Overload with Wing Pass

least three players to shift to ball side. Three defensive positions are predetermined and thus are entirely predictable: the wing, low post, and weak side must be covered regardless of how the rest of the defense is played. Most zone-defensive teams prefer to keep two players back to cover the rotation passes to weak side, but if you create a *four-player overload* (say, by cutting 05 to high post and sending 03 to the ball-side corner), they will adjust by bringing a fourth defender over. When that occurs, the remaining defender—X5 in Figure 5–9, usually one of their big men—may have great difficulty in containing the remaining weak-side player within his expanded area of responsibility.

Admittedly, the cross-court pass shown in Figure 5–10 is risky, but the rewards can be enormous if you have an excellent passer at 02 and an outstanding shooter at 01.

5. Send cutters through the zone defense or into its interior or seams. This serves to alter matchups as well as creating defensive confusion.

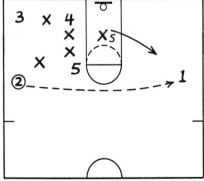

Figure 5–10 X5's Zone of Responsibility in a Four-Player Overload

Against man-to-man defense, altering inside matchups usually requires screening to force defenders to switch; against zone defense, however, all that's necessary is to interchange the two post men, since the switches are automatic.

Post interchanges are most effective against teams with a weak inside defender: Once you've identified the weak defender, match him up against your best inside or baseline scorer and work the ball to that scorer for the shot you want to take.

Cuts should be purposeful, not random. They can be made behind defenders to hide their movements or between defenders to attack the seams where defenders' responsibilities overlap. If two defenders converge on the cutter, someone else will be open elsewhere. Cuts to the weak-side perimeter should be followed by quick rotation passes around the zone—but not *through* it. Attempting to pass over a zone defense is inadvisable; attempting to pass through it is insane.

6. Attacking a zone defense requires rapid ball movement. It is difficult, if not actually impossible, to attack a good zone defense slowly. Once the defenders are set in their positions, quick ball movement via fast, accurate passes is the only way to force defenders out of position. Dribbling, holding the ball, or making long, looping passes allows the defenders ample time to shift, get set, and adjust to cutters into or through the defense. Rapid ball rotation, on the other hand, is always difficult to defense because the ball can be moved faster by passing than the defenders can move by sliding or running.

7. Zone offensive patterns should contain elements of continuity that permit a flow of ball and player movements without having to pause to reset the offense. Set plays have traditionally been an effective means of combating man-to-man defense, due largely to the ease with which they can be designed to attack a specific defensive weakness. Against zone defenses, however, set plays offer limited options to attack weaknesses that may be hidden within the zone coverage—and every time the offense pauses to reset itself, the defense will be doing the same thing. This gives the defenders an extra advantage, since they already begin with an initial edge: They don't have to worry about protecting the ball or committing turnovers while they're moving.

Another advantage of continuous ball movement is that, because the defenders' basic court positions and adjustment to other positions are prearranged and based on ball location, their movements also tend to become automatic as the ball and offensive players rotate from one side of the court to the other and back. The longer you move the ball, the greater your chances become of taking advantage of these patterned defensive movements by breaking your offensive pattern, especially by passing inside from the point as the ball rotates from one side of the court to the other. Players at the point should always glance inside before relaying the ball to weak side, and post men should always be prepared for the inside pass whenever they cut into or across the lane in ball rotation.

When the post man receives a pass in the lane or at the post, he must shoot quickly or pass outside to avoid double-teaming. Zone defenses are more post oriented than man-to-man defenses: Like bees swarming an intruder when their queen is threatened, zone defenders react quickly to inside threats. Thus, quick jump shots without fakes are more likely to succeed against zone defense than are hook shots, which require more preparation and space.

8. Dribbling is generally an ineffective method of dealing with zone defenses. As a means of moving the ball around the perimeter, dribbling is infinitely slower than passing the ball. And as a means of attacking the defense, if the dribbler happens to avoid double-teaming and beat his man, he still has to contend with the rest of the defense.

In fact, dribbling generally has only two effective usages within a zone offense, namely, resetting a pattern that has gone completely haywire or forcing a double-team so that a passing lane to a teammate can be created (called *pinching*) (see Figure 5–11).

9. Screening can sometimes free players for high-percentage shots. In the set play shown in Figure 5–12, 1 passes to 2 and moves to the edge of the free throw lane extended as the defense adjusts to ballside. 5 picks for 4 cutting across to weakside after 2's return pass to 1, and the ball is quickly rotated to 4 just outside the lane. Screening in the lane requires precise timing, since 4 will not be open if he cuts too soon and 5 must clear the lane quickly to avoid a three-second violation.

Other screens can be devised that occur outside the lane—for example, 2 and 4 setting a double screen on X4—but screening is generally less popular than other zone-offensive techniques due to the length of time required to hold the screen during ball rotation and defensive adjustment.

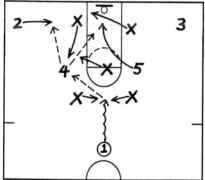

Figure 5–11 Pinching in the V Offense, Initial Moves

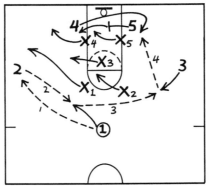

Figure 5-12 Screening in a Zone Offense, Set Play

10. Attacking a zone defense requires patience. As we mentioned earlier, all zone defenses have weaknesses of one kind or another. But while zone coverage concedes certain things, the defense is usually able to dictate what is given up, and where. In terms of shooting, the defense can pretty much dictate which shots they give up by the way they arrange their coverage. If, for example, a fundamentally weak defender is unable to seal off the ball-side low post, they'll double-team the post and reduce coverage somewhere else—say, the baseline if they don't think you can beat them from there, or the top of the circle if your point guard isn't a good outside shooter, or the weak side perimeter, and so on. But they won't concede that low post shot, no matter what else they have to give up.

Two salient points emerge from this analysis: First, since the chief priority of almost every form of zone defense is to keep the ball outside, they aren't likely to let you take the ball inside on them consistently; thus, to create any kind of continuing inside threat, your shooters must take—and *make*—outside shots at least occasionally. It's the *only* way to loosen up a tight zone defense.

Second, since the defense may be able to dictate where your shooting openings will arise (in the initial stages of your offense, anyway), your players should avoid the temptation to take the first available shot. Patient ball and player movement in your zone offensive pattern should create better shots for you than whatever shots the defense wants you to take.

—— MODIFYING YOUR OFFENSE TO FIT YOUR PERSONNEL ——

For years we've heard educators criticize rote learning—memorization through repetition—as an ineffective way of teaching, and we've wondered how so many otherwise intelligent people could be so wrong. We learn to walk through repetition. Doing reps—repetitions—in the weight room increases our strength. We acquire basketball skills in the same manner.

As coaches, everything we do in our daily practices is geared toward repetition, because repetition enhances neuromuscular efficiency. Using the whole-part method of teaching—showing the whole system, then breaking it down into its component parts—we teach our offenses and defenses through repetition.

As coaches, all of us are more or less at the mercy of the personnel on hand; thus, it is imperative for us to get the most out of the players we have. Players can be taught new skills, but they cannot be changed into something they are not. We can fit players into our offensive system up to a point—but we cannot completely change their playing style. We must also be realistic enough to modify our patterns or playing style to use our players' talents to best advantage. We can and should use the strengths that individual players have to offer; we cannot use as strengths abilities that they do not possess. Good coaches will use particular players to their best advantage by modifying the offense to exploit their unusual talents.

Basketball is a game of habits. We try to teach our players good habits while correcting any bad habits they might have acquired along the way. Offensively, shot selection is a habit—hopefully, a good one—but in team terms, at least, *execution* and *timing* are the two most important habits to establish.

Every offensive system is based on proper execution of fundamental skills to create scoring opportunities, and coordinating players' movements to get the ball to them *while they are open*. Teaching these aspects of any offensive system is time consuming, but it is also critical to the teams's success offensively. Modification and variations of basic offensive patterns require additional teaching time and can be achieved successfully only after the basic patterns are mastered.

Guidelines for Offensive System Modification

The previous line of reasoning introduces a key point: Because modifications are necessarily time-consuming, they should not be made frivolously. Every experienced coach has struggled with the question of whether or not to add a new option that could help the offense. If left unchecked, this natural tendency to improve an offense by constantly revising it can lead to confusion and chaos, especially when the players' notebooks have more offensive options, modifications, and keys than General Eisenhower's battle plans for Operation Overlord in World War II.[10] Thus, we offer five guidelines for modifying an offense:

---

[10]And need we point out that what looks like a beautiful pattern on paper can be a complete and utter flop when it is tested on the court with actual players rather than Os and Xs?

1. In a pattern offense, five options (with normal freelance opportunities off of each) are sufficient. Beyond that point, emphasis is focused on the options rather than on the scoring opportunities they are intended to create.

2. Be cautious about revising your basic offense. When you discover something new, study it at length and from every possible vantage point before trying to install it. (We usually wait several weeks, using that time as a "cooling off" period during which far more ideas are discarded than implemented.)

3. Consider each player's strengths and limitations in relation to his ability to execute the new pattern. Try to put yourself in his place in deciding how he will respond to his new assignment.

4. Try to avoid confusing the players. They must understand precisely what to do in the new pattern and then be drilled in it until they do not have to think about their movements and timing, but respond automatically out of habit.

5. Each option in a pattern must have its own signal or key—and each signal should be clearly distinct from the signals used to key other movements.

A PROGRAM APPROACH TO OFFENSE

Program is everything. (And, conversely, everything you do is your program.) Players win games, but programs win championships. Successful coaches keep on winning after key players graduate. Such coaches build winning programs the same way that successful artists paint masterpieces: with care and precision, one stroke at a time; with attention to detail and understanding of the elements involved. Luck can play a fleeting part in producing a superior program if you happen to have a Kareem Abdul-Jabbar or two somewhere along the way, but lasting achievement and success in coaching are more matters of skill than chance.

We noted earlier that it's important for a coach to select an offensive style that is compatible with his basic philosophy of how basketball should be played—and having made that decision, to stay with that basic style that he believes in. But let's take that concept a bit farther to see how it can be productive for a coach to stay with that basic system (including yearly modifications to suit his personnel) for, say, a decade or more.

Let's assume that you're enterprising enough to extend your program concept to include all of the schools (and recreation programs, as well) that make up your feeder system; what if all of the teams on those lower levels of play ran the same offenses, defenses, and drills that your varsity teams use? Would *that* simplify your coaching and speed up player development?

Think of the time you spend every year teaching the same old drills to new players coming up through your feeder program. It's not *wasted* time—well, not exactly—but it *is* time that could be spent doing other things if the players already knew your drills and understood both the terminology and the techniques involved in your team offense and defense.

The royal road to such good intentions begins and ends with communication between you and the coaches and players involved. First, tell the coaches involved what you want—a unified, cohesive program that produces superior basketball players and outstanding teams every year on *all* levels of play, not just at the varsity level—and then tell them how, by working with you, that process can be initiated and maintained. (The key words here are *with you*: If you approach the coaches in your feeder program with a "Here's-what-I-want-to-do-to-help-you" attitude, they'll listen—at least, the *good* ones will—and they'll appreciate your interest in their programs.)

What can you do to help the coaches in your feeder program? Well, for starters, your occasional presence even for a few minutes at their practices or games is visible evidence of your interest and support; it means a great deal to the players as well as the coaches. You can also speak at their awards banquets; provide coaching clinics on various aspects of your team preparation (drills, teaching techniques, team offenses and defenses, etc.); offer summer camps for the players, using the coaches as instructors; hold frequent get-togethers for the coaches (e.g., one night a week at a local steak house, which is budgeting money well spent); if you have a weekly radio program[11] you can occasionally invite those coaches to be your guests; you can have brief rec league, middle school, and/or junior high intrasquad scrimmage games or ballhandling exhibitions at halftimes of your home games; and most important of all, you can maintain positive lines of communication with the coaches by talking with them regularly about their problems—and by *listening* as well as talking. Communication is a two-way street.

Another important phase of the "we're-all-in-this-together" attitude that you're trying to create is to solicit the coaches' assistance with *your* program, too, whether by asking them to videotape varsity games, keep stats on the bench, call in scores to newspapers after games, scout opponents with or for you occasionally—at your expense, of course, not theirs—or even help with your varsity practices occasionally if you or your assistant coach are temporarily under the weather and there's no conflict in practice times with their own teams. If your feeder program is large, you can rotate your requests among the various coaches in turn. While their assistance may or may not prove invaluable, depending on the nature of the tasks and their ability to fulfill them, they probably will appreciate the opportunity to become involved in your varsity program. The only way to find out for sure is to ask them.

---

[11]Have you tried to get one? If not, do so. It's great p.r. for your program. If you've tried before, try again—but before you do, talk to a few local businessmen about sponsorship. It's not as hard to line up sponsors as you might think.

"But how [you may be asking yourself] am I supposed to get them to run my offenses and my defenses? What's to stop them from using a style of play that has absolutely nothing in common with what we're doing on the varsity level?" First, of course, you may be able to insinuate yourself into the process whereby new coaches are selected, which should give you a natural "in" here.[12] If not, well, in this case there may be another way to skin the cat. Let's answer the question indirectly by asking a few other questions.

1. How much time do you have to spend every basketball season revising your offenses and defenses, preparing practice schedules, and finding or creating drills to teach the fundamentals and your style of play? (Even a hastily contrived daily practice schedule without time allotments will take twenty to thirty minutes to prepare; doing a thorough job of preparation normally takes about ninety minutes daily.)

2. How much time would you have to spend doing all of those tasks if someone were to hold a series of Saturday morning coaching clinics during the spring or summer and teach you his *entire* offensive and defensive system, including all of the drills he uses, and give you a complete set of his daily practice schedules for the upcoming season, with time allotments, teaching hints, drills, and everything else you'll need to conduct your daily practices (including player notebooks for your players)? Would the prospect of saving about 150 hours of planning time every basketball season appeal to you? And would your players like to learn the offensive and defensive systems and drills now that they'll be using later when they get to high school?

Of course, it's not just a matter of going by the middle-school gym and just happening to ask the coach, "Oh, by the way. Here's a set of my practice schedules; how about running your program *my* way this season, just as a special favor to *me*?" We're referring, rather, to building positive relationships with all of the coaches in your feeder program—friendships and close working relationships that permit a continuing flow of ideas between you and every one of these coaches. If you don't have the kind of control within your system that permits you to dictate what offenses and defenses are used at the lower levels of play, persuasion in the form of the kinds of reciprocal assistance we described previously is the next best thing.

In a very real sense, we're talking about building the same sort of team spirit among the coaches in your feeder program that you create on your own teams. For example, we firmly believe that if your players know that you care

---

[12]Especially if you're the high school's or school system's athletic director. If your school or system already has an athletic director, make her your friend; if not, urge the creation of such a position and take it even if it's unpaid. What it doesn't pay in dollars may be more than compensated for in *control*.

about them personally as well as professionally they will consistently astonish and amaze you with the intensity of their work habits, loyalty, and determination to play the game however you want it played. If they know that you love them, they won't let you down.

That same principle is a cornerstone of all effective leadership: People will rise to your expectations when a personal relationship based on mutual respect has been established. On a strictly personal level, once the coaches—and their players as well, incidentally—understand that you're genuinely concerned about them (as opposed to using them purely for your own selfish interests), they will at least listen to what you have to say. And on a strictly professional level, once the coaches discover via your coaching clinics and your conversations with them that adopting your system can save them an incredible amount of time and energy in terms of daily preparation and planning, they'd be fools not to at least consider the merits of trying it out for at least one season.

When that happens, all that's left to do is to follow through on the promises you've made and be the kind of leader for them that you are for your players: Someone they can trust and count on to do what's best for them.

As any coach who has used a program approach will tell you, it's well worth the effort.

SECTION 6

Determining Which Defense Is Best for Your Team

You have to have the defense to start with because you have to keep from losing before you can win.

—*Paul "Bear" Bryant*[1]

It's easier to build a solid defense than it is to build a dependable offense, for two very good reasons: First, while shooting, dribbling, passing, and catching the basketball require a certain amount of hand–eye coordination, the only prerequisites for playing tough defense are receptivity to coaching and willingness to work hard. And second, it's easier to control opponents defensively than offensively because on defense you don't have to worry about protecting the ball or committing a turnover or violation.

In deciding what type of defense is best for your team, there are two areas of concern to be addressed: personnel considerations and personal philosophy.

---

[1]Paul W. Bryant and John Underwood, *Bear: The Hard Life and Good Times of Alabama's Coach Bryant.* (Boston: Little, Brown, 1974), p. 328.

75

—————————— **PERSONNEL CONSIDERATIONS** ——————————

Team Speed

Quickness is the single most important attribute a basketball team can have. In terms of game tempo, for example, it's easier to dominate slower opponents by outrunning them than it is to control faster opponents by playing at a deliberate pace. The tortoises may win battles every now and then, but the hares win most of the wars. Speed can offset superior height via fast-breaking and full-court pressing, and it can adversely affect opponents' shooting skills by denying the ball to good shooters or taking away their preferred shots.

With superior team speed, press opponents full-court using aggressive zone techniques to trap the dribbler. Use run-and-jump or turn-and-double (i.e., trapping) techniques if you prefer man-to-man pressing. Whichever you use, though, keep constant pressure on the ball. On a half-court basis, you can do whatever you want to defensively, given sufficient team speed. The greater your overall quickness, the more likely you are to steal the ball or force your opponents into mistakes or turnovers before they can get off a shot.

With average team speed, you might consider using half-court pressing defense. That way you won't get burned as badly when they beat your traps. By definition the term *average* refers to the middle range of abilities. Therefore, with, say, 40 percent to 60 percent of your opponents faster than you are you may prefer a generally passive, or protective, approach to team defense, or at least a defensive style that allows you to choose when you're aggressive and when you're not. (An excellent half-court defense of this sort is the 1–3–1 trap zone, in which traps are sprung only in certain areas such as one corner or the other. Another is matchup zone defense, which requires alert, basketball-wise players but may be played aggressively or passively.)

With poor team speed, use pressing defense sparingly and passively if at all, to slow down opponents or to give them something else to think about, a new look. With slow players, you're best advised to use zone defense, or at least a man-to-man with zone principles, in your half-court defense.

Height

Because most high school lineups do not feature six-feet-ten-inch players, coaches tend to build their teams around the skills and limitations of their tall players. For example, teams with one big man tend to play zone defense to (1) keep him inside for rebounding purposes, (2) curtail his range of movement to combat fatigue and/or immobility, and (3) provide defensive assistance to keep him out of foul trouble. The most notable exception to this tendency occurs when the big man's teammates are so quick, aggressive, and talented that it is affordable to risk the problems associated with his playing man-to-man defense.

While any team can use man-to-man defense, depending on such factors

Figure 6–1. ZONE-DEFENSIVE ALIGNMENT TENDENCIES

Type of Team	Zone Preferences (Reason)
5 small players	1–2–2 (Keeps 4 players inside for rebounding purposes)
1 tall player	2–1–2, 2–3, or 1–3–1 (big man is aligned in the middle and stays inside)
2 tall players	2–1–2, 2–3, 3–2, 1–2–2, or 1–3–1
3 tall players	2–1–2, 2–3, or 1–1–3
4 tall players	1–3–1 *trap zone* (tall players can play the passing lanes and force lob passes that facilitate trapping)
5 tall players	1–3–1, probably (this versatile alignment can be played in any of several ways to accommodate players' skills and limitations)

as coaching preferences and players' defensive skills or quickness, zone-defensive alignments tend to mirror the team's size (see Figure 6–1).

One way that many teams use their big man effectively is in covering the inbounds passer in full-court pressing defense, especially when the big man has a wingspan like a 747 jetliner.[2] And when the ball is rebounded successfully, the big man traps the receiver to repeat the process.

Experience

While the term *experience* may also encompass such factors as maturity, leadership, and the ability to remain calm in pressure situations, we're using it in the more basic sense of "familiarity with the team's defensive style of play." The more experienced the players are within a given defensive system, the more aggressively they will be able to play without losing control. For inexperienced players who still have to think about what to do before doing it, defense can be a mystery ranking up there with Stonehenge and the surface features of Jupiter. That's why inexperienced teams *always* use one form or another of passive defense. Toddlers learn to walk before they learn how to tap dance or run high hurdles.

---

[2]We had a junior high point guard who stood six feet one inch but played at six feet five inches because his arms were so long he could practically scratch his knees without bending over. He averaged three steals a game in our press *off inbounds passes alone!* (He wasn't really that good, of course: Great coaching was the only reason why the kid averaged 27 ppg. for the season.)

─────────────── **PERSONAL CONSIDERATIONS** ───────────────

Young coaches starting out in the profession tend to use styles of play that they are familiar with, without regard to personnel considerations. After a decade or more of coaching they may look back and wonder how they managed to survive those early years while they were learning what basketball and coaching is really all about. Their philosophies normally change—and broaden somewhat—over the years as they discover new and exciting ideas and approaches to the game. Practically the only thing that never changes for most good coaches is their commitment to defense as the bottom line where winning is concerned.

Defensively, basketball philosophy involves making decisions regarding four situations: whether to use an aggressive or passive playing style; whether to use zone or man-to-man defense; if using zone defense, what sort of alignment to use; and whether (or how) to press.

Aggressive vs. Passive Defenses

There are at least two ways to distinguish between these two general approaches to basketball defense:

1. Passive defenses are basket oriented; aggressive defenses are ball oriented. Passive defenses are designed to protect the posts and basket area from offensive attack by compressing individual defenders' areas of responsibility toward the posts and lane and away from the perimeters of the half-court. Aggressive defenses tend to focus on the ball, whether to influence it toward or away from certain areas or to take it away from the opponents before they can shoot it.

2. Passive defenses are reactive; aggressive defenses are active. This statement clearly reveals the difference in attitude and intent between the two defensive styles. Passive defenders are like medieval knights protecting their castle from enemy attack; aggressive defenders are those same knights storming the walls of an enemy's castle. One group waits to respond to whatever tactics the enemy adopts, and the other group tries to dominate or control the action by attacking the ballhandler and/or the most likely pass receivers.

Points to consider in adopting a passive or aggressive style of play:

- The success of any aggressive defensive style depends on three factors: team speed, the players' familiarity with the defense (including understanding their own roles within the larger framework of the team defense and being able to adapt to new situations without abandoning or weakening the average), and their desire to make the defense work through attentiveness and hard work. While the same also holds true for *all* defenses, it is critical in the case of aggressive defenses, since every physical or mental shortcoming dramatically increases the risk involved in playing that particular defensive style.

- Playing defense aggressively is not the same thing as using an aggressive defensive playing style: While the former refers to a level of intensity or concentration that *all* players should strive for on defense at all times, the latter refers to certain specific, high-risk defensive styles designed to force turnovers or take the ball away from the offense. You can make players aggressive defensively by using competitive drills involving rewards and punishments in your daily practices—but that doesn't necessarily mean that the players will function best under game conditions in an aggressive defensive style.

- Aggressive defensive styles cease to be aggressive when players have to think about what they are supposed to do before they do it.

- Aggressive defensive styles usually work best against slower teams, teams with weak ballhandling, or teams with limited depth. They are least likely to control teams with good overall speed and capable ballhandlers.

- Passive defenses may be used by any team—fast or slow, tall or short, experienced or inexperienced. Passive defensive styles are most effective for tall, slow teams or against teams with poor outside shooting, and are least effective in catch-up situations when the opponents would like to run out the clock to preserve a win.

To sum up: The overall strength of your team should dictate whether your basic defensive style is passive or aggressive. The stronger your team is, the more it stands to benefit from trying to win games via an aggressive playing style, since the players' skills will more than compensate for their occasional mistakes. Conversely, the weaker your team is, the more conservative your defense should be. As Bear Bryant liked to say, "If you cut down on your mistakes, you might be able to steal a win or two just by luck."

Zone vs. Man-to-Man Defense

We hardly think it's an exaggeration to say that the decision to use man-to-man or zone defense is one of the most critical options facing a coach: Although every zone defense contains elements of man-to-man coverage and vice versa, the two approaches to defense are so dissimilar, and so exclusive, that their usage should always be carefully studied and thought out beforehand.

Man-to-Man Defense—Strengths. Man-to-man is the only form of team defense that offers simultaneous inside–outside control possibilities and pressure. While this form is easily adaptable to passive defensive techniques, it also offers outstanding possibilities for aggressive play. In its aggressive form, it can be used to disrupt *any* offensive pattern or style of attack. Man-to-man coverage is as basic to basketball as blocking and tackling are to football, since all basketball defense eventually reduces to one-on-one confrontations. Man-to-man defensive responsibilities are generally more clear-cut, constant, and easily defined than zone defensive responsibilities. Man-to-man offers the best way to deal with delays, slowdowns, and freezes.

Where maintaining an up-tempo attack is concerned, man-to-man defense maintains more constant pressure on the offense than zone defense does. Due to the defensive concepts involved, someone is always open against zone coverage—not necessarily in prime scoring areas, but at least open somewhere along the perimeter. As a result, zone coverage tends to slow the tempo somewhat and permit the opponents' big men to catch their breath while their teammates pass and cut around the perimeter. Pressure man-to-man permits no such resting, since inside *and* perimeter passing lanes are denied.

To repeat: While you can fast-break from transition in *any* defense, you cannot dictate the tempo at both ends of the court by using a half-court zone defense.

Man-to-Man Defense—Limitations. Man-to-man coverage requires that all five players be fundamentally sound defensively, since even one weak link in the defensive chain can tax the other players to their limits and beyond. The physical demands of playing man-to-man defense are greater and more constant than those of zone defense. Slow teams are generally ineffective in man-to-man coverage, although rare exceptions exist. Man-to-man is generally less effective than zone defense in combating screens, covering cutters, and controlling superstar-caliber players. Rebounding is less organized in man-to-man than in zone defense since the big men, whose court positions are less static and predictable in man-to-man, can be drawn outside by cutters. Although pressure man-to-man offers excellent transition possibilities, fast breaks are difficult to organize because the players' locations relative to the lanes are not predictable. And if man-to-man defense fails to contain the opponents as a team's primary defense, switching to zone defense is unlikely to improve matters except in terms of slowing down the tempo. It's easier to switch from zone to man-to-man than the reverse.

Zone Defense—Strengths. The basic movements and responsibility relative to ball position in zone defense are easy to teach and easily learned by most players. Playing zone defense doesn't require highly skilled or experienced players, tall players, or even quick players. Zone coverage tends to keep the tall defenders inside, with additional manpower available to guard the posts and lane and reduce dribble-penetration possibilities. It can be used to hide certain individual or team weaknesses (e.g., players in foul trouble or weak in defensive fundamentals). Zone defense tends to slow down up-tempo offenses, while at the same time enabling a more organized transition from defense to offense because zone defense is position oriented rather than player oriented. Zone defense allows big men to rest when the ball is at the perimeter and no one is in their zones. It is an excellent defense against weak outside shooting, poor ballhandling, or teams that use screening or cutting patterns. Zone defenses are extremely versatile: Although certain alignments tend to enhance certain strategies (e.g., the 1–2–2 zone and rebounding, the 1–3–1 and trapping), zone coverage can literally be as varied as a coach's imagination or a team's needs. (A coach we know swears that his teams use his 1–2–2 zone defense in any of eleven different ways, depending on the game situation.) And whereas some strong defensive teams play man-to-man defense and others play zone, *all* weak defensive teams play zone. It's the only defense that gives weak teams any chance at all.

Zone Defense—Limitations. Although zone defense can be used to hide some of a team's weaknesses, it cannot hide all of them. Passive zone coverage can be played lazily, since defensive movements in response to ball rotation tend to become automatic and players get to rest when no one is in their zone. Whereas defensive matchups in man-to-man can be altered by the offensive team only by setting screens, all that's necessary to create favorable one-on-one matchups against zone defense is to send a cutter through the lane or interchange the posts.

Because areas away from the ball are left relatively unprotected, openings always exist somewhere in zone defenses, especially along the seams, where players' responsibilities overlap. Zone defenses are generally ineffective against good outside shooting and slowdowns and delays. While techniques such as overloading can create severe pressure on outnumbered ball-side defenders, weak-side defenders may have zones of responsibility stretching from the middle of the lane to the sideline.

CHOOSING THE RIGHT DEFENSE FOR YOUR TEAM

Having taken the previous information in this section (and Section 4 as well) into account in considering your team's defensive potential, you can put it all together by considering the breakdown of defensive styles in Figure 6–2; it's just a matter of identifying your preferences in relation to your team's needs, strengths, and limitations.

Passive Defenses

The best times to use a passive approach to team defense are when your players are unable to control either the ballhandler, the posts and lane area, or both through aggressive defensive techniques. It is also useful when you're

---

Figure 6–2. DEFENSIVE STYLES

I. PASSIVE DEFENSES
- A. Man-To-Man
  1. Sinking
  2. Switching
- B. Zone
  1. Basic
  2. Help-and-recover
  3. Matchup

II. AGGRESSIVE DEFENSES
- A. Pressure man-to-man
  1. Sideline-influence or funneling
  2. Run-and-jump
  3. Turn-and-double (trapping man-to-man)
  4. Sliding (fighting through screens)
- B. Zone
  1. Trapping
  2. Amoeba (matchup with pressure on ball)
  3. Combination (pressure man-to-man on certain player(s)

---

trying to protect a lead and prefer not to take chances. Conversely, the worst time to use passive defense is when your team is behind and trying to catch up, or at any other time when your chances of winning hinge on keeping a fast game tempo.

Assuming that a passive defensive style best fits your team's needs, the first two questions that need to be addressed are, Should we play man-to-man or zone? and Do we want to keep pressure on the ball or establish a defensive perimeter and wait for the ball to come to us? (The question of *whether* the posts and lane will be guarded is unimportant; the only question is *how* they will be guarded.)

Passive man-to-man defense is the safe way to use man-to-man techniques—at least, it's "safe" in the sense that it doesn't challenge the offensive team by taking away the perimeter passing lanes. We use sinking man-to-man at AUM: turning the offense to the middle (where help is available) but never letting players drive the middle. We play tight on the man with the ball and drop off as far as possible when away from the ball. Our normal front-line position is one step out to the top of the circle. Our post defenders front their men out to the notch and the weak side protects on the pass over to their post man.

We do *not*, however, use switching techniques to combat screens. We prefer to slide through and help so that we can maintain our defensive assignments. We feel that this style promotes aggressiveness on an individual basis and offers support on a team basis.

We used to play sideline-influence pressure man-to-man at AUM—but on the college level, at least, that style isn't really workable anymore, not with every kid you meet capable of executing 360 degree spin-dribbles with either hand and given that the last time a ref called a palming violation was in 1969. You just can't keep the dribbler from reversing to the middle, so we decided to do it the other way. We don't play it passively, of course—at least, not on an individual basis. You have to play aggressively within the context of whatever defense you're using to have any chance of being successful.

There are four ways to play passive zone defense: two basic styles, help-and-recover, and matchup.

With the exception of trapping and combination defenses, all zone defenses are virtually alike until the ball is established on one side of the court. Once that occurs, the two main considerations for teams using basic zone defenses are denying the offensive team access to ball side low post and keeping the ball away from high post and the lane area. All other areas of the half-court—including the ball side wing and corner, the top of the circle, and weak side—are less urgent concerns than defending the posts: That specific strategy defines the use of basic zone defense.

In Figure 6–3, the low post is single-guarded with the ball at the wing; in Figure 6–4, the low post is double-teamed and only one defender is back to guard weak side. (Both styles double-team low post with the corner pass as shown, since X2's sinking movement is both natural and easy.) Which style a coach selects depends on whether a single defender can contain the low-post man when the ball is at the wing. Double-teaming the low post virtually ensures control of that area in most cases—but it leaves weak side drastically undermanned when the ball is at the wing. Single-guarding low post as shown in Figure 6–3 is weaker on ball side (corner coverage is difficult) but stronger in terms of combating quick rotation passes to weak side.

Teams that use basic zone defense usually use *help-and-recover* tech-

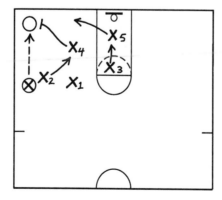

Figure 6–3. Low Post
Single-Guarded

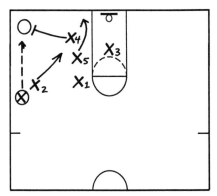

Figure 6–4. Low Post
Double-Guarded

niques to cover the rotation passes (see Figure 6–5). With two players to guard in Figure 6–5, the best X3 can hope for is to stall the point guard long enough to allow X1 to take over. X3 does this by taking a hard jab step toward the ball as the receiver catches it and squares to the basket. Then, in virtually the same motion, X3 retreats quickly toward the open player on weak side as X1 arrives to cover the receiver in case the relay pass is not made.

If you've never used help-and-recover techniques, you'd swear that they wouldn't work in a million years. Figure 6–5 does no justice to it because, frankly, help-and-recover looks lousy on paper. In practice, though, it can be a devastatingly effective form of outside coverage. After all, all that's necessary is to delay the pass receiver's penetration, rotation pass, or shot for even a part of a second for X1 to move into position.

Help-and-recover can be used effectively by any team, although experienced players will learn the techniques involved faster than neophytes. All that's necessary to practice it in breakdown form is to overload the weak-side

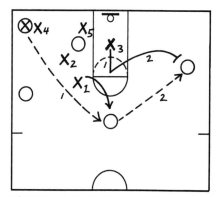

Figure 6–5. Help-and-Recover
Techniques

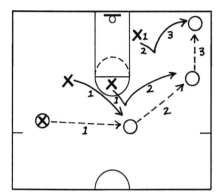

Figure 6–6. Weak-Side Overload

perimeter with more offensive players than defenders in a manner similar to that shown in Figure 6–6.

Matchup coverage is used by teams that like to play man-to-man type defense from the relative security of a zone alignment. In matchup defense, the initial defensive alignment shifts to match that of the offensive team (Figure 6–7), thus setting the matchups and defensive responsibilities. Although ball location along the perimeter does not affect the matchups, they usually change with every cutter into or through the zone in a manner similar to switching man-to-man defense. If the offense overloads with four players, the defense will have an equal number of defenders on ball side; if the overload features only three offensive players on ball side—say, at wing, low post, and the corner or high post—the defenders will keep two players back to guard the lane and cover weak side.

Matchup defense requires alert defenders who are capable of maintaining effective coverage in the face of constantly changing offensive alignments. It also requires that the players be fundamentally sound in man-to-man defensive techniques or else matching up will be useless. Inexperienced players may have to spend too much time thinking to make matchup coverage

Figure 6–7. Matchup Defense

practical—although in a sense *every* zone defense is a matchup defense, at least in terms of guarding the ball. It's the players and cutters who don't have the ball who make matchup defense difficult for beginners.

Still, you'll find that almost without exception, teams that play matchup defense are excellent defensive teams; after all, they wouldn't be matching up if they didn't think that the matchups favored their team. They could always use basic zone coverage or something else. Matchup zone defense is too difficult to be used frivolously.

Aggressive Defenses

Although all teams use one form or another of aggressive defense at least occasionally, not every team can or should use an aggressive defensive playing style on a regular basis. Aggressive playing styles are ball oriented, not basket oriented; whenever momentum toward the ball fails to contain the ball, the result is usually points on the scoreboard for the opponents. Aggressive defense is gambling defense—the defense is gambling that it can take the ball away via a turnover or steal before the offensive team can shoot— and the quicker and more highly skilled the defensive players are, the more likely the gamble is to pay off.

While game situations frequently dictate their use (e.g., combating delaying or slowdown tactics or trying to catch up when trailing on the scoreboard), aggressive defensive styles are simply too difficult and risky for many teams to use profitably. They are best used by players who are fundamentally sound, quick, and mentally aggressive. Given those attributes in sufficient abundance, the only question remaining for a coach to resolve is which style of aggressive defense is best for her team.

Perhaps somewhat surprisingly, the defining characteristic of *pressure man-to-man defensive styles* is not pressure on the ball, but instead the amount of pressure exerted on the next receivers along the perimeter passing lanes. *All* forms of team defense feature pressure on the posts, whether directly or inferentially[3]—and any defense can be modified to feature constant pressure on the ball. Such moves can hardly be said to entail any great risk. But when you take away the support personnel by sending defenders out to play the passing lanes, you're inviting a world of trouble if your on-the-ball defender cannot contain the ball by himself. Therein lies much of the risk involved in pressure man-to-man defense.

To stabilize the odds by reducing the offensive team's options and effective playing space, pressure man-to-man defense is generally played either of two ways, by influencing the ball toward one sideline or the other and denying penetration by dribbling or passing to the middle (see Figure 6–8), or by

---

[3]For example, by off-guards sinking toward high post in 2–1–2 zone coverage or players pinching in the middle to cover high post in 1–2–2 zone defense.

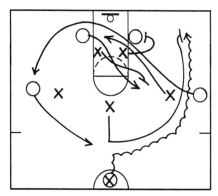

Figure 6–8. Containment

influencing the ball toward the middle without giving up the drive. Both styles are physically demanding and difficult to execute with precision. They require players who enjoy playing hard, are in superior condition physically, and take considerable pride in their ability to control opponents in one-on-one situations. And because stealing the ball is so much more easily achieved through pressure man-to-man defense than in most other forms of team defense, it is perfectly suited for up-tempo teams who like to fast break and maintain triple-digit scoring averages.

The greatest advantage of the sideline-influence style lies in its disruptive potential: No matter what the offensive team tries to run, the only avenues open to them will be dribbling toward the sideline or trying to pass to teammates cutting backdoor to the basket. All other passing lanes and dribbling routes will be overplayed and denied, including the posts. The greatest deterrents to its effective usage have been that, with spin-dribbling no longer a violation, it is difficult if not downright impossible to stop kids from reversing to the middle and attacking the defense at its weakest point; and that, without superior team speed on defense, neither the dribbler nor the lanes and posts could be controlled.[4]

At any rate, having influenced the dribbler one way or another or otherwise set him in motion, there are three aggressive methods of dealing with him. The defender can (1) contain him along the sideline or in the middle, which is what every coach prefers; (2) use run-and-jump techniques to stop

---

[4] Coach Bill Haubrich of Concorde High School in Concorde, New Hampshire, has suggested workable solutions to both of these problems in his book *DEFENSE WINS!!!*, by: (1) allowing the point guard to choose which way he wants to go before influencing his dribble toward the sideline, and (2) allowing perimeter passes that do not advance the ball closer to the basket or scoring position than it already was. With the addition of those simple, but certainly not minor, changes, Coach Haubrich has freed the sideline-influenced style from the speed prerequisite that had rendered it impractical for all but the quickest of teams.

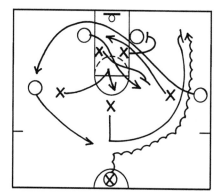

Figure 6–9. Run-and-Jump
Techniques

his advance; or cut him off and turn him toward a trapping teammate's double-team. The three techniques are shown in Figures 6–8, 6–9, and 6–10.

As is true of *help-and recover* and *trapping* techniques, *run-and-jump* defense doesn't look like much on paper, since at least one offensive player is always open while the technique is being applied. The defensive equalizer in all three techniques is the defenders' court awareness and familiarity with the process through long hours of intensive drill in specific situations in daily practice. The defenders know when and where the run-and-jump will be applied, for instance, and who shall apply it; the dribbler, driving headlong along the baseline toward the basket, has no such advance warning. He may be so preoccupied with the ball and his defender that he cannot see or react to the defensive switch in time to avoid a charging foul or turnover—and even if he does, he probably will be unable to find his open teammate in the heavy traffic around him. At any rate, he is dead in the water if he picks up his dribble.

What makes run-and-jump defense so effective is that it looks and is run exactly like trapping except that instead of setting the trap, the two defenders simply switch players—and if the dribbler slows down his drive to a con-

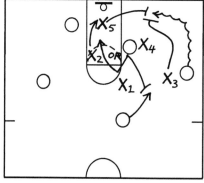

Figure 6–10. Double-Team Trap

trolled speed in anticipation of the run-and-jump, his defender should be able to stop his drive without resorting to run-and-jump at all.

Because only certain situations (e.g., full-court pressing man-to-man, defensing baseline drives) are conducive to run-and-jump, players must be experienced enough to recognize the situations appropriate for run-and-jump as they arise; skilled enough to perform the technique quickly, aggressively, and correctly; and smart enough to play effective man-to-man defense in all other situations. Using run-and-jump or turn-and-double (i.e., man-to-man trapping) techniques is the equivalent of using two defenses at once—the aggressive style combined with another, more basic form of man-to-man when the run-and-jump or turn-and-double cannot be applied. It takes intelligent players to recognize which technique should be applied in any given situation.

On a half-court basis, at least, *turn-and-double* is the most underused form of man-to-man defense, partly because double-teaming is riskier than the switching movement associated with run-and-jump, and partly because the court positions where traps can be sprung vary with the offensive patterns that each team runs. If you want to trap more often than occasionally in your half-court defense, the *best* way to do it is to use a 1–3–1 laning-zone alignment that literally forces teams to set up 2–1–2 if they want to avoid matching up with you and thus to set a player in the corner where he can be trapped (see Figure 6–11).

Still, *trapping* is undeniably the most aggressive defensive technique in basketball. If you play man-to-man with defensive players who are capable of trapping without getting beaten like water flooding through a screen door, we suggest that you simply substitute trapping in your run-and-jump situations. (Incidentally, how seriously you apply your turn-and-double will be shown by X1's response to the baseline drive in Figure 6–10: If he chooses the safer alternative—retreating to the lane and staying there to cover the weak-side perimeter pass—the turn-and-double will not contain the ball. Only by cutting off the primary ball-side passing lanes to high post and the wing can the defense realistically hope to cause a turnover or steal the ball.

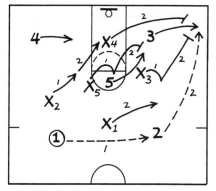

Figure 6–11. Trapping Movement

There are three possible ways to deal with screens, all of which are shown in Figure 6–12. Of the three, going behind the screen normally is least productive due to the distance it creates between the ballhandler and his defender; its only effective usage probably lies in situations in which the screen is set on weak side and the cutter is not an immediate threat to get the ball and score.

Regarding the other two methods, sliding through—the aggressive approach—is harder to do and carries greater risk of fouling but allows the defenders to maintain their original matchups. Switching—the passive approach—is easier to perform and may be either automatic or called. Unlike sliding through, switching techniques for combating screens can be learned quickly and easily by players at any stage of their development; whether they can handle the altered matchups is another question entirely.

During the 1963–64 college basketball season, coaches all over the nation watched in awe as an obvious impossibility became commonplace, culminating in UCLA's startling 98–83 dismantling of a very good Duke team, the first of ten NCAA titles for the Bruins in the twelve years between 1963 and 1975: Coaches discovered that it was possible for *three* defenders to guard *four* offensive players throughout 4700 square feet of floor space while the other two defenders were harassing the ballhandler. And if the intervening years since then and now have jaded your regard for the visionary aspects of that incredible discovery, all that's necessary to restore your respect is for you to sit down and diagram a full-court zone trapping situation in which none of the ballhandler's four teammates is wide open when the trap is sprung.

Precisely for the reason cited above, zone trapping styles and techniques still constitute a potent force on all levels of play even after all these years. Quick or slow, tall or short—teams of all kinds have trapped successfully; the only limiting factor in its usage appears to be *experience*. Since (as we've noted) a player is always open when the ballhandler is trapped, it is critical to the defensive team's success in trapping that every player carry out the duties and responsibilities of his position fully. Even a momentary lapse in

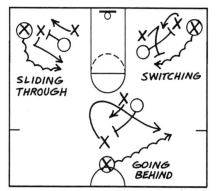

Figure 6–12. Dealing with Screens

concentration may be all that's necessary for the opponents to elude the trap and mount an offensive attack of their own. Thus, to reduce the odds against them, most trapping teams will do so only in certain situations, such as when the ball is in a certain location (e.g., the corner) or when a particular player has the ball. At other times they play their regular zone defense, whatever it may be, while waiting for the next trapping situation to arise.

The trapping movement shown in Figure 6–11 works best against a right-handed player; a left-hander would more likely be trapped successfully in the opposite baseline corner—assuming in both cases, of course, that X4 first denies the baseline drive, his second responsibility is to *turn the ballhandler away from the baseline and toward his trapping teammate* (X3 in Figure 6–11). At the same time, X1 moves in position to intercept any return pass to 2, X5 covers whatever ball-side cut 4 or 5 makes, and X2, who is responsible for both 4 and 1, watches how 3 responds to double coverage in the corner: If X4 turns 3 toward X3—or if 3 indicates by eye contact or arm movement that he is about to throw the diagonal crosscourt pass to 1—X2 will move out to intercept the pass. It's a gamble, of course: While 4 apparently is wide open at weak-side low post, his openness is largely illusory since X4, X5, 5, and the basket are all hindrances to 3's finding 4 and delivering the ball to him.

The laning process (e.g., X1 playing between 1 and 2 and X3 moving between 2 and 3 in the corner) is necessary to force lob passes that will give the defenders time to close the trap, which they could never do if the offensive players were allowed to use chest passes. Whenever the defense elects *not* to trap, they will maintain their laning techniques on ball side and sinking, or support, defense on weak side. As we've noted, they'll trap only when and where they feel the opponents are most vulnerable—usually, in the corner(s), where the passing angles are most confined, or when your weakest ballhandler has the ball. The one thing you can bank on is that they *won't* do it when or where you want them to.

The *amoeba defense* is essentially a combination of basic and matchup

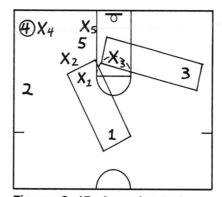

Figure 6–13. Amoeba Defense

zone defense with pressure applied to the ball. It can be a tenacious defense to deal with offensively when it is applied aggressively.

Like its namesake, the free-flowing amoeba defense changes its shape almost at will, not only in response to altered matchups or to intensify defensive pressure, but also to challenge the offense. For example, consider the defensive possibilities that arise with the pass to the corner in Figure 6–13:

1. It can be played as shown (which is basic zone defensive strategy).

2. Instead of dropping back to double-team at low point, X2 can double-team the ball in the corner with X4. (That would be trapping defense, not amoeba.)

3. X2 could stay out at the wing, forcing X4 to make the longer pass to the point or to weak side. (This is a favorite amoeba technique, inviting the long cross-court pass.)

4. X1 can cheat outside toward the passing lane with the return pass to the wing to disrupt or steal the rotation pass to the point (in which case X3 is responsible for high post and X5 will cover the weak side pass). Or X1 can simply stay at high post.

5. If X1 covers high post, X3 can slip outside to contest or steal the rotation pass from the wing to the point—or he may not. Amoeba coverage is flexible and based on keeping the offensive team off-balance. Even when players don't really intend to cut off passing lanes, they'll fake it every now and then just to keep the ballhandler guessing.

6. If necessary, help-and-recover techniques can be applied to slow down ball rotation to weak side long enough for the defense to adjust to the new matchups or restore the old ones.

7. No matter what kind of defensive techniques or strategy are used, the defense is already matched up: X4 and 4, X5 and 5, etc. (The coverage will change from matchup to basic when 4 passes back to 2.)

Only highly experienced, highly aggressive players who are thoroughly familiar with a broad range of zone-defensive techniques are capable of using amoeba defense to full advantage. It works best with quick, mobile defenders—what defense doesn't?—and at least two big men (one to guard low post and one to cover the corner, on each side). Its basic zone-defensive aspects do not suggest its use for teams of less than average height, since the inside matchups will likely favor the taller opponents. And while speed and quickness are valuable assets for any defensive team, they are not essential to success with amoeba defense, given adequate height to deal with opponents' inside games. In many cases, the unpredictability and seemingly haphazard nature of the coverage serves to make ballhandlers unduly cautious about their passing, thereby slowing down the offense accordingly.

Combination defenses are overrated. There, we've said it, and we're glad. If your team is good enough to play combination defense effectively it's also good enough to find ways to adjust your regular defense to the presence of one or two superior players, rather than wasting your valuable time teaching your players a defense that they won't use but once or twice a season.

Yeah, we know the arguments *for* using combination defense. It theoretically keeps the ball away from the opponents' best scorer—and when he gets the ball, he has to beat not only the man guarding him, but also the zone defenders as well. And it requires special preparation by the opponents to combat its effectiveness, too—or so the theory goes. But if special preparation is so important, why not make combination defense your *regular* defense? That way, you could guarantee that every opponent has to prepare differently for your team than for any other team on its schedule.

Here's the truth about combination defenses:

1. The "ball-denial" aspect works only when your man-to-man defender is at least as quick as the player he's guarding; the rest of the time, you can expect the defender to trail his man like a bloodhound following a week-old scent—and with about the same rate of success, too!

2. Even if you manage to largely eliminate the opponent's big scorer, your zone defense, which necessarily must be conscious at all times of the whereabouts of the scorer, likely will have gaps in its coverage that you could drive an eighteen-wheeler through. For one thing, the defenders' zones are larger than if all five of them were playing zone; as a result, it's easier to confuse the coverage by overloading or sending cutters into or through the seams; if (as is likely) the zone defenders stay inside to protect the lane and posts, the offensive team will get so many open fifteen-foot shots that they'll feel like they're having spot shooting drills; and if the zone defenders extend their coverage, they will be highly vulnerable to penetrating ballhandlers, given the expanded zones of responsibility.

The bottom line: Good teams don't need combination defense, and weak teams won't profit from the "quick fix" short-term aspect of using a gimmick defense—at least, not in the long run.

When all is said and done, the best thing you can do is teach your kids a defensive style that fits their talents and hides their individual weaknesses as much as possible and that you and they can believe in, whether it be a passive or aggressive defensive style, and hitch your wagon to *that* wishing star until such time as it becomes a reality for you and them. Don't waste your time and theirs working on gimmicks that they don't really need.

SECTION 7

Finances and Paperwork

You can only spend it once.

—The Basic Law of Budgets

Spiraling costs of athletic uniforms and equipment. Increases in ticket prices. Cutbacks in athletic funding and staffing for athletic teams.[1] Almost everywhere, tight budgets are making life uncomfortable for coaches and players alike. In most schools, the day is long past when the athletic department provides players with basketball shoes or gives senior players letter jackets; nowadays, players are lucky if they don't have to pay a participation fee of, say, $15 to $50 to be permitted to play for their school team.

The latter practice, although necessary at certain schools to help defray their athletic expenses, is particularly unfortunate because, while sympathetic fans or boosters may be willing to kick in the necessary bu¢k$ to subsidize superior, economically deprived athletes (especially on the varsity level), marginally skilled athletes on lower levels of play—say, third-string B-team or jayvee players—who also happen to be poor may not be so fortunate, having to forfeit their opportunity to play if they can't pay the fee. Anyway, it doesn't seem kosher to expect kids to pay for the honor of warming the bench during games, or for serving as student managers or student trainers.

Still, many coaches and players who have faced the dilemma will tell you

---

[1] In New York, only head coaches receive supplements; assistant coaches are unpaid volunteers, many of whom have no other connection with education beyond coaching. (Matt Winkeljohn, "Hyder: Budget-Cutting Widespread Problem," *Atlanta Journal–Constitution* [April 21, 1991], p. E24.)

95

that even $50 per player is a small price to pay when the alternative is dropping the basketball program altogether on the interscholastic level. Admittedly, it hasn't happened on a widespread basis yet because basketball, along with football, has traditionally been a revenue-producing sport that supports other sports. But if you think it can't happen because it hasn't happened already, you're like the nonswimmer who wasn't worried when his boat began taking on water because the leak was at the other end of the boat.

What can you do to avoid having your program become embroiled in financial difficulties? First and most important you should be aware of your school's, athletic program's, and basketball program's financial status, both now and for the foreseeable future.

In January 1991, Governor Zell Miller announced in his State of the State message that Georgia was in fine shape financially; by July 1991, plans were underway to fire hundreds of state employees as part of $600 million in cutbacks necessary for the state to meet its financial obligations without raising taxes. Burying your head in the sand may be all right for ostriches or earthworms—but not for governors or basketball coaches.

Along with knowing what's going on, you must be willing to be honest with yourself about your prospects for building or maintaining a strong program with acceptable continuity in terms of players, support personnel, and financial solvency. If you already have a strong program, then perhaps you don't have a great deal to worry about in this regard because you're already getting healthy fan support. Behind every successful interscholastic sports program in the U.S. are a good coach and the money brought in via admissions—the fans in the stands.

Fans everywhere want to back a winner, and they will turn out to support winning teams. If you can't build a winning program where you're at—or if you're already winning but not receiving the kind of support that's necessary to keep your team fiscally solvent—find a coaching job elsewhere. Life is too short to spend it trying to butt down doors that are six inches thick and padlocked on both sides.

FISCAL RESPONSIBILITY

Where finances are concerned, a fine line exists between responsibility and irresponsibility. Responsibility involves not just the ability to distinguish between *necessities* and *luxuries* in budgeting, but also deciding when quality is more important than cutting corners, and vice versa.

Example: Say $2,250 has been allocated for buying new uniforms. Do you buy: (1) ten full uniforms (home and away jerseys, home and away trunks, warmup top and pants) of proline quality at $225 per set, (2) twelve full uniforms of good but not superior quality at $187.50 per set, or (3) fifteen full uniforms of lesser quality at $150 per set? (Bear in mind that the number of uniforms determines the number of players you can dress out, not just this year, but every year until you buy more uniforms.)

When we were confronted with that problem, we immediately dismissed option (3)—and since we wanted a uniform that would last for five to seven years, we also eliminated option (2) as well. We ended up buying fifteen pro-line uniforms consisting of home and away jerseys, *one* pair of trunks that complemented both jerseys, and a warmup top (no pants). We considered it a successful compromise: Although we *wanted* the whole uniform, we got what we *needed* at the same price, without sacrificing quality.

PURCHASING/FINANCIAL GUIDELINES

1. Don't leave your program in the red at the end of the school year. Bear Bryant used to say that you should never leave a program when the talent has run out because it's not the classy thing to do. We always considered that statement to be hogwash; first, because there are so many reasons both positive and negative why a coach might decide to leave a school, and second, because every coach's first obligation should be to do what's best for himself or herself and his or her family, irrespective of available player talent or any other factor.

What we *do* think is important and classy, though, is to leave your program in sound financial shape. You don't owe it to the next coach to win games for him by developing a program that is so strong that he can't possibly find ways to lose games—but you owe him the courtesy of not having to pay off athletic debts that *you* created while coaching at that school. Aside from major projects such as the construction of a new gym or laying down a new floor or playing surface, it's not wise to incur large debts that can't be paid off by the end of the school year.

2. Don't make unauthorized purchases—ever. You may or may not be fired for losing games more consistently than certain people would like, but there's no uncertainty about the next statement: You *will* be fired for fiscal irresponsibility if it's discovered that your program is heavily in debt and you haven't been playing by the rules (i.e., requesting and receiving administrative approval) in your purchasing policies. People can stand poor coaching a whale of a lot longer than they can accept even the hint of a suggestion that a coach's fiscal high jinks are leading the school or its athletic program down the path toward financial disaster.

Most of the school systems that we're familiar with have adopted policies requiring purchase orders to be signed by specific administrative officials (e.g., the athletic director or principal) before purchases of athletic equipment or materials can be made. Some systems do not reimburse their employees for articles bought without a purchase order, considering such purchases to be personal expenditures.

Know the policies you're working under before you go shopping—and never exceed the limits of your athletic budget. Whether it's one $1,000 purchase or a thousand different $1 purchases, it's all the same if you're $1,000 over your budget.

3. You don't need first-class plane tickets to get from Minneapolis to St. Paul. (All that's necessary is a single step, since their city limits adjoin.) You don't always need the very best of everything for your program, either. Uniforms, shoes, basketballs, and athletic tape are four areas where we think it pays off to go first class; in staying overnight on the road, however, lodgings at, say, a Day's Inn or Marriott Courtyard will be just as comfortable as those of, say, a top-of-the-line hotel such as a Marriott Marquis—and at far more affordable prices.

4. Don't expect to buy first-rate quality products at third-rate quantity prices. Admittedly, the quality/quantity problem can be vexing. And because quantity and quality are, in many cases, mutually exclusive where cost is concerned, our guideline is to shop for bargains where quantity is a higher priority than quality, and buy name brands when buying, say, uniforms or basketball shoes.

Name brands often are no better than other brands where quality is concerned—and they're always more expensive than the lesser-known brands—but what you're really getting for that extra money is not just merchandise from an established, reputable firm but also assurance that problems with the merchandise will be resolved quickly—without hassles, delays, or unexpected announcements such as "We regret to inform you that the jersey you sent us cannot be replaced because that line of clothing has been discontinued by our company." Providing a quality product and reliable, prompt, hassle-free service is how firms become established as "name brands" in the first place. All the advertising dollars in the universe cannot compensate for an inferior product or erratic service policies.

As for other, non-name-brand merchandise—well, the Latin phrase *caveat emptor* ("Let the buyer beware") was coined for precisely such situations.[2] The importance of high-quality, professionally fitted basketball shoes cannot possibly be overstated; but on the other hand, is it really important to consider name brands in buying towels, air freshener, shoe laces, basketball nets, or the like?

Always return defective equipment promptly. Save all receipts, bills, guarantees, and so on. In this, the era of *planned obsolescence* in which manufac-

---

[2]A friend of ours bought a cute little red Italian sports car—and later, when he tried to order touch-up paint, the dealer had to order it from Italy. The whole process of getting the paint took a year, by which time the car's original color had faded from red to orange.

turers purposely design products with a built in longevity of fifteen minutes longer than the warranty that covers them, we're lucky if new basketballs don't literally come apart at the seams even before they're fully inflated.[3] Damaged or defective equipment should be returned promptly, together with copies of receipts, bills, invoices, and the like, when dealing directly with supply houses rather than going through local or area sporting goods retailers.

FUND RAISING

We cannot stress the point often enough: *The proper function of coaches is coaching.* If you had wanted to become a professional fund raiser, you'd have gone to work for Jerry Lewis or one of the political parties. Unfortunately, though, fund raising is usually required in most schools to offset whatever gaps and limitations exist in a school, sport, or athletic department's budget.

The best solution to the problem is, of course, to have a dynamic, actively involved booster club, whether specifically for basketball or covering several (or all) sports. When confined to either or both of their two valid functions, raising funds to supplement the basketball program and offering moral support for the team, booster clubs can exert a highly positive influence on a team or sports program.

If you have an active booster club in your school, be grateful for it. In its absence, the head coach or athletic director must function as chief fund raiser. Work with the members of your booster club and support their efforts to enhance your program—but *don't* let them run your program or influence your coaching. You're better off not having a booster club at all than to be answerable to its members for the way you coach your team or the decisions you make. (A coaching acquaintance once turned down use of a rent-free house and complimentary car in his new job because of strings attached to them by their donors, the basketball boosters. It was, he said, a classic case of the Golden Rule in action: they had the gold, so they wanted to make the rules.)

Your booster club can become affiliated with Booster Clubs of America, by writing to that organization at 200 Castlewood Road, North Palm Beach, FL 33408. The club's regular newsletters keep members abreast of current financial trends and developments in athletic programs across the nation and offer a wealth of ideas and resources for money-making strategies and techniques.

---

[3]Considering the rapidity with which the leather strips peel off at the edges in many new expensive, game-quality basketballs, we've privately wondered if the sporting goods manufacturers aren't using the same glue that the U.S. Postal Service uses on its stamps.

Fund-Raising Guidelines

1. Plan early and carefully—and apply early, especially if other groups will have similar fund raisers. In many schools, a given club, organization, or sport is allowed to undertake a maximum of *one* fund raiser per year. Such a strategy is hardly surprising, since a large high school may have fifteen to twenty-five different sports teams alone, to say nothing of the various other clubs and organizations in the school, many of which will want to raise funds to finance their activities during the year.

Thus, careful planning and early application to whatever approving agency is used for this purpose (e.g., principal, Board of Education) is mandatory. Successful fund-raising groups suggest that the best approach is to select an activity that can be repeated year after year.

2. Be sure that the activity doesn't violate local or state laws, or educational guidelines. Selling candy to students at school, or installing candy or soft drink vending machines in hallways or the gymnasium, may violate state nutritional standards; and charging admission for students to attend a movie on school time—which is what *we* used to do back in the good old days because high schoolers would pay *any* amount to get out of class, especially to sit in the dark with their boyfriends and girlfriends for ninety minutes—may not be acceptable under state standards, either.

3. Be aware that, in most cases, you have to spend money to make money. The ideal, of course, is a totally profitable activity with nothing invested but time and effort—but there just aren't many such activities. If you're going to sell bumper stickers, for example, you're going to have to *buy* them before you can sell them.

Fund-Raising Activities

The Booster Clubs of America is far better equipped to arm you with viable money-making projects than we are. Our intention here is simply to alert you to the various types of projects that you might use:

- *Continuing projects (projects that you can pursue year-round):* collecting aluminum cans (and possibly newspapers) for recycling.

- *Basketball-/or athletics-related activities:* offering season tickets at reduced prices; selling reserved seats in designated areas with owner's name painted on the seat; selling chances at games to win prizes by making shots from various distances; sponsoring a schoolwide (or even community-wide) "hot shot" type contest, or one-on-one, two-on-two, or three-on-three tournaments, or free-throw contests—all with awards for winners and entry fees for all contestants, of course (varsity and/or jayvee players not allowed in one-on-one, two-on-two, etc.); soliciting pledges to support a marathon basketball game; renting out wall space in the gym for advertising;[4] selling basketball or athletic spirit T-shirts, sweatshirts, license plates, bumper stickers, or other promotional items; sponsoring dances after Friday night home games; having a "roast" for a local sports celebrity and inviting well-known local, state, and professional athletes or celebrities to participate; auctioning off old game films at class reunions; and auctioning off sports gear that has been used, worn, or autographed by well-known sports figures.

- *Group sales/activities:* selling candy, doughnuts, pizza, flowers, or school promotional items such as key chains, pennants, magnetic note holders, or other novelties; holding barbecue, spaghetti, or pancake suppers; and sponsoring activities such as car washes, and cake or cookie sales.

FINDING WORKERS

In a sense, the healthiness of a given basketball program can be gauged by the number of workers and amount of services involved in the coach's efforts to administer his program. A listing of his auxiliary workers and tasks might include:

- Medical personnel (team physician, team dentist, team chiropractor, team trainer, at least one student trainer, emergency medical personnel)
- Scorebook keeper (for home and away games)
- Clock operator (home games only)
- Public address announcer
- Concession stand/ticket sales and collection.[5] Your best bet here is to have the basketball booster club in charge—or in the absence of a viable booster club, to have the athletic director administer the concession stand and ticket sales. That way, at least, the profits stay in the athletic program (which is not the case if, say, the PTA or another school-affiliated club operates the concession stand). Other methods that we've seen include: a school requirement that every faculty member sign up to work at least two basketball home games; paying faculty members to work voluntarily; and athletic department policy requiring players' parents or guardians to sign up to work at one or two home games. Cleaning up is usually done the next morning due to the late hour at which games are completed and the slow rate at which fans vacate the bleachers.

---

[4]May be unlawful if state funds were used to build the gym.

[5]A reproducible worker master list and sign-up sheet are included in the Appendix.

What you want to avoid at all costs is having to find the concession and ticket workers yourself. We can tell you from experience, it's a difficult and frustrating task that detracts from your preparation time for upcoming games, no matter how organized you think you are. People back out at the last minute—or else they don't show up at all—and in either case it's an aggravation that you should avoid if at all possible.

- Security officer. In times like these, having an off-duty police officer on the premises before, during, and after games is money well spent. Referees control games; police officers or deputies control rowdies, troublemakers, and drunks. (Standard fee usually is about what you pay each referee, less mileage.)

- Statisticians. We use student managers to keep stats. It's just an idiosyncrasy of ours, but we wouldn't think of asking an assistant coach to keep stats. (In situations where our managers have been unable to keep stats, we've used jayvee or B-team players.) We simply feel that the proper function of coaches is coaching, not keeping stats.

- VCR operator. A manager can do it—but because we're talking major bucks if the VCR camera happens to suffer damage, you may prefer to have an adult take the responsibility for filming your games.

- Bus driver. We quit driving athletic buses for good the night when, absorbed in our mental preparations for the upcoming game, we drove the varsity bus through two red lights and a railroad crossing in Louisville, Georgia, without slowing down or even looking either way.

PAPERWORK

As a coach, you're expected to be a leader, motivator, teacher, counselor, parent pro tem, tactician, and scout—but there is one other role you must fill that may be the most important role of all, namely, that of *administrator*. As head coach, you bear ultimate responsibility for seeing that what needs to be done, gets done.

Administration is likely the least exciting and most thankless part of a coach's job: If done well, no one notices that you've done it at all; if done poorly, everyone finds out about it when the feces eventually hits the ventilator.

The abbreviated nature of this section in no way diminishes the role of paperwork in a basketball coach's daily life: Many of the coach's paperwork responsibilities (e.g., preparing scouting schedules, scouting reports, game plans, daily practice schedules) are addressed in other sections of this book.

Insurance

"It was my first day of coaching," the veteran high school coach told us, "and although I was only twenty-two years old I already had it firmly established in my mind that I was gonna be the toughest, hardest-nosed [expletive deleted] ever to coach basketball. So I set out the very first day trying to make Bobby Knight look like Shirley Temple. I mean, I even had last year's returning managers running wind sprints and suicides after practice.

"It wasn't long before I noticed that one of the managers, this sickly looking, puny little guy, was sucking for air like a beached fish, and the next thing I knew he'd slowed down to a walk in the middle of a suicide. I decided to make an example of him right then and there and show the others how mean I could be when I got riled. So I ran over and got in the kid's face and started yelling I don't know what all kind of nonsense at him, and pretty soon my face was as red as his was. He took it, though, and just stood there quietly with his head hanging down and a hand pressed against his heaving chest while I roared and bellowed at him. Finally, a player came over and tapped me on the shoulder. When I turned to see what he wanted the player leaned over and whispered in my ear, 'Uh, Coach, you may not know this, but he's had open-heart surgery three times.'

"You know," the coach went on, "it's true what they say about things like your life flashing before your eyes in moments like that. Only what I thought of was Jerry Clower's friend Marcel Ledbetter, up there in that tree with a bobcat and hollerin' for somebody on the ground to shoot up at them through the darkness because one of them needed some relief. I just knew that, if the kid didn't keel over and die, *I* was going to. Overcoming the urge to pick him up and carry him, I casually suggested that we walk over to the bench and discuss his problem.

"As it turned out, he hadn't mentioned his heart problem because I hadn't asked, and when we started running he thought he could handle it.

"Turned out that he had insurance, too. That was good news. The bad news was, I hadn't even bothered to ask if any of the kids were covered by insurance. It was a scary way for me to learn a very important lesson during my very first day as a basketball coach. I've made a million mistakes in my coaching over the years since then—but I've never made that one again. Believe me, once was enough. *Nobody* practices until I find out that they're insured."

A reproducible insurance coverage verification form for parents is located in the Appendix.

Physicals

The same applies to physicals, of course. The quick and easy way to do it is to schedule a time before practice begins that's acceptable to the team physician when you can load up the players on a bus and take the whole kit and kaboodle of them for checkups and flu shots—coaches, managers, trainers, cheerleaders, and all of the players on the girls' and boys' teams.

Because our state simply requires a physical examination but does not offer a standardized form or specify precisely what it should consist of, we haven't bothered to create a form for the doctor and nurses to fill out; instead, we simply use the doctor's standard physical examination form, the same one he uses for workers who are required to have annual physicals. Copies of the physical results are kept on file at the school.

Player Information Sheets

Basic information about individual players should be compiled and updated every year by the players. In addition to providing information about how to contact players at home or where to find them at school, information sheets can, when combined with stat sheets from last year or the season in progress, provide background data for use in media guides or athletic profiles in local or school newspapers.

A reproducible "Player Information Sheet" appears in the Appendix.

Classroom Progress Reports

There are two sides to the question of whether (or how closely) to monitor players' classroom performances. Of course, monitoring on a regular basis (say, weekly) *does* tend to identify grade slippage in a given course before the grade can plummet or bottom out—which in turn may provide time to remedy the situation by one means or another. But on the other hand, some teachers may resent the work involved in filling out the progress reports—which usually is minimal—or worse, they may use the threat of poor reports to browbeat certain athletes, especially if behavioral difficulties are involved. Finally, we've all known teachers who resent *all* athletes (and coaches as well); giving such teachers student progress reports to fill out likely will produce nothing more revealing than the depth of the teacher's bitterness, disgust, or dislike for athletes or sports in general. (But at least you'll have the evidence in writing if the teacher's comments are too stridently negative, malicious, or personal.)

At any rate, we've included a reproducible "Classroom Progress Report" in the Appendix.

Incidentally, while we're on the subject of grades and studying here's a nice twist to the idea of conducting afternoon study halls for basketball players while they're waiting for other team practices to conclude: At Griffin (GA) High School, student athletes of both sexes arrive at school an hour early every morning to tutor other athletes whose progress reports or report cards indicate that they need extra help. The program is not confined to one sport, but is open to all athletes in the school.

Student athletes helping student athletes . . . an unbeatable combination!

Eligibility Reports

Every state high school association has its own eligibility reporting format. In Georgia, individual and team eligibility information must be filed with the state office at least two weeks prior to the team's first game. That information includes a team roster and individual forms listing specific background information about any new players who have not already had eligibility reports filed on their behalf at that school, whether in basketball or in any other sport or extracurricular activity governed by the GHSA.

About those forms: List returning players on the team form by using last year's eligibility sheets as a guide. Double-check both the team and individual forms for factual and spelling accuracy, because there is absolutely *no* margin for error here. Any sort of mistake—even a typographical error—will result in the form being returned with the player in question marked *INDEFI-NITELY INELIGIBLE*.[6] A factual error, if deemed to have been done maliciously for purposes of deception, can result in a coach's being suspended from his coaching activities by the state association for a period of up to several years. And even if it was an honest mistake, if you waited until the last minute to file your report you'll have to file a corrected report (and possibly hand-deliver it to the state office as well) to correct the error and restore the player's eligibility before the first game.

Game Contracts

The various state high school associations produce and distribute their own game contract and player eligibility forms. Where game contracts are concerned, your most pressing need is to understand that such contracts have the same degree of validity within your state association as your contract to buy a car has with your local and state government. You're bound by the terms of the contract; failure to comply with or fulfill the contract can bring stiff fines and suspensions. You may be able to get away with occasional mistakes in scheduling non-revenue-producing sports—once, on our way to play a road baseball game, we passed the other team's bus taking them to play at *our* place—but if a basketball team fails to show up for a game (or worse, forfeits an unfinished game by walking off the court and quitting before the game is concluded), you can expect to find the school being fined (up to $2,500 in GA)

---

[6]One year a player of ours was declared ineligible because his name was listed out of alphabetical order on the team form. We made the correction in time . . . but you see the problem involved.

and someone's hide nailed to the wall unless the offending coach provides a compelling reason for his failure to fulfill the contract.[7] It won't be *your* hide baking in the sun if you pay attention to every detail of the contracts.

When you prepare contracts, you should carefully check the locations and dates against the calendar at least twice before signing them, taking them to the principal for his or her signature, and then mailing them yourself; and when the other coach prepares the contracts, you should check the information at least three or four times before completing the signings and returning one copy to the other school.

If you've never filled out a game contract before, there are only two areas that are not self-explanatory: (1) In the space allotted for financial terms or agreement write "Home and Home," which stipulates that, while the visiting team is responsible for its own travel and other expenses, the home school will retain all monies collected via gate and concessions and will be responsible for all game-related debts such as paying the game officials; and (2) in the space allotted for officials, simply write the initials of your state high school association to indicate that the referees will be registered and certified by that governing body. It is acceptable—although unnecessary—to name the specific officials' association (e.g., Montgomery Co. Officials' Assn.) in your game contracts.

Scheduling

There are a lot of factors to consider in preparing a season schedule. First and most important, *start early* because it can be a laborious, time-consuming process. League opponents are mandatory, and because league games determine postseason standings and matchups they should be given scheduling priority over nonleague games. Most coaches like to play a few games against nonleague opponents before embarking on their league schedule.

In scheduling nonleague opponents, factors that may affect priorities include long-standing rivalries, travel distance involved, conflicting open dates, potential gate (Will they bring a large number of fans—paying customers—with them?), and competitiveness (the stronger a team is expected to be, the stronger its schedule should be and vice versa).[8]

As we've indicated elsewhere, we hope you don't have to find workers to sell tickets and run the concession stand at your home games—but in case you do, we've included reproducible forms in the Appendix to help you keep up with who's signed up to work which games. (*Note:* You'll have to fill in your home schedule on the sheets and then reproduce copies of the pages with

---

[7]A game may be cancelled—or shortened—without penalty if both schools agree to it.

[8]The "Scouting Schedule" (Figure 10–1 and in the Appendix in reproducible format) may also be used in scheduling opponents for next season, in a manner similar to that described in constructing a scouting schedule.

schedules on the individual sign-up sheet. The same individual sheet with your *road* schedule on it can be used for bus drivers if you don't have the same driver every time.)

Scheduling gym use at the high school level normally does not entail any great difficulties—at least, it hasn't for us. Top priority always goes to varsity home games, of course—but that's usually no problem since most jayvee teams have the same game nights as the varsity, following the familiar 4:00–5:30–7:00–8:30 format. If the school happens to have B teams as well, the B-team games and practice schedules can be coordinated with those of the junior high teams.

Prioritizing daily practice times among the jayvee girls' team varsity girls' team, jayvee boys' team and varsity boys can follow the game-day format of ninety minutes of daily practice for each team—but we've never liked the idea of students practicing basketball at night if it can be avoided. And while after-school study halls can make a plus out of what we think is a potentially negative situation, our particular solution to the problem has been to combine the jayvee/varsity practices into two two-hour time slots.

You may or may not agree, but we *like* the idea of having the two girls or boys teams practicing together at the same time at opposite ends of the court, especially if the gym is equipped with four side goals for separate full-court practice. It takes precise planning, coordination, and coaches working together to avoid mix-ups and communication problems, but hey, isn't that what we're supposed to be doing anyway? The only problem we ever had was that, occasionally in dual full-court scrimmaging, players on one court would react to whistles on the other court. But the instant access to the jayvee squad can be a definite plus for the varsity players, particularly in terms of trying out new plays, techniques, or skills and seeing how they are intended to work (which isn't always the case when opposition is provided by other varsity players who already know how the play goes and thus can find subtle ways to counter it by overplaying). The jayvee players benefit similarly by their daily interaction with the varsity players, both in terms of watching superior players execute skills and techniques with precision and in seeing the intensity with which the varsity players apply themselves to daily practice.

In a nutshell: If you're constantly around good people who have good work habits, you'll probably develop good work habits yourself. However, it works in reverse regarding varsity players whose influence, effort, and attitude is negative: If you have players like that on your varsity, you probably *won't* want the teams to practice together, at least not until such time as you can get rid of the rotten apples in your bunch.

Inventory

Every school system has its own equipment inventory form; the one we've provided in reproducible form in the Appendix is typical.

Computers

The old saying "To err is human; to really foul things up, you need a computer" notwithstanding, computers are playing an ever larger and more important role in today's world. Computer games, business computers, personal computers, word processors—all are having a profound effect on our lives. In kindergartens across the nation, youngsters are learning how to use computers, not merely as a means of playing Nintendo™ games but as functional learning tools as well. Computers provide fast and accurate computations and analyses of complex problems, and their enormous storage capability and fast retrieval of prodigious masses of information (along with their ability to zero in on selected phases of a problem and provide high-quality paper printouts) can be a blessed timesaver for basketball coaches.

There are literally thousands of companies who specialize in producing educational computer software. Although athletics is a relative newcomer in the software field, most educational software companies are rapidly expanding into the lucrative sports market. Many of them have software programs available that are designed specifically for basketball coaches. Since every coach's needs are highly individualized, you'll have to shop around to find the program that fits your needs; still, here are a few ways in which computers may be able to reduce the paperwork associated with your job:

- Storing personal information about each player (including grades and classroom progress reports) with easy access, quick retrieval, and virtually unlimited expansion potential
- Equipment inventories
- Team rosters (including opponents)
- Schedules
  —season (yours *and* your opponents)
  —work (concession stand, ticket takers, bus drivers)
  —gym use
  —preparing scouting schedules
- Detailed, comprehensive individual and team statistics
  —totals, averages, and percentages in various categories
  —single-game, season, and career stats
  —career-best performances, including (but not limited to) school, league, and state records
- Scouting reports (including analysis of trends in various situations)
- Game plans
- Daily practice schedules

Imagine never having to write up another daily practice schedule; instead, you simply call up the particular practice schedule you want on the terminal screen, then make a printout of it. (This feature can be achieved on almost any word processor.) You can also make changes on it before making printouts.

Of course, someone has to put the information into the computer so it can be stored, analyzed, and/or retrieved—after all, the data isn't going to leap into the computer on its own—but even if you're as computer illiterate as an Amazonian Jivaro headhunter, your school has student computer whizzes who can make a computer do everything but tap dance while playing "Swanee River" on a banjo. If you can't get them to computerize your basketball program for course credit in *Computer Science 301* or whatever, maybe you can persuade one of them to do it for a few bucks here and there along the way. It's well worth the effort.

SECTION 8

Team Tryouts and Preseason Practice

Many are called, but few are chosen.

—Matthew 22:14

Basketball is a paradox. We call it a game, but learning to play—or coach—it properly is very hard work.

Another paradox is almost as fundamental, namely, that while we as coaches draw our players from the general school population, we don't want them to *be* like the general school population.

To become a basketball player, a youngster must be willing to step out of the crowd and sacrifice large chunks of his free time doing things that the average nonathletic student wouldn't dream of doing. Rigorous physical conditioning. Endless repetitions of drills that demand intense concentration. Submission of ego to the demands of the coach and the needs of the team. All these things and many more—all prerequisites for becoming a skilled basketball player, with no shortcuts to success except, as Bobby Knight observed, being seven feet tall.

And the process begins, whether you're Michael Jordan or Joe Blow from Idaho, with trying out for the team.

IDENTIFYING CANDIDATES FOR YOUR TEAM

Except possibly for your first year at a school, you should have a pretty good idea who is coming out for your basketball team before tryouts even begin.

If you've done your job properly, you probably already know everything you need to know about the players who will be coming into your program next year, having established close ties and good working relationships with the coaches and players in the schools that make up your feeder program.

In your own school, other coaches and p.e. teachers are excellent sources of information regarding potential players—but your consistently best source will be your players. In addition to (and even more important than) informing you of possible candidates for the team, they will also spread the word around the school regarding the kind of person you are and the kind of program you run.

The key word here is *loyalty*: Players who are loyal to you and your program will urge their friends to try out for the team—and because birds of a feather *do* tend to flock together, those friends who make the team are likely to be similarly loyal. They in turn will attract other candidates, and your program will grow accordingly. Somewhere down the line, you find yourself coaching the younger brothers or sisters of players who have already passed through your program—a built-in supplement to your program continuity.

Meanwhile, you're doing everything possible to attract players into your program. You'll post notices concerning tryout dates in the gym and other prominent places around the campus such as the cafeteria, school office, library entrance, and the halls. You'll ask the principal to announce over the intercom several days in advance of the tryouts that students are encouraged to attend the tryouts. And you'll personally contact every basketball prospect in the school about trying out for the team, whether by talking with him or sending personal letters to his home and following up with a telephone call.

GUIDELINES FOR CONDUCTING TEAM TRYOUTS

Duration

The tryouts should be long enough for you to thoroughly evaluate the candidates' ability and potential—but not so long as to infringe on the team's preseason practice. Three to five days should be sufficient for tryouts, depending on the number of participants. (That number usually declines with each passing day as the players discover that there's more to basketball than practicing slam dunks or standing around tossing up forty-foot prayers for an hour or so.)

Whatever the case, everyone should be told at the beginning of the first session how long the tryouts will be held, and how team members will be selected.

Length of Tryout Practices

We prefer short practices that are highly organized and physically demanding—the same characteristics that we strive for in our daily practices.

Tryout sessions usually last from one and a half to two hours—again, depending on the number of candidates—and never more than two hours. (With a large turnout, we may take four or five days but we *won't* make the practices longer.)

Practice Organization

Our tryout sessions mirror our regular practice sessions in most respects[1]—that is, brief but intensive drilling in the phases of the game that we want to cover.

An effective method of dividing practice time might be individual offensive skills (ballhandling, dribbling, passing, shooting, and rebounding), thirty minutes; defensive drills and conditioning, fifteen minutes; simple two- and three-man movement sequences (e.g., figure 8s, screen-and-roll, give-and-go, etc.) and competitive drills in one-on-one, two-on-two, and three-on-three situations, fifteen minutes; and scrimmaging, thirty minutes.

Beyond demonstrating skills, we do relatively little teaching and correcting flaws during tryouts; at this stage, we're more interested in observation and evaluation than in instruction. The teaching will come later, after they've made the team. (*Note:* While physical conditioning should not be a primary goal in the tryouts phase of your program, a certain amount of repetitive high-speed, full-court drills is necessary for two reasons: First, to let the players know that conditioning is an ongoing and important part of your daily practices, and second, to separate the serious candidates from those who think they might look good in your uniform.)

Evaluation

Quantitative measurements such as height, standing reach, vertical jumping, shuttle run or other quickness tests, and strength tests are, or can be, important factors in determining a player's athletic potential or ability. We're always on the lookout for good athletes—and the younger they are, the better their chances of making the team. Similarly, players who are fundamentally sound in basketball's basic skills are always welcome. We evaluate both quantitatively for athletic ability and qualitatively for basketball skills. Those who possess neither (or both) are easy to spot; it's the others who require the closest scrutiny.

The Appendix contains the "Player Evaluation Form," that may be helpful in assessing candidates' athletic ability and basketball potential, both quantitatively and qualitatively. About the form: (1) *Wingspan* refers to the distance between fingertips with the arms fully extended to the sides at

---

[1]Except for the absence of work on team offensive and defensive patterns.

shoulder height. (2) The shuttle run is an excellent gauge of foot speed, quickness, and explosive power, whether you use the President's Council fitness test version or simply count the number of times the players cross the lane and touch the floor in twenty seconds. (3) We've included two familiar basketball skills tests: free throws made in twenty seconds and the dribbling suicide, which is nothing more than a regular timed suicide or ladder drill in which the contestants dribble while they're running. (The problem with quantifying basketball skills is that the players may require more than one try to overcome the learning factor. Still, we've left ten blank spaces for whatever athletic or basketball skills you want to test). (4) The parentheses beside each blank are for ranking the players, in case you want to use that evidence in explaining to unsuccessful candidates why they didn't make the team and what they need to work on.

Choosing the Squad

Our priorities as to whom we should keep and who must be let go include the following considerations:

- Unathletic *and* unskilled upperclassmen are likely to be your lowest priority, since you *won't* make athletes out of them and you only have two years at best to teach them the skills they should already possess. Freshmen and sophomores who are unathletic and unskilled may in some cases be used to fill out the B-team or jayvee rosters.

- Upperclassmen who are either unathletic or unskilled (but not both) are less important to your program continuity than underclassmen who possess the same traits. This is especially true of tall players who have not yet achieved physical maturity.

- Guard candidates should be more physically mature than the forwards and centers, who may be awkward or lacking in strength due to rapid growth rate. The guards' basketball skills should be more highly developed for the same reasons.

- Tall underclassmen who work hard are *always* a high priority—but not necessarily for your varsity squad if it means relegating them to bench duty most of the time. If they aren't likely to get much quality playing time on the varsity level, maybe a year of B-team or jayvee basketball will speed up their development.

- Don't just take our word for it: Jerry Tarkanian feels the same way, that *quickness* is the single most important skill in basketball. Quickness can make up for a lack of height in ways that height cannot compensate for a lack of quickness. (Of course, *tall* quickness is even more beneficial; you'll never have trouble identifying such players as prime candidates for your team.)

To recap: Among players of roughly equal ability or skills, take the one who has the most eligibility remaining. (That's why we put the ABCs—age, birthday, and class—on the evaluation sheet.) Look for tall players who are coachable and willing to work. Look for quick players—guards with the speed to burn opponents in your pressing defenses, and forwards who can fill the fast break lanes in transition. Look for players who are fundamentally sound, and players who *listen* and *think*. Don't worry about jumping ability: If they're quick they'll be good leapers too, since the quadriceps development that gives them explosive acceleration in running does the same thing for their vertical jumping; and if they are fundamentally sound but don't possess outstanding jumping ability (think: Larry Bird), they can compensate for it by concentrating on anticipation, positioning, and timing.

MAKING THE CUTS

Some coaches prefer to announce or post cuts every day at the end of tryouts to reduce the size of the group to a more manageable number. Such a policy is all right if you're taking a week to pare the squad down to size and begin making cuts after the third day—but not if you intend to start earlier than that. (It usually takes two days for the players to learn the drills and become acclimated to the practice environment.)

While it's easy to identify within the first fifteen minutes of tryouts some of the ones who won't make the team, the fact that they're there at all merits consideration. And while some coaches feel that keeping them even for three days is either a waste of their time and ours or a form of mental cruelty in the sense of raising the players' hopes unnecessarily, we disagree with both viewpoints. We strongly believe that every player who comes out for the team deserves to be treated with respect, regardless of his or her chances of making the team. A girl may not make a single shot during the three days of tryouts—but we'll give her her chances, which is what she wanted in the first place—and we won't single her out by releasing her at the end of the first practice session, regardless of her lack of skills or her poor attitude.

We prefer to make all cuts on the same day, if at all possible. Of course, if we have eighty-five candidates vying for fifteen varsity spots we may have to space out the dismissals over the last three days of tryouts so we can talk with the players individually and discuss the reasons for their dismissal and their prospects for playing in the future. But we won't post names on a bulletin board or call out the names of those who don't make the team, because those methods are too impersonal.

Failure is always a deeply personal matter to those who have failed, whether they show it or not. The professional way to handle it is to thank the player for his love for the game and for his desire to be a part of the program—and where young players are concerned, it is also important to point out that failure is not a permanent condition and can in fact be a springboard to future success in basketball, given a proper attitude and good work habits.[2]

Most coaches agree that dismissing players in preseason tryouts is the single most difficult task that we face. Yet it must be done, and if we approach the task as professionals who are concerned about the youngsters who try out for our teams, we can gain fans and supporters for our program who might otherwise have become embittered enemies.

Incidentally: if you have a player who won't make the team but loves the game and is loyal to you, you might consider asking him to be a team manager. And if he's young and potentially talented, continued exposure to your daily practices may show him the way to become a player in your program someday.

PRESEASON PRACTICE

First things first.

Before you embark on another seasonal date with destiny, there are numerous administrative tasks to be completed and preparations to be made. Some tasks should be done in the spring (e.g., ordering new uniforms) to allow plenty of time for their preparation; others, such as painting the dressing rooms or updating the player handbook, can be done at any time during the off-season.

In the reproducible form that appears in the Appendix, we've divided the preseason tasks and preparations into two phases: those that should be attended to before practice starts, and those that should be done prior to the first game. While the importance of the various tasks may be relative to your coaching situation, we've endeavored to list them according to the need for their early resolution.

The Coach, Conditioning, and Legal Liability

In this era of quick and easy litigation, it is important for a coach to protect himself from lawsuits by every means possible. In your case, this could mean requiring players to have physicals and show evidence of insurance coverage before you let them participate in *any* team-related activity.

---

[2]While in college, eventual NFL Hall-Of-Famer Alex Karras was dismissed from the squad at the beginning of his junior year at Iowa for being overweight; he came back the next year to make consensus All-America. And, as a youngster, Michael Jordan didn't make his junior high team, and—well, you know the rest of the story.

In July, you might want to send out letters to your returning players and possible candidates for the team, outlining the running and weight training schedule you will expect them to follow in preseason—assuming, of course, that they aren't involved in football or other fall sports. You should also schedule your physicals as soon as possible after school starts, with preseason running, exercise, and weight training beginning immediately afterward. If it sounds as if you've already selected the team before tryouts begin—you haven't (although you should have a pretty good idea who most of the players will be): The conditioning phase of your preseason program should be required for your veterans and prospects from your feeder system, but it should also be open to anyone else who wants to try out for the team.[3]

In addition to the obvious benefits of strength and endurance conditioning, there are two other reasons why we feel it is important to get the players involved early: First, a gradually accelerated conditioning program drastically reduces the number of blisters suffered by the players; and second, because their influence on each other is positive and supportive, we like the idea of keeping the players together as much as we can during the school year.

Organizing Preseason Practice

On the high school level or below, coaches generally have four to five weeks in which to select and prepare their teams for the upcoming season. And if, like us, you prefer short, concentrated practices, even with three-day tryouts your tight schedule has little room for error; it will require precise scheduling if you're going to cover everything that needs to be covered prior to your first game.

How Do I Practice Thee? Let Me Count the Days. The first step in planning your preseason practice schedule is to count the available days for practicing, and then subtract the number of tryout days. What you're left with will be your total number of practice days. For example, assuming that you have twenty practice days between October 15 and your first game and you use three of those days for tryouts, you're left with only *seventeen days* to get your team ready to play![4]

But there's a fly in the ointment that can rob you of valuable practice time if you aren't prepared for it: The time spent going over new rules, taking shoe orders, filling out eligibility reports and player information sheets, tak-

---

[3]A copy of AUM's strength and conditioning program for men's basketball, by head athletic trainer Shelby Searcy, as developed and modified for purposes of this book to include high school athletes, appears in the Appendix.

[4]That's another reason why we prefer pretryout conditioning exercise and running, and scheduling physicals and flu shots for players, managers, and coaches in that same time frame.

ing the team to have physicals, and giving out and going over the player handbooks (team rules, philosophy, offenses and defenses, etc.) with the players. Here are some time-saving shortcuts to consider:

• Always keep copies of the individual players' eligibility sheets that you send in to the state high school association. If you fill out your returning players' sheets during the summer, the only ones you'll need in the fall when tryouts are completed will be those for the new players—and you can work on those before or after practice.

• The same holds true for the player information forms that you'll use in compiling player profiles for local newspapers or other media. Although they need to be updated every year, you'll have plenty of time for the players to work on them during pretryout conditioning.[5]

• While it's imperative to go over new rules with the players and discuss the player handbook with them in detail, there's nothing that says you have to do it during the week. An alternative method that we've used with great success for years is to have full-dress game scrimmages every Saturday morning during preseason, complete with referees (who also discuss this year's rules changes in far greater detail than we could ever do). Preseason Saturday intrasquad scrimmages are good for everyone concerned: Our fans get a sneak preview of what this year's team will be like, the referees use the scrimmages for getting in shape for the season, the coaches gain weekly insights into the team's progress, the players love scrimmaging under game conditions—and all of the necessary paperwork can be attended to without interrupting daily practice.

Having determined the number of available practice days, the next step is to determine what needs to be covered in practice prior to your first game. Those areas basically include (1) endurance conditioning, (2) fundamentals, (3) individual defense, (4) team defense, (5) individual offense, (6) team offense, (7) rebounding, (8) transitions, (9) free-throw situations, and (10) out-of-bounds situations.

An extended reproducible outline of those areas appears in the Appendix.

Preparing and Implementing Your Practice Schedules

Knowing what must be covered and exactly how much time you have available to cover it in, all that remains is to devise practice schedules that organize your practice time efficiently. With four weeks or less to prepare your

---

[5]A reproducible form appears in the Appendix.

team, you not only cannot afford to waste time on nonessentials, but you should also look for shortcuts that save time. Here are a few techniques and ideas to consider regarding preseason practice organization and administration:.

• **Have a set time for working on your practice schedules every day, whether alone or with your assistant coach**. Immediately after practice is concluded may be acceptable for evaluating that day's practice but not for preparing the next day's schedule. You need time to unwind mentally before thinking ahead, which suggests either (1) after supper, when you've had time to relax somewhat from the rigors and demands of the day's teaching and coaching, or (2) the next morning, while your mind is fresh and creative. Planning periods are good times to work on daily practice schedules—if, that is, you're lucky enough to have one.

• **Organize your preseason practices in terms of priorities—and don't try to do everything at once**. "To everything there is a season," wrote the author of Ecclesiastes, "and a time for every purpose under heaven." Thus it is with basketball coaching: So many phases of the game to prepare for, so little time to do it. For example, working on individual fundamentals can be somewhat frustrating when you consider how many other aspects of the game must be covered; still, it must be done because, like conditioning, learning to execute basketball's basic skills with precision cannot be hurried. It requires patience, and seemingly endless repetitions. Few shortcuts exist, beyond the realization that working on fundamentals is *never* a waste of time. The time you're "wasting" on fundamentals now will save you time in the future, if you stick to your priorities.

How long will your practices be? During early preseason, ours are anywhere from 90 to 105 minutes; and during late preseason (i.e., the last two weeks before our first game), from 105 to 120 minutes. We may vary our lengths within those figures, but not beyond them, because practice length is an important priority for us: It forces us to be super organized to avoid wasting time.

How should practice time be allotted? That's hard to answer, because it depends on your priorities—where you are now versus how far you have to go. In early preseason, practices tend to feature conditioning and development of individual skills; later on, as the first game date draws near, aspects of team play normally take precedence. And while we'll have more to say about that later, we'll note that, generally speaking, our preseason practices are divided as follows: one-third shooting drills and practice (including free throws), one third offense, and one third defense. And although percentages may vary somewhat depending on the overall skills level and experience of our players, we may spend up to half of our preseason daily practices working

Figure 8–1. PRESEASON DAILY PRACTICE SCHEDULE

THOUGHT FOR TODAY:
FATIGUE MAKES COWARDS
OF US ALL.

DAILY
PRACTICE
PLAN
FOR: _____
(Date)

Time	Activity	Points to Stress
2:30–2:45	I. Dress	A. P.e. locker room
		B. Lock all outside doors
2:45–3:15	II. Warmup shooting	A. Competitive shooting
		B. Rotate baskets
3:15–3:25	III. Squad meeting	A. Center circle
	1. Announcements	B. Check all forms
	2. Quiet time	C. No practice unless physical examination
3:25–3:40	IV. Ballhandling drills	A. 8 balls, 8 lines
	1. Fingertip control	A. Up and down length of body
	2. Around the body	A. Left then right
	3. Figure 8	A. Through legs—left then right
	4. Dribble figure 8	
	5. Pretzel drill	A. Half-court and back
		B. Start and whistle
3:40–3:50	V. Dribbling drills	A. Eight balls, eight lines
	1. Stationary	A. Right hand then left
	2. Control	A. To half-court
		B. Change hands on dribble
	3. Speed	A. Full-court
		B. Change hands on dribble
3:50–4:00	VI. Pivoting and passing drills	A. Eight balls
		B. One count stop with reverse pivot (left foot then right)
		C. Include dribble
		D. Step with proper foot on pass
	1. Two count stop two hand chest pass	A. Use forward pivot
		B. Back foot—pivot foot
		C. Always step as you pass

4:00–4:15	VII. Passing with movement	
	1. Chest pass—"Two-man drill"	A. Six lines—3 balls B. Two man advancing ball C. Half-court and back
	2. Three-man drill	A. Advancing ball full-court B. One ball in each group of 3 C. Keep lines spread D. Shoot layup E. Middle man stop at free-throw line
	3. Figure 8 drill	A. Full-court B. Middle man stop at free-throw line
4:15–4:25	VIII. Defense	
	1. Step–slide (two 40-second periods and one 1-minute period)	A. Mass formation B. Broomstick fashion C. Feet spread, knees bent, tail down, back straight, head and shoulders up; elbows in
	2. Sideline cut off drill	A. Three slides and drop step
4:25–4:30	IX. Scrimmage Line 1 vs. Line 5	
4:30–4:35	Line 2 vs. Line 4 Line 3 vs. Line 6	
4:40	Squad meeting	A. Brief comment on today's practice B. Thought for today C. Take up all forms D. Check new people E. Dismissal

primarily on individual- and small-group-related drills and activities before we put it all together in team-oriented preparations such as scrimmaging.[6]

---

[6]For definitional purposes, we are referring to *scrimmaging* as "any five-on-five repetitive activity or drill that involves a single phase of the game" (such as practicing a zone offensive pattern). Other forms of scrimmaging include *game scrimmages*, playing under simulated game conditions; and *controlled scrimmaging*, five-on-five play that is limited to *two* phases of the game (such as half-court offense and pressing after scores).

• **If time management is important to you (as it should be), organize your daily practice sessions into time-blocks in a manner similar to that shown in Figure 8–1—and stick to the schedule!** Allot *x* number of minutes for each drill; have your manager time the drills, whistling once when one minute is left and twice when it's time to change drills; and require your players to sprint everywhere between drills. If a given drill is going particularly well, you can stop early and go on to the next drill, thus giving you extra time to work with *that* drill, if necessary—but you should resist the temptation to "borrow" time from the next drill when things are *not* proceeding smoothly with a given drill; in our experience, at least, those borrowed minutes never seem to get repaid and we wind up going thirty minutes beyond our allotted practice time. And while no physical damage is done, it's easier to stay focused on what you're trying to accomplish when you stick to the practice format that you originally devised.

• **If you can't find the right drill, invent it.** Other coaches' drills, while helpful in many instances, were designed for other coaches' teams; they may not work as intended for *your* team or *your* players. If that's the case, don't hesitate to create new drills that meet your team's specific needs. And if those drills don't work, either, keep trying—and keep looking elsewhere—until you come up with the drill you need; after all, you wouldn't want your players to give up whenever *they* try something that doesn't work.

• **Drill your players in the specific individual fundamentals they will use in the various phases of the game.** Do this in addition to working on fundamental skills such as ballhandling, dribbling, shooting, and defensive stance/footwork (which should be practiced separately on a daily basis), by breaking down your team offenses and defenses into their component parts, and do it weeks before you even start to install your team offense or defense! Here's how we do it:

We give out our player handbooks early, and we expect the players to begin studying them and learning the offense and defense immediately, even though our daily practices are oriented almost exclusively toward individual development—conditioning and skills—at that stage.

After giving out the handbooks, we take the players to the locker room and show them our half-court offenses and defenses, diagramming them on a chalkboard. We don't really care whether they understand the entire offense and defense; all we want them to know at this point is that *the drills we will be practicing every day are taken directly from the offensive patterns and defensive techniques we will be using when the season starts.*

We've found that this process—giving the players a glimpse at the overall picture, followed by repetitive drills in one-, two-, and three-man segments of those patterns—greatly enhances the players' awareness and appreciation of our short-range and long-term plans for the team. And besides speeding up the transition from individual skills to team skills, the game-related nature of the drills lends a sense of importance and urgency to the drills that improves players' concentration and inspires them to work harder on their individual skills than if we were using unrelated drills to practice those same skills. We know, because we've tried it both ways. This way is better.

• **If you're really pressed for time and your first game is not a league game, stick to your most important priorities and don't worry about getting everything in.** For instance, if your team is young and inexperienced and you have only seventeen practice days to prepare your team, you may have to spend more time than you'd like on fundamentals and developmental skills. If so, you may have to hold off introducing certain relatively nonessential phases of your team preparation such as special situations, and keep the variations of your basic offense and defense to a minimum. You don't *want* to do it that way, of course, but as every coach knows *circumstances dictate strategy.* You do the best you can with what you have to work with, and hope for the best.

Incidentally, that's one reason why most high school coaches schedule nonleague games early whenever possible: those games don't count against your league record if you happen to lose them.

• **Don't forget to prepare your players to beat the press.** While conditioning and fundamentals drills are your two most important individual priorities, beating the opponents' presses should be your most important priority in terms of team preparation. You may have devised the greatest half-court offense in the history of basketball, but it won't be worth the paper you used in designing it if your players can't advance the ball safely into your offensive half-court.

• **Prepare several copies of your daily practice schedules**—one for the locker room bulletin board, one for yourself and each assistant coach, and one for your manager on the clock.

• **Coaches should be on the floor at least fifteen minutes before practice begins**—and thirty minutes early if you have to do your own taping.

• **Trainers, managers, and players to be taped should arrive thirty minutes before practice.** All equipment (e.g., balls, clock, towels) should be ready and the gym floor freshly dust-mopped before any of the players take the court (see Figure 8–2). The "Managers' Game Duties Checklist" appears in reproducible form in the Appendix.

• **Don't allow interruptions or distractions.** Daily practice is the heart, soul, and backbone of your coaching. It should be run in a businesslike manner, with a minimum of interruptions or distractions. In our age of thirty-second attention spans, it takes very little to distract players from what they're doing. As a result, most of the very best coaches allow little or

---

Figure 8–2. MANAGER'S DAILY RESPONSIBILITIES AND DUTIES

General

1. Be at the gym thirty minutes before practice every day, forty-five minutes before departure on away games, ninety minutes before home games.

Daily

1. Clean the coach's office, varsity dressing room, and visitors' dressing room. Sweep the floor. Pick up trash, clothing, etc., off the floor. Empty trash cans. Tidy up to make the rooms as neat as possible. Flush the toilets, and be sure that toilet tissue and hand towels are available. *Be sure that the coach's office and dressing rooms are locked during and after practice.*

2. Clean the gym floor with a dust mop. Sweep the bleachers and pick up trash.

Practice Procedures

1. Get copy of daily practice schedule from the coach. Study it to find out where and how you'll be used during practice.

2. Turn on gym lights and scoreboard thirty minutes before practice.

3. Inflate basketballs if necessary; have basketballs, ball rack, portable chalkboard, erasers, chalk, towels, practice jerseys, scoreboard controls, and any other mechanical aids to be used in practice available and ready for use.

4. During practice, the senior manager will time drills on the clock. Other managers will assist with drills as needed, or keep stats.

---

no casual conversation during practice, whether by players, coaches, or spectators in the stands if practices are open to the public. The same applies to phone calls during practice: Unless they are emergencies, they should be treated as unnecessary distractions and handled by the managers.

Another familiar distraction is players who show up late for practice. When this happens, the best way to handle it is to have a standard rule that players arriving late go ahead and dress out, do stretching or limbering up exercises on the sidelines until the next shooting drill or water break, and then report to the head coach to discuss the reason for their tardiness. If their excuse is valid, they can join practice; if not, they are dismissed for the day (and possibly the next day as well). But in all cases the problem should be dealt with quickly, quietly, and forcefully. Chronic tardiness is a valid reason for suspension or dismissal from the team.

• **Notify players in advance when you or an assistant coach want to work with them individually before practice.** It's not realistic to expect a player to read your mind and show up early for practice if he hasn't been told to.

• **If you have your players do stretching exercises on the floor—and it's amazing how our pulled muscle injuries virtually disappeared at AUM after we began using them—have them do their stretching routines as soon as they arrive on the floor.** If another team is using the gym before you, the players can do their stretching or limbering up while waiting for the other team to conclude its practice.

• **Put your gym space, equipment (e.g., rebounding machines), and available goals to maximum use.** That's why you have them. Station drills and small-group activities keep players actively involved rather than standing around in long lines, contemplating their navels and waiting for something to happen. As Bobby Knight has pointed out, even if you're working alone without assistant coaches, you can effectively oversee several small groups working simultaneously if your drills are specific and you've organized them properly.

• **Keep your drills brief.** The function of drills is to provide repetition of selected skills; keeping the drills brief focuses attention on those skills without the players' becoming bored by the constant repetitions.

• **Evaluate your daily practices—and keep the schedules and evaluations.** The easiest way to do it is to jot down notes as to what worked, what didn't, and why, on your practice schedules, and then file them away for future reference. Doing this every day will help you, not just in preparing tomorrow's schedule, but in next year's daily practices as well.

PRACTICE PLANNING

Murphy's Laws of Basketball Practice: 1. If it works on paper, it won't work in practice. 2. If it works in practice, it won't work in games.

Chapman's Addition to Murphy's Laws of Basketball Practice: If it works in games, someone will suggest a few minor adjustments that will make it work even better.

Warren's Addendum to Chapman's Addition to Murphy's Laws of Basketball Practice: If you try out the adjustments, they won't work in practice or in games. Neither will the original pattern.

THE MASTER PLAN

If we were so adventuresome as to consider sailing solo around the world in a tiny boat, one of the many things we'd need would be accurate charts and nautical maps to guide us on our way. First, of course, we'd want a world map to use in planning our general route—but because world maps are necessarily limited in detail, our subsequent planning would also require progressively more detailed maps covering smaller areas of the world's oceans. A variety of maps would be far more valuable in keeping us on a safe course from day to day throughout our trip than any one map would be.

In planning for an upcoming basketball season, a coach needs to be aware of two things, *where he's going* and *how he intends to get there*. Your "world map" is your Master Practice Schedule covering the phases of the game your players need to work on during the course of the season. Those phases include:

1. Conditioning
2. Fundamentals drills

3. Individual offense and defense (including rebounding)
4. Team defense (zone and/or man-to-man)
5. Team offense (zone and man-to-man)
6. Beating the presses (zone and man-to-man)
7. Fast-breaking
8. Delay game
9. Out-of-bounds
10. Last-shot or special scoring plays

Breaking Down the Master Schedule

Although invaluable as an organizational reference tool, a master plan is too broad to provide the basis for day-to-day practice planning. Each category must be broken down into its component parts—and those segments correlated to the team's offensive and defensive playing style, patterns, and so on—before it can be applied to daily practices. For example, breakdown analysis of aspects of team preparation to be accomplished prior to a team's first game was shown in Figure 8–1—but much of that breakdown can be used effectively only in relation to the specific offenses and defenses that the team will use. If you don't intend to use pressing defense in your first game, you don't need to break it down or even include it in your yearly master schedule unless you intend to put it in later in the season.

Monthly Practice Planning

Preseason practice is always hectic because there's so much to prepare for in so little time. Based on the assumption that a high school, jayvee, junior high coach, and so on, has about a month of daily practices before his first game, the team preparation chart shown in Figure 8–1 is also likely to be the team's first monthly practice plan.

Because you can't accomplish everything at once, monthly practice planning is essentially a matter of organizing your practice schedule in terms of priorities. Every daily practice should accomplish certain specific goals in terms of preparation—but because emphases differ from week to week within the month, those goals should not be the same for every practice or every week.

After the first game, monthly practice planning tends to change radically. While preseason planning is naturally compressed to cover every phase of team preparation, the regular season offers broader possibilities for emphasizing various aspects of the game at a relatively more leisurely pace. For example, the time between the first game and the beginning of league play (or the end of the Christmas holidays, whichever comes first) is ideal for practicing the phases of team preparation that may have received less attention than you would have liked during preseason: special defenses (e.g., combination) or offenses against them; delay patterns; jump balls; free-throw situations (offensive and defensive); late game and last-second plays and strategies; bring-in plays from various court positions (e.g., back-court baseline); and incorporating, in breakdown fashion, elements of up-coming league opponents' offensive and defensive patterns into daily practice drill segments.

The latter technique will undergo further analysis elsewhere in this section, since it can greatly reduce the difficulties associated with prepar-ing for two or more different opponents every week during the season.

Beyond that, monthly preparations may not be terribly important ex-cept in terms of practice length and a few practical considerations:

• As noted in, Section 8, team tryouts normally last from 1½ to 2 hours daily for most teams. In early preseason, we'll go from 90 to 105 minutes daily, and during the last two weeks we'll extend it to 105 to 120 minutes. We'll stay at 2 hours until midseason—that is, after the Christ-mas break—and then cut back our practice time to 1½ hours. And as the playoffs draw near, we'll practice for 1 hour daily, or maybe even just 45 minutes.

In preseason and the early stages of the regular season, practices need to be longer because the players have a lot to learn while their legs and minds are fresh. As the season progresses, however, the new things to be learned are gradually reduced to refinements of basics that they already know, and our main concern then becomes keeping the players mentally fresh, rested, and eager to play. (This doesn't mean that we have easy practices or daily shoota-rounds, of course; as Tark the Shark puts it, *"You never want to have easy practices, just short ones."*)

• By midseason, most of our offensive practice is spent working on op-tions within our plays and patterns, and working against our next opponent's defenses. Conversely, the majority of our defensive practice involves working against our next opponent's offense.

• Beginning at midseason, we like to give our regulars a day off from practice every now and then. They love it, and it gives us a chance to focus our attention on the reserves to a far greater extent than is possible at regular practices. We always hold abbreviated game scrimmages on the starters' rest days.

• At least once during the late season before the playoffs begin, we'll give the entire team a day off from daily practice. And while that may not seem like much, the players greet such announcements with the sort of enthusiasm normally displayed by lottery winners—not because they don't love basket-ball, but because they need occasional respites from the rigors of daily prac-tice to recharge their batteries mentally and physically.

Weekly Practice: Preseason

Assuming a month or more of preseason practice, time allotments in the first week normally are weighted heavily toward the basics: conditioning and fast-break drills; offensive and defensive fundamentals; one-, two-, and three-man drills incorporating various aspects of the team offensive and defensive style; and perhaps a scrimmage at the end of the week to evaluate the players' progress.

The second week of preseason practice usually features more of the same, but with reduced time allotments, allowing time for the introduction of the basic team defense (half-court), with a scrimmage at the end of the week to evaluate progress. Additions during the third week of preseason practice normally include the team offense (half-court zone and man-to-man, and beating the presses) and full-court defenses—again with corresponding reductions of the fundamentals/small-group segments of practice. (*Note:* If your reserves are not capable of offering more than token defensive resistance to the starters at this point, you can up the ante by having the starters go five-on-seven, or even five-on-eight if necessary.[1]

The fourth week of practice can be used to review the offenses and defenses, to install whatever special situations patterns and techniques you intend to use, and to practice against your early-season opponents' offenses and defenses if you've scouted them or otherwise know what they're going to do.

Weekly Practice Schedules: Regular Season

In making out a weekly practice schedule, simply list the goals you want to accomplish that week and the drills you plan to use to accomplish them. It's important to avoid trying to cover too much in a given week, however, lest you confuse the players or take them farther than they're ready to go at that point in time. Try as we might, we can't rush the development of young players, because learning takes time. It proceeds at its own pace. As basketball teachers, the best we can do is *specify, simplify,* and *repeat, repeat, repeat* (via drills).

Our definition of *overcoaching* is "trying to cram a month's worth of practices into a single week, or a week's worth of practices into a single day." It's a natural tendency that many of us have as coaches, due in part to our love for the game and the missionary zeal with which we approach daily practices, and also our fear that, unless resolved immediately, our weaknesses will defeat us next game. Such unflagging devotion or unbridled fear can be self-defeating, though, like attempting an inside-the-park home run without

---

[1]You can also do the same thing in reverse with your zone defenses by placing seven offensive players on the court at one time (or six if you're playing man-to-man).

touching the bases along the way. Properly designed weekly practice schedules serve to control our overambitious impulses.

The best way to organize weekly practice schedules is to highlight a different phase of the game every week. For example, for the nine weeks that normally fall between New Year's Day and the first week in March, you could feature *full-court offense and defense* (fast-breaking, beating the presses, and pressing defenses) in weeks 1, 4, and 7; *half-court defenses* in week 2, 5, and 8; and *half-court offense and special situations/strategies* in weeks 3, 6, and 9.

Of course, you would still be practicing other phases of the game such as fundamentals, individual offensive and defensive techniques, and preparations for upcoming opponents—but emphasizing a different area every week permits greater in-depth treatment and flexibility than can be achieved by other methods. Changing the emphases every week keeps the daily practices from becoming predictable and stale.

Weekly Practice Schedules: Late Season and Playoffs

Practice ends when teams are eliminated from post season play; until then, late-season and playoff practices tend to be increasingly brief and directed largely toward preparing for the next opponent and fine-tuning the team offense and defense.[2] As a result, weekly schedules are likely to be important only if the coach continues to highlight certain areas of team preparation such as fast-breaking, and the like.

———————————— **DAILY PRACTICE** ————————————

Whatever you would make habitual, practice it; and if you would not make a thing habitual, do not practice it but accustom yourself to something else.

—Epictetus (A.D. 50–120)

No matter how good your team is, you cannot afford to waste practice time.

—Larry Chapman

Everything you do in daily practice should have a purpose. Just as a TV set or a lawn mower contains no unnecessary parts, your daily practices

———————————

[2]*Late-season* refers to the last two weeks of regular season play.

Figure 9–1. EARLY SEASON PRACTICE SCHEDULE

THOUGHT FOR TODAY:
THERE IS NO "I"
IN TEAM.

DAILY
PRACTICE
PLAN
FOR: _____ OCT. 16
(Date)

Time	Activity	Points to Stress
2:30–2:45	I. Dress	A. P.e. locker room B. Lock all outside doors at 3:00 P.M.
2:45–3:15	II. Organized shooting 1. Correct grip and flip of wrist (5 min.)	A. Everyone 25 times B. Concentrate on release
	2. Jump shot drill	A. Divide into groups
	a. Stationary (15 min.)	B. 10' jump shots
	b. Moving (10 Min.)	C. Competitive
3:15–3:20	III. Squad meeting	A. Today's practice B. Quiet time
3:20–3:40	IV. Layup drill	A. Divide squad into two groups
	1. Straight-in (10 min.)	A. Both sides B. Two balls
	2. Crossover (10 min.)	A. Proper dribble B. Proper crossover C. Proper approach to basket
3:40–3:55	V. Defense 1. Stance (5 min.)	A. Mass formation B. Good body position C. Proper base D. 30 sec. periods
	2. Reaction drill (5 min.)	A. "Hey" drill
	3. Step–slide defensive drill (5 min.)	A. Mass-squad formation B. 1 min. twice C. 1 min. 30 sec. once D. 30 sec. periods
3:55–4:10	VI. Fast-break drill	A. Three men advancing ball

	1. Three-man drill (5 min.)	B. Middle man stop at FT line
	2. Figure-8 drill (10 min.)	C. Move to side passed to
4:10–4:15	Conditioning	A. 15 sprints
		B. 2 suicides—30 sec.
4:15–	Squad meeting	A. Post practice comments
		B. Thought for day
		C. Dismissal

Figure 9–2. MIDSEASON PRACTICE SCHEDULE

THOUGHT FOR TODAY:
YOU DON'T PUT SKILL ON
LIKE A COAT—
YOU BUILD IT
DAY BY DAY.

DAILY
PRACTICE
PLAN
FOR: _____ DEC. 12
(Date)

Time	**Activity**	**Points to Stress**
2:30–2:45	I. Dress	A. Issue practice equipment
		B. Check in game uniforms
2:45–3:15	II. Preseason warmup	
	1. Jog two laps	A. Around playing court
	2. Stretching exercises	A. Two 8-second takes
	3. Juggling exercise	A. 50 attempts without a miss
	4. Shooting square on wall	A. Stress shooting form and follow-through
	5. Mikan drill	A. 25 shots with each hand
		B. Hold ball in both hands
		C. Turn toe in and don't let ball hit floor
	6. Partner Shooting	A. Shoot 10 and change
3:15–3:20	III. Squad meeting	A. Leave for Smith's Station at 5:15
		B. Play Smith's Station
		C. Quiet time
3:20–3:40	IV. Pre-game	

		warmup	A.	Two teams
	1.	4 basic layups	A.	Two balls
	2.	Star-shaped drill	A.	One ball
	3.	Defensive slide	A.	Go through twice
	4.	Partner shooting	A.	Shoot 10 and change
			B.	Juggle once and move to midcourt
	V.	Free throws	A.	Use six baskets
			B.	No talking
3:40–3:55	VI.	Team concepts	A.	Vs. ½-court freelance offense
	1.	"10" defense	B.	"B" team on offense
			C.	Next receiver pressure by wing men, force back door
3:55–4:10	2.	"23" Defense	A.	Two teams
4:10–4:30	3.	Man-man offense	B.	Rotation to weak side
	a.	1–4 attack		
	b.	"Stack"	A.	Fast-break down
	4.	All-purpose drill	B.	Swing and complete fast-break attack
			C.	Run zone attack
			D.	Three-on-two back
4:30–4:40	VII.	Free throws		
4:40	VIII.	Squad meeting	A.	Thought for day
			B.	Leave at 5:15
			C.	B-team scrimmage tomorrow & Fri.
			D.	Film in classroom

should contain no unnecessary elements. Every practice should be planned in advance and adhered to down to the last minute.

The way we see it, the only reason for taking time to devise a practice schedule is to follow it. Doing things spontaneously may be easier, but it does not ensure that what needs to be done actually gets done. The only way to use your practice time effectively and efficiently is to start on time, stay on time, and finish on time.

A reproducible "Daily Practice Schedule" form appears in the Appendix. Figures 9–1, 9–2, and 9–3 offer sample practice schedules.

PRACTICE ORGANIZATION

No matter what else you do at practice—and no matter how long or short your practices are—here are five things you should always include in every

Figure 9–3. LATE SEASON PRACTICE SCHEDULE

THOUGHT FOR TODAY:
CONCENTRATE ON WHAT YOU
ARE DOING—THEN YOU WON'T
HAVE TIME TO TENSE UP
AND WORRY.

DAILY
PRACTICE
PLAN
FOR: _____ FEB. 26 _____

(Date)

Time		Activity		Points to Stress
2:30–2:45	I.	Dress		
2:45–3:00	II.	Prepractice Warmup	A.	One ball for each varsity player
		1. Jog 2 laps	A.	Immediately on arriving on gym floor
		2. Stretching exercises	A.	Two 8-sec. takes
		3. Mikan drill	A.	25 shots with each hand
3:00–3:15	III.	Pregame Warmup		
		1. 4 basic layups		
		2. Star-shaped drill		
		3. Defensive slide		
		4. Partner shooting		
3:15–3:25	IV.	Squad meeting	A.	Preview practice
			B.	Quiet time
3:25–3:40	V.	Team Concepts	A.	Against passive B-team defense
		1. Man–man offense (all options)		
		2. Zone Offense	A.	Against 1–2–2 zone
		a. 1–4 regular		
		b. Post to corner		
		c. 2 attack		
3:40–3:50		3. Zone press offense	A.	Against 1–2–1–1 Press
			B.	B team play defense
3:50–4:05		4. Free throws	A.	Shoot 2 and change
			B.	No talking
4:05–	VI.	Squad meeting	A.	Thought for day
			B.	Leave at 6:30 Wed.
			C.	Tonight's game at 7:00

practice session you conduct (except game-day walk-throughs and shoota-rounds):

1. Warmup drills or stretching exercises
2. Fundamentals drills
3. Shooting drills
4. Defensive stance and footwork drills
5. Fast-breaking

• *Warmup drills/stretching exercises.* For years, we began our daily practices with the two-ball Cincinnati layup drill and four-corner passing drill. They were our "limbering up" exercises; they "warmed up" the muscles by increasing the heart rate, and thus the blood supply to the muscles—as if the muscles were not constantly receiving freshly oxygenated blood anyhow!

Today, although we still use layup activities within the context of our daily shooting practice, we no longer use them to "warm up" the muscles. Muscles don't need to be warmed up for basketball, they need to be *stretched* to give the athlete flexibility and looseness. Our players always do a series of stretching exercises on the floor for 15-20 minutes before practice.

• *Fundamentals drills.* For the sake of interest, the drills you use can and should be changed from time to time—but not the fundamentals themselves. Players never outgrow their need to practice the fundamentals. With highly skilled players, we simply increase the difficulty of the drills—say, by performing a simple between-the-legs walking dribble drill at a jogging or running pace, or going two-on-three in rebounding drills.

• *Shooting.* We don't list shooting as a fundamental activity because its importance merits special consideration. We devote fully a third of our practice time to structured shooting practice and free throws.[3] During that time, we work on layups (driving and power), tip-ins, post shots, jump shots off the dribble or coming off screens, perimeter shots—and free throws, of course.

• *Defensive stance and footwork.* Individual defense provides the foundation for *all* effective team defense. The importance of proper stance and footwork to a team's success defensively cannot possibly be overstated. We use step-slide drills *every day* to extend the limits to which our players can operate comfortably in the low, broad-based defensive stance[4] that although fatiguing, is critical to success in attacking or responding to offensive tactics.

---

[3]In a two-hour practice, we'll spend ten minutes shooting free throws, thirty minutes working on various shots, forty minutes working on various phases of individual and team offense, and forty minutes working on individual and team defense. Scrimmage time is considered as half offense and half defense.

[4]The defensive stance: feet spread, knees bent, tail down, back straight, head and shoulders up.

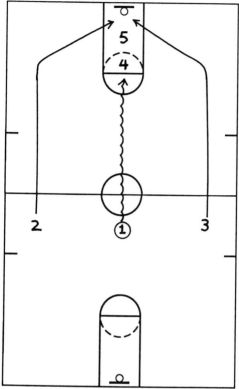

Figure 9–4. FIVE-MAN FAST-BREAK DRILL (THREE-ON-TWO)

• *Fast breaking.* Regardless of how often your team fast-breaks or what style of fast-breaking you use, the only way to reduce the ballhandling risks involved in fast-breaking is to practice it every day.

In addition to our regular five-man pattern (see Figures 9–4 and 9–5) and other fast-break drills we use, we also practice fast breaking against full-court pressing defenses because half-court offense begins only when you've beaten the opponents' press.

At AUM, we devote one third of our daily practice time to shooting, one third to offense, and one third to defense. In a two-hour practice, that translates into forty minutes for each phase of the game.

Offensively, we'll spend five minutes on each of our five options (twenty-five minutes), and fifteen minutes on ball rotation and pattern continuity, freelancing, fast-breaking from defense, and fast-breaking from free throws.

Defensively, our forty minutes will be allotted among some (but not all) of the following areas: footwork, sliding, switching, post coverage, team man-to-man, team switching, zone defense, fast-break defense, foul-line defense, jump balls, situation work (offense and defense), and opponents' offenses. Which areas we highlight in a given practice will depend on our breakdown of weekly practice goals.

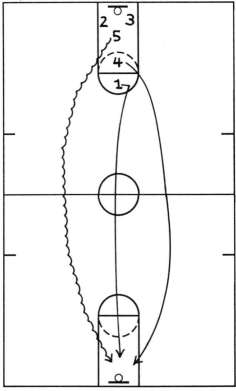

Figure 9–5. FIVE-MAN FAST-BREAK
DRILL (TWO-ON-ONE)

• ***Drills.*** In small-group form—say, three to five players working on a given activity within brief time blocks of five to ten minutes each—drills provide quick, constant repetition of isolated skills. When combined with other related drills, they teach basic skills and team concepts in a highly efficient manner. The five-man fast-break drill shown in Figures 9–4 and 9–5 is an excellent lead-up drill to team fast-breaking.

There are many types of drills, of course: conditioning drills, fundamentals drills, individual and small-group drills and activities, team offensive and defensive drills—all are important in building individual and team skills. But because drills are necessarily—and intentionally—repetitious, they can also become boring to the players involved.

No matter how highly motivated players are, they tend to become inattentive and lax in their performances when drills are extended too long. Using brief drill segments with quick changes between drills (or stations) is one way of dealing with the problem; two other ways are to make the drills competitive whenever possible and to alter the drills (or find new ones) to give the activity a new look.

A final thought about drills in general: *When you simulate game conditions in practice, make the drills harder than actual game conditions will be.*

Three examples (among many such drills that could be used): bad-pass drills (in which players turn one way or another on signal and field poorly thrown passes); step–sliding movements practiced daily over a period of several weeks until players are capable of staying down in their defensive stance for six to eight minutes or more at a time without standing erect; and one-on-two rebounding or inside offensive play, with the coach or a manager either shooting or passing to one of the three players to initiate sequences. Practicing two-on-three, three-on-four, four-on-five, or five-on-as many players as you want to use—all are variations of this same overloading technique. It's based on the idea that, through careful and intense drilling, players can be taught to handle situations that are more difficult than they will face in games—and as a result they will be better equipped to handle and adjust to actual game conditions.

Installing Your Offense Through Breakdown Drill Sequences

We recommend a nine-step approach to installing an offensive system:

1. Teach your players the basic pattern or movement sequences by walking them through it until everyone is thoroughly familiar with it. Although timing, execution, and options are critical to the success of any offensive system, your most important concern initially is for the players to learn the positions and sequence of passes and cuts involved in the basic pattern or design.

Let's say you want to install a flex-type passing game or continuity pattern. (It can be used equally well in either capacity.) Assuming further that you have a big man that you want to keep inside—5 in Figures 9–6 and 9–7—let's consider a variation of the flex in which the outside cutters execute two screens on their way to weak side.

As 1 brings the ball up, 2 screens for 4's outside cut to receive 1's pass. 2

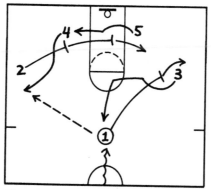

Figure 9–6. FLEX OFFENSE, BASIC MOVEMENTS

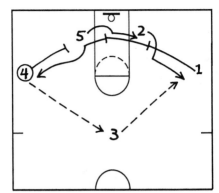

Figure 9–7. FLEX OFFENSE, BALL AND
PLAYER ROTATION

screens for 5 cutting to ball side low post and clears to weak side. 1 and 3 interchange, whether by screening as shown or simply by cutting (Figure 9–6). In the rotation, 4 passes to 3, 1 screens inside for 2's cut to the wing, and 1 continues into the lane to screen for 5's cut to low post. 4 moves inside to screen for 1's cut to the wing in the next ball rotation. After 3 receives 2's pass (not shown) and relays the ball to 1, 3 and 2 will interchange.

And that's the basic pattern. There's more to the flex offensive system than that, of course, but that's what the players need to learn first in this particular flex style. (Other styles exist: For example, 2 and 4 could set up in a low double stack to allow 2 to receive 1's pass, in which case 2 could pass inside to 4, or 4 could screen in the lane for 5's cut to ball-side low post. Or 3 could screen for 5's outside cut to reverse the pattern, if you don't mind having both 4 and 5 venturing outside occasionally.)

2. Drill the players in isolated segments of the basic pattern. Because the flex is primarily intended to create favorable one-on-one matchups, its basic breakdown drills are simple and easy to learn. Simplicity is a major

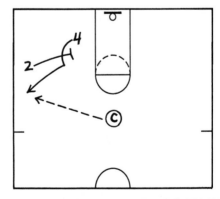

Figure 9–8. FLEX BREAKDOWN DRILL 1:
INITIAL MOVEMENT

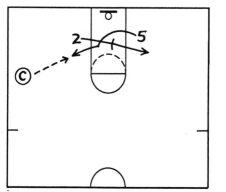

Figure 9–9. FLEX BREAKDOWN DRILL 2:
SCREENING IN THE LANE

reason why so many teams use flex patterns as the basis for their passing game offenses.

While Figures 9–8, 9–9, and 9–10 show two-man drills, they can be expanded to include three or four players—for example, by combining the movements of 2, 4, and 5 in Figures 9–8 and 9–9 to make a three-man drill, or replacing the coach with 1 and adding 3 at the weak-side wing to combine the movements in Figure 9–8 with those in Figure 9–10 to make a four-man drill.

3. Add defense to the drill sequences, but don't let the defenders overplay the pattern—at least, not yet. Even mediocre defenders can disrupt the pattern by overplaying the passing lanes when the offensive players haven't practiced the options. What's important at this stage is to give the offensive players a sense of what the basic pattern looks and feels like against defense.

4. Introduce options to the pattern one at a time in walk-through fashion. The balanced nature of the 1–2–2 alignment offers virtually unlim-

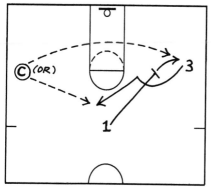

Figure 9–10. FLEX BREAKDOWN
DRILL 3: ROTATION PASS

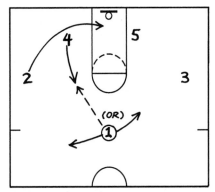

Figure 9–11. FLEX OFFENSE, FLASH TO
HIGH POST AND BACKDOOR CUT

ited quick and easy access to scoring options not found in the basic pattern.
For example, either 4 or 5 can flash to high post, with the wing on their side
cutting backdoor (Figure 9–11). If 2 doesn't receive the ball, his clearout to
weak side will give 4 more than enough room to work his man one-on-one—
or 2 can set a double screen with 5 for 3's wheel-type cut into the lane. 1's
movement either way is intended to occupy his man; he could as easily
interchange with 3 or down screen for 5.

In Figure 9–12, 4 and 2 have interchanged—but instead of cutting to
low post, 5 cuts to *high* post off 2's screen. (After passing to 5, 4 will either
cut to the basket or flare to the corner.)

In Figure 9–13, 2 V's back to receive 1's pass. 4 moves into the lane to
screen for 5 and, finding the defenders switching, cuts back to post up for 2's
pass. (If the defenders don't switch, 5 will be open when he cuts around 4's
screen.) After passing inside, 2 will flare to the corner—and 5 may continue
outside to screen for 3 cutting to the basket. (And if the defenders on 5 and 3
switch, 5 will cut toward high post.) Or 1 may screen for 3's cut to the high
post area. Or 4 may simply work his man one-on-one.

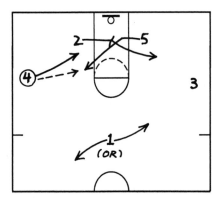

Figure 9–12. FLEX OFFENSE, HIGH-POST
CUT VARIATION

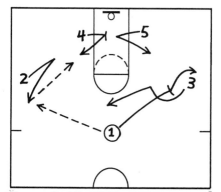

Figure 9–13. FLEX OFFENSE, FALSE
POST INTERCHANGE

2's down screen for 4 in Figure 9–6 normally will be successful because most defenses are basket-oriented; while they will overplay from inside-out to protect the post, they usually will give up the pass to 4 cutting to the wing.

When teams *don't* play it that way—when they use pressure man-to-man to overplay the outside passing lanes—the screen by 4 and backdoor cut by 2 can set up an easy layup for 2 as shown in Figure 9–14. (Even if 2 doesn't get the ball, 4's roll off the screen will set up the same kind of one-on-one confrontation at high post that existed in Figure 9–11.) If 1 passes to 4, 2 will clear to weak side and 5 will either stay where he is, flash into the lane, or screen for 3's backdoor cut to the basket.

5. Break down the options into drill segments. Since the basic purpose of the flex is to take advantage of favorable matchups, pattern often is incidental to the freelance possibilities arising out of the alignment and basic movements. For example, the 1–2–2 alignment offers splendid inside power-game opportunities for 4 and 5. If the team is using power-game principles, 4 and 5 will stay inside working to free themselves for entry passes from the

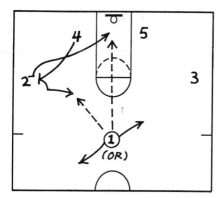

Figure 9–14. FLEX OFFENSE, OUTSIDE
SCREEN AND BACKDOOR CUT

point or the wings. If it can be accomplished from the point by 4 or 5 cutting to high post, that's what one or the other of them will do; and if not, they'll work for the pass from the wing, whether by establishing inside position as 4 did in Figure 9–13, 4 interchanging with 5, or 5 cutting to ball-side high post with or without a screen from 4.

To break down the options into two-, three-, or four-player segments all that's necessary is to decide where you want the options to occur (i.e., wing pass to low post, wing pass to high post, or point pass to high post), how many people are involved in getting the ball there, and begin the drill with the entry pass to the desired area and end it with the attempt to score.

With the flex power game, it's even easier. Start with penetrating and driving drills for 1, 2, and 3 from the point and wings. Add one- and two-man drills in the movements shown in Figures 9–10 and 9–13 to create leads in the perimeter passing lanes. And for the heart of the offense, teach 4 and 5 how to use each other and their own skills as well to work themselves free in the paint and at the posts.

6. Add passive defense to the options drill segments. Players should get used to seeing the defenders as they evaluate their options.

7. Practice the basic pattern, option, and automatics, first in breakdown drills and then in team form.

8. Add full-scale defense to the breakdown drills and team runthroughs. Let the defenders play it however they want to. Offensively, emphasize five points:

 a. Anticipation
 b. Timing
 c. Execution
 d. Pattern
 e. Breaking the pattern to catch the defense off-guard or take advantage of mismatches or freelance scoring opportunities.

9. Whenever you encounter problems, go back to the breakdown drills in practice. Often, it's something minor such as timing or positioning that causes the offense to misfire; if so, breakdown drills can usually pinpoint the difficulties quickly and easily.

Of course, you don't *have* to use breakdown drills at all—but if your car has a flat tire, all you need to repair is one tire, not all four.

Installing Your Defense Through Breakdown Drill Sequences

The same principle applies equally to offensive- and defensive-system installment: Like the postseason banquet meal, they are more easily consumed one bite at a time, and in small bites.

Whether offensively or defensively, the teaching process is the same: Show them the overall picture, then break it down into smaller segments that permit intensive, repetitive practice of the techniques associated with that segment of the overall pattern. Then build back to the full team by adding players to the drills.

In teaching your defensive system in walk-through fashion, your main concern should be the players' gaining an understanding of their defensive responsibilities in terms of ball and player movement. Specific techniques for carrying out those responsibilities will be revealed in the course of practicing your breakdown drills.

Regardless of the style of man-to-man or zone defense being used, your breakdown drills will be directed toward any or all of the four following areas: on-the-ball coverage, ball-side responsibilities, post coverage, and help-side or weak-side responsibilities.

Drills are an efficient, time-saving method of teaching skills—but they are only a means to an end, not the end itself. When players master the skills involved in the two-, three-, or four-player breakdown drills, they are ready to put those skills to use in team drills or scrimmaging.

Preparing for League Opponents Through Breakdown Drills

If you know beforehand via scouting, past experience, and the like, what your league opponents like to do offensively and defensively, you can begin preparing for them early by breaking down their offenses and defenses into drill segments and incorporating them into your daily practices long before you play them. For example, you can work on down picks in the flex and how to play them, screens on the block and how to play the cutter, double-down screens and how to play them, and whatever else your league opponents might do—and later (say, two days prior to playing them), when you introduce the opponents' offenses and defenses, your players already will be familiar with the techniques and methods necessary to combat them.[5]

Scrimmaging

As noted earlier, *scrimmaging* is a broad term that is variously used to describe five-on-five play that's (1) full-court, under simulated game conditions with referees; (2) either full- or half-court, practicing one phase of the game, such as zone offense; or (3) either full- or half-court, practicing two phases of the game, such as zone offense and fast-breaking in transition. In our present context, we're using it simply to refer to *any* competitive five-on-five basketball drill or activity.

---

[5]You could do the same thing for nonleague opponents on your schedule, too, of course—but time considerations and the fact that league games are more important than nonleague games usually limit this practice to league opponents.

Every coach has his own philosophy regarding scrimmaging. Some coaches like to start out scrimmaging the very first day of practice and devote part of every daily practice to scrimmaging. Other coaches believe that you should build to it gradually. We believe in starting out with the fundamentals and working on them until they become habits that the players use naturally without having to think about doing them. At that point, the players are ready for scrimmaging.

Two points about scrimmaging: First, the more fundamentally sound your players are, the more time you can afford to spend on scrimmaging or working on team aspects of your offense and defense. And second, full-court scrimmaging under game conditions makes your practices interesting for the players once you've established your style of play and installed your offense and defense. We believe in scrimmaging as much as possible once the team is ready for it—say, twice a week, on Wednesday and Saturday.

During the early season and up to midseason, our scrimmages will go for twenty minutes on the game clock: eight minutes playing man-to-man offense/defense, six minutes zone offense/defense, and six minutes with our presses. Later in the season we'll have longer scrimmages, with half of the scrimmage time allotted to team offense and the other half to team defense.

Perhaps a word or two of caution should be added here, namely, that while it is enjoyable for the players and easier to prepare for in terms of daily practice planning, *scrimmaging should not be considered a substitute for drills*. Scrimmaging—especially full-court under simulated game conditions—does not provide the kind of immediate, constant repetition that builds individual skills the way that drills do, nor is it useful in terms of correcting mistakes. The function of scrimmaging is to *complement* the drills you use, not to replace them.

SECTION 10

Scouting

Be prepared.

—Boy Scout motto

There are two widely divergent schools of thought in basketball circles regarding the importance of scouting opponents prior to playing them.

At one end of the spectrum are coaches who, by virtue of having powerful teams capable of controlling the tempo of games and dictating what opponents can and cannot do, consider scouting to be relatively unimportant—or at least less important than developing and maintaining their own strengths to overpower opponents.

One such coach was UCLA's John Wooden, whose confidence in his players and his style of play was such that he preferred to let opponents worry about beating UCLA rather than the reverse.

Coach Wooden's philosophy was that, regardless of what opponents tried to do, UCLA was going to make them play to the Bruins' strengths. And that was usually the case, too. With teams whose weaknesses were minimal, Wooden considered his time best spent in constantly drilling his players in the aspects of their game that rendered them virtually unbeatable during the mid-1960s and 1970s—full-court zone pressing defense, half-court man-to-man pressure defense, fast-breaking, and a half-court offense built around the prodigious talents of such players as Walt Hazzard, Gail Goodrich, Lew Alcindor, Bill Walton, Keith Wilkes, Sidney Wicks, and Curtis Rowe. Wooden considered scouting opponents to be a waste of time in his case—which indeed it was, considering that the Bruins won ten NCAA championships between 1964 and 1975, including seven straight titles, and had winning streaks of 88, 60, and 47 games during that incredible span.

Two factors must be taken into account for Coach Wooden's philosophy to be workable in other situations: First, the team's weaknesses must be minimal and its strengths considerable if it is to consistently negate whatever strengths and tactics an opponent might use against it without having prior knowledge of what those strengths and tactics might be; and second, the coach must be—as Wooden was—an excellent game coach, to adapt as necessary when his players and style of play fail to contain the opponents or dictate the flow of the game. When those factors work in a coach's favor, however, he may be entirely correct in considering scouting to be important only in terms of scouting *his own team*.

Because most basketball teams possess weaknesses, however minor, that adversely affect their ability to consistently overpower opponents without regard to the opponents' strengths and weaknesses, most coaches consider scouting to be an important aspect of game preparation. Scouting provides advance information regarding how a team uses its strengths and hides its weaknesses; it also reveals styles of play, strategy, tactics, and individual skills that can help a coach determine how effective his own strengths, style of play, strategy, tactics, and individual skills are likely to be against that opponent.

Armed with such knowledge, a coach can adapt or alter his strategy and tactics prior to the game, for example, by using deliberate play against superior up-tempo teams or by full-court pressing slow teams with poor ballhandling, to use two familiar examples. The old adage "forewarned is forearmed" applies aptly: If you know in advance how an opponent is likely to play you, you may be able to devise ways to attack his weaknesses or control if not nullify his strengths—and in either case to reduce the effectiveness of what he does best and force him to alter his original game plan. Such strategies are based on the familiar coaching principle that *the farther a team strays from its original game plan, the more error-prone its players are likely to become.* Every team prefers to do what it does best—and when those avenues are denied, players tend to become confused and lose confidence and concentration.

Of course, a given opponent may be so strong that nothing short of divine intervention will defeat them, given the level of our own players' skills. In such cases, the goal is to find ways to keep the game close enough to salvage pride if not to give our team a chance to win in the final quarter. Scouting can provide valuable clues regarding the best way to win or to keep the score respectable without waiting for the opponents to do so after they have built a forty-point lead.

——————— WHICH TEAMS SHOULD YOU SCOUT? ———————

It's often impossible to scout every opponent on your schedule prior to playing them, especially on the high school level, where games usually are played on Tuesdays, Fridays, and Saturdays. You can scout opponents on your open dates, of course—and you can double up by sending your assistant coach to scout other games.[1] At AUM we have the same coaches scout the same teams every year. Still, you may not be able to scout every team in advance. Leaving aside for the moment the possibility of indirect scouting, or gathering information about opponents without actually seeing them play, the problem arises: Which teams should you scout? The answer depends on what you want your scouting to accomplish and the relative importance you place on defeating certain opponents. The following principles may be helpful in defining your scouting priorities:

• ***Scout the teams that are most important for you to defeat.*** League rivals are always important when the final standings determine postseason tournament seedings and pairings. Likewise long-standing or intense rivalries with opponents who may or may not be in your league, since winning those games may influence your longevity at your present school. Beyond such considerations, your scouting priorities are likely to involve the relative strengths of your team and your opponents.

• ***With a strong team, scout your strongest opponents.*** Although upsets occur occasionally among even the best of teams, scouting weak opponents can be a waste of time when you fully expect to beat them soundly anyway. Thus—with the exception of faraway opponents for whom direct scouting may be impractical or impossible—your chief scouting priority is likely to be seeing the best teams on your schedule. To do so, however, it is imperative for you to have a copy of each of your opponents' schedules—and while swapping schedules is traditional, coaches sometimes have to press the issue by keeping after certain coaches to send along a copy of their schedules.

Once you have a complete set of your opponents' schedules, sit down with your assistant coach and prepare a scouting schedule, using a calendar and your own schedule for reference as well as your opponents' schedules. Your goal may be—as ours has been—to see every opponent play before your team faces them, if possible, and to scout every home-and-home opponent at least once before the end of the Christmas break. (We like to scout the better teams on our schedule regardless of whether we've played them or not, to see how they react to other playing styles, strategies, and tactics.)

Normally, scouting tends to tail off as the season progresses. Still, we think it's important to look in on opponents occasionally to see what sort of changes they've made, if any; after all, we not only play most of them twice per season on a home-and-home basis, but we also may meet them again in

---

[1]We've even had our players scout local games that they were going to attend on open dates anyway—and they've done a remarkably fine job, once we told them what to look for and what information to collect.

Figure 10–1 SCOUTING SCHEDULE

	Date	Teams (circle team being scouted)	Location	Game Time	Scout
F-SA	11-16/14-17	Woodbridge Inv. Tour			
Tu	11-20	(Martin Co.) Trinity H.S.	Martinsville	8:30	
F	11-23 *	Woodbridge H.S.	Away		
SA	11-24	(Mayesville) Barton Co.	Mayesville	8:30	
Tu	11-27	(Dobbs Co.) (Oak Creek H.S.)	Oak Creek	8:30	
F	11-30 *	Martin Co.	Home		
SA	12-1	Bradley H.S.	Home		
Tu	12-4 *	Woodbridge H.S.	Home		
F	12-7	(Stanton H.S.) Martin co.	Stanton	8:30	
SA	12-8 *	Dobbs Co. H.S.	Away		
Tu	12-11	(Hillcrest) (Oak Creek)	Oak Creek	8:30	
F	12-14	(Mayesville) (Woodbridge)	Mayesville	8:30	
SA	12-15				
Tu	12-18	Northbridge Invit. Tour			
		(Polk Co.) (Bradley H.S.)	Glendale	TBA	
F	1-4	Hillcrest H.S.	Away		
SA	1-5				
Tu	1-8 *	Mayesville H.S.	Home		
F	1-11	Bradley H.S.	Away		
SA	1-12	(Sherwood Acad.) Trinity H.S.	Magdeton	8:30	
Tu	1-15 *	Martin Co. H.S.	Away		
F	1-18 *	Oak Creek H.S.	Away		
SA	1-19				
Tu	1-22	Hillcrest H.S.	Home		
F	1-25 *	Dobbs Co. H.S.	Home		
SA	1-26				
Tu	1-29 *	Sherwood Acad.	Home		
F	2-1 *	Polk Co. H.S.	Away		
SA	2-2	Oak Creek - Martin Co.	Oak Creek	8:30	
Tu	2-5 *	Mayesville H.S.	Away		

* = Region game

F	2-8	* Oak Creek H.S.	Home	
SA	2-9	Polk Co. – Woodbridge	Woodbridge 8:30	
Tu	2-12	Stanton H.S.	Home	
F	2-15	Dobbs Co. – Sherwood Acad.	Ripley 8:30	
SA	2-16	* Sherwood Academy	Away	
Tu	2-19	Stanton H.S.	Away	
F	2-22	* Polk Co. H.S.	Home	
SA	2-23			
	2-27/3-2	Subregion Tournament	TBA	TBA

PREPARING A SCOUTING SCHEDULE

1. Using a calendar and blank Scouting Schedule forms, list every Tuesday, Friday, and Saturday date for the entire season (including Thanksgiving weekend and the Christmas holidays), beginning with the first game played by your team or anyone on your schedule and ending with the last regular season game for your team or your opponents.

2. Fill in your own schedule (and mark those dates off your opponents' schedules if you don't plan to send an assistant coach to scout on your game days). The remaining dates will be your available days for scouting.

3. Using a blank sheet of paper, list the open dates on your schedule—and for every open date, list every game involving your opponents on that day. (In many cases, several teams will be playing on the same day: include all of them, because at this point you haven't decided which game to scout on any given open date.) Underline the home teams (in case travel distance is a factor), highlight the teams you may want to scout, and circle all games involving opponents you can scout prior to playing them.

4. Fill in any open dates on your Scouting Schedule in which only one opponent is playing (e.g., a Saturday game).

5. After considering your scouting priorities, fill in the remaining open dates on your Scouting Schedule with the games that you most need to see *at that time* (preferably, just before you play a given opponent), making sure that you see every team on your schedule at least once before you play them, if at all possible (or necessary).

6. If open dates still remain—which likely will be the case, especially in the latter part of the season—you can fill them with games featuring teams you want to scout again—or else you can use them as occasional holidays from scouting, or time to catch up on whatever daily practice or game preparations you need to attend to.

postseason play. And once we know for sure that we'll be advancing to higher levels in postseason play, we'll do our dead-level best to see our likely opponents' tournament games.

Every year, the various state high school associations send out an updated bylaws and procedural book—referred to in Georgia as the "White Bible" because it's a white paperback book—that contains, among other things, state basketball tournament schedules and dates for completing region tournaments as well. A phone call or two will tell you when and where the tournaments you want to see are being held. And if you can't attend the tournament yourself, maybe you can send a jayvee coach or local junior high coach to scout the games.

On the high school level, we've occasionally entered into agreements with other coaches in our league that whoever loses out in region competition will scout other games for the winners—and, even more rarely, we've been able to schedule our own region tournaments in such a manner as not to conflict with other tournaments, to facilitate scouting.

• *With a weak team, scout your weakest opponents.* When wins are likely to be few and far between, it makes little sense to scout the best teams on your schedule if it means passing up opportunities to watch the teams with whom you have a realistic chance to compete. Winning games breeds far more confidence than reducing an opponent's potential winning margin from, say, 50 points to a more respectable 25.

• *With an average team, scout the average-to-weaker teams on your schedule.* We aren't saying that you shouldn't scout stronger opponents, of course; it's merely a question of establishing priorities. Our personal view is that, with a team of average ability, your Number One priority is to make absolutely sure that you beat the teams you're supposed to beat. If you fail in this regard, your average team may fall to below average or worse, with a resultant decline in morale confidence, and productivity against *all* teams. Your second priority is to win the close games by finding winning edges—and scouting can be an important means to that end. Winning the close games elevates the average team to above-average status, which offers psychological edges in terms of morale and confidence that may help your team when you face teams that are clearly superior to yours.

INDIRECT SCOUTING

Question: "If the season hasn't begun yet, how do I know how good my opponents are going to be?" Answer: You don't know for sure until you've seen them play, of course, but there are several ways you can make educated guesses with a fairly high degree of precision. All are based on indirect methods of gaining information about your opponents.

Scorebook, Scouting Reports, and Game Plans

If you were coaching at the same school last year, you probably already have a great deal of information about this year's opponents that you played last year: your scorebook, scouting reports, and game plans. (And if you filmed last year's games, you can also refer to those videotapes.)

• *Scorebook.* If you've made it standard operating procedure to have your scorebook keeper find out and record the grade levels of opposing players, you already have a pretty good idea who's returning, except for transfer students, academically ineligible students who have regained their eligibility since last season, and underclassmen who have moved up to the varsity. (Regarding the latter, you can get that information from the B-team or jayvee scorebooks—provided, of course, that you were able to persuade those coaches to record grade levels in their scorebooks, too.)

• *Scouting Reports.* You may not learn much about a team's playing style from last year's scouting reports if a given opponent has changed coaches, since the new coach's philosophy and approach to offense and defense may be wildly different from that of the previous coach. If the coach hasn't changed, though, your scouting reports may still be valid for the most part, since coaches tend to stay with a given system that they and their players understand and believe in. Exceptions exist, of course, but by and large it doesn't pay quick dividends to make drastic changes in a team's playing style unless last year's model was a real clunker.

At any rate, you can still use last year's scouting reports and game plan evaluations to help you evaluate returning players' strengths, weaknesses, and playing tendencies.

• *Game Plans.* Like scouting reports, last year's game plans are most likely to be helpful against returning coaches who are predictable in their adherence to a given style of play. For example, we know a football coach who doubled as a high school girls' basketball coach for more than two decades without ever using any half-court defense other than a 2–3 zone. (And if you find that unusual, you tell us: What defense will Bobby Knight's Indiana Hoosiers use next season?)

Newspapers

Newspapers usually offer their readers a preview of local and area teams. If your school is in a metropolitan area, the sports section of your local newspaper may be a goldmine of information about opposing teams and players—

especially if you double-check the facts for accuracy against last year's scorebook, scouting reports and game plan.[2]

Talking with Other Coaches

Talking with other coaches is probably the most popular indirect method for obtaining information about opponents. Coaches aren't likely to discuss their own teams with us (except in negative terms, that is)—and we'd be fools to believe them if they did—but most coaches will at least talk about other teams if requested to do so. A warning, though: such discussions are often less revealing than might be expected, due to the fact that the coach's perceptions are clouded by *his* team's ability to deal with that opponent.

—————————————— **DIRECT SCOUTING** ——————————————

Obviously, the best way to scout a team is to see it in person, whether by yourself, with an assistant coach, or by sending the assistant coach to scout a particular game while you're scouting elsewhere.

While no method of scouting is likely to reveal *everything* that you need to know about a team—to cite two examples, if the game is a rout you won't see the opponent's last-second shot strategy, and if the coach knows that you're scouting her team she may try to show you as little as possible of what she plans to do against *your* team—direct scouting offers insights regarding the team's preferred playing style and ample opportunities to study what the team and its individual players do well—and poorly. Regardless of the lengths to which a coach goes to conceal her preferred offenses and defenses, she cannot hide her players' skills and deficiencies except by benching her starters. Direct scouting always reveals players trying to do what they do best, whether or not they actually succeed.

Techniques for Effective Scouting

1. Verifying the game. Call the host school on game day to verify that the game hasn't been postponed, canceled, moved to another location, or had its starting time altered. We learned this lesson the hard way many years ago, by driving twenty-five miles to scout a high school game that had been postponed because of snow.

2. Materials to be taken. Before leaving, make sure that you have everything with you that you plan to take along—roadmaps and directions

———————————————

[2]While budgetary considerations may prohibit the practice on the high school level, many college basketball coaches subscribe to their opponents' local newspapers as a way of staying plugged in to what their opponents are doing.

for getting to the school (if you need them), your coaching pass, clipboards, scouting forms, scratch paper, shot charts, and plenty of pens or sharpened pencils. Repeat the process before you enter the gym to scout the game.

3. Thorough scouting/charting. If you plan to scout both teams—or if you plan to keep shot charts—take someone along with you (e.g., assistant coach or spouse) to help compile the information you need. You can do it all by yourself if need be, of course, but not as well or as accurately as two or more people can do the job by simple division of labor. Two or more pairs of eyes and hands can record at least twice as much as you alone can do—and they also see things that you might miss by yourself.

4. Travel and early game preparations. Leave early enough to account for such potential problems as traffic and parking, minor car trouble, or stopping to pick up a snack along the way.[3] You need to arrive early enough to watch the teams warm up and to get a comfortable seat with a clear view of the whole court. Get everything that you'll need ready and close at hand as soon as you're seated. You don't want to be fumbling around looking for a pencil while the scouted team is calling offensive signals or trying something new that you've never seen them do before. And you probably don't want to sit near the pep band or in the student section, where communication or vision may be obstructed.

5. Programs. Buy a program if they're available, and save it for your file on the team you're scouting.

6. Statistics. If you have someone keeping shot charts (see Figure 10–2), he can also record free throws, the score by quarters, rebounds, or whatever other stats you consider important.

7. Pregame scouting. (See Figure 10–3.) If you'll be playing the host team later in the season, the first aspect of your scouting should be to note any unusual or potentially troublesome features of the gym and playing area, such as:

• *Dim lighting.* We once scouted a high school team whose unpainted rims on its home court were practically invisible from more than ten feet from the basket, due to poor overhead lighting and a background that featured gray walls and an ancient backboard that had lost much of its transparency through age and constant use. (In our game plan for that gym, we stressed our inside power game exclusively on offense and ignored all shots from more than ten feet out, no matter how open our shooters might be.)

• *Unusual court dimensions or features.* If the court is small (i.e., a "matchbox"), you'll want to note whether (or how) the teams press each other

---

[3]If you're being paid mileage, you'll want to record the odometer readings at both ends of the trip.

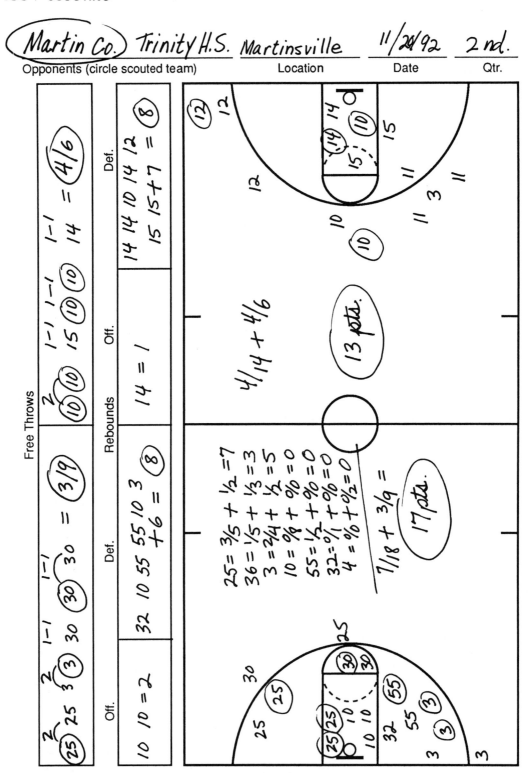

Figure 10-2 SHOT CHART

Figure 10–3 PREGAME SCOUTING FORM

⟨Martin Co.⟩ Trinity H.S.   Martinsville   11-20

Teams (circle scouted team)   Location   Date

I. GYM CONDITIONS

A. Lighting _Old gym with 3 overhead lights out, dark bleachers & dark red-brick walls (poor shooting background)._

B. Unusual court dimensions/features (e.g., short or long court, wide or narrow court, sideline/baseline space floor surface, baskets/backboards, special ground rules, etc.)

Faded paint on rims add to shooting problems & home court advantage. Wood floor (look for dead spots when we play there). Court size similar to ours.

II. INDIVIDUAL PLAYERS (e.g., shooting form, jumping ability, left-handedness, injuries, etc.)

25 - 5'7"-5'8," muscular, outstanding leaper (had 3 slam dunks against Polk Co. last yr). Very fast (quick start, long, powerful stride). excellent shooting form & range (practices shooting from dribble, reverse pivot, and stationary). Averaged about 27 ppg. last yr. A senior (THANK goodness!)

30 - About 6'1" thin, good speed. White, with freckles. Shoots jump-stop jumper (good form) with quick release, but form breaks down beyond 15'-18.' (prob. due to poor arm strength). Shoots better off the dribble then stationary. Smooth, good ballhandler, Senior.

3 - 6'2" redhead, excellent rotation on jump shot, appears to be good perimeter stationary shooter. Slow, pudgy, doesn't jump well for a forward. (Too slow to be a guard.) Practices shot.. fakes to draw defender into air. Prob. plays well without ball. Senior.

Figure 10-3: Pregame Scouting Form, continued

32 . About 6'3" (2nd tallest), slow, poor leaper. Not a perimeter shooting threat. Prob. doesn't shoot much: takes too long preparing shot, watches ball while dribbling. Junior

4 . 6'1"-6'2", fast but awkward, thin. Not a shooter: no backspin, poor form, no follow-through. Shoots FTs from right side (not center) of line. Decent vert. jump (24"-26"). Used rt.-hand dribbling exclusively in warmups. Senior.

10 . About 6'4" BIG (220-225 lbs.), slow. Moves like an off. lineman, not a BB player. Poor shooter, but prob. strong off. rebounder (only ave. vert. jump). Put him or #4 on the line at the end of the game if we have to foul somebody. Sophomore, prob. played JV ball last year.

55 . About 6'1", bulky (smaller version of #10). Better inside moves & shot than #10 (Effective range: 10'-12'.) Slow, but has quick release of jump shot. Wears knee brace (???) Only a fair leaper. Senior.

Overall - Martin Co. wasn't in our region last year, but I saw them beat Polk Co. by about 30 pts. (Don't remember any of their players except #25 & 30, and a 6'7" center who must have been a senior.) They're small, both in size & number (only 8 players dressed out), with excellent speed at guard, slow elsewhere. Used a 3-guard lineup last year, prob. will this year too. Word is, if you beat their press and hold #25 to his average, the rest of the team won't beat you -- but that may be easier said than done. (They're well-coached.) No left-handers.

© 1992 by Parker Publishing Company

and beat the presses—and to consider your own team's capabilities in those regards as well. Small courts are ideal for fast teams and full-court pressing defenses, whether zone or man-to-man—and as a result they can create considerable problems for slow teams trying to beat the press. Against double-teams, your ballhandlers may have to resort to longer passes than they're accustomed to making to beat the presses on regular courts, due to the reduced midcourt area.

The same sort of restrictions apply to older courts that are standard length but narrow. You may want to consider trying to center the ball on baseline inbounds passes rather than inbounding to the corner, to open up the midcourt areas or beyond for passes. And in your half-court offense, you may want to run your regular offense from an exaggerated spread rather than using a four-corner type of delay or slow-down if that tactic becomes necessary, since the narrow court brings the defenders closer together and makes cross-court passes even more risky.

On a half-court basis, small or narrow courts tend to favor the defense rather than the offense: Perimeter coverage is more easily achieved because the perimeters are not so distant as on regular courts, and defenders can clog the middle without conceding the perimeter shots. The key to defeating half-court defenses on small or narrow courts is to use a series of short, crisp passes to set up scoring opportunities (as opposed to, say, making long passes over or around the defense).

Long—or wide—courts, on the other hand, tend to reduce the effectiveness of quickness and trapping full-court defenses by enlarging the individual zones of responsibility for players away from the ball. As a result, half-court pressing defense is likely to be more effective than full-court pressing on big courts, whether in stealing the ball, forcing turnovers, or reducing the opponents' quick-strike potential when they beat the press. And big courts usually offer excellent opportunities to spread half-court defenses to their limits, whether to slow down the tempo of the game or to set up individual confrontations favoring the offensive team.

• *Sideline/baseline space.* If the area between the bleachers and the sideline is limited, you may want to talk to the referees or the home team's coach about the ground rules, if any, regarding sideline bring-ins. You could wait until your team plays there to discuss it, of course—but in some cases the ground rules may be bizarre, and if you find out now you can prepare for it by setting up benches or chairs on your court to practice your sideline bring-in plays under similar conditions before you play there.

• *Other considerations.* Are the rims level? You can check it out by standing in the bleachers with the rims at eye level. (We once scouted a high school game in which one of the rims appeared to be tilted upward. We asked the referee to measure it when we played there, and sure enough, it was in fact three quarters of an inch off. Someone—guess who?—had slipped several washers onto the nuts that affixed the basket to the backboard, presumably to keep the ball on the rim longer for his fast-breaking team to rebound missed shots in three-on-two situations.)

More important, are the rims tight or loose? New rims especially tend to be so rigid that even marginally imperfect shots have little chance of bouncing or rolling in. Constant use "deadens" the rims somewhat and softens the impact of errant shots; until then, however, rebounds are likely to be longer than usual and shots require a slightly higher trajectory to compensate for the rims' rigidity.

Are the nets tight? New nets tend to hold the ball longer, and thus to delay getting the ball out quickly for fast bring-ins.

Are the team seating areas satisfactory? Except possibly for postseason tournament play, there's no rule that we know of that says your team has to sit in chairs along the baseline or along the side of the court away from the scorer's table—yet we've encountered such seating arrangements on the road many times. (Rather than cause a scene, we merely arrange a place for our team and our gear in the bleachers near the scorer's table.)

Is the weather outside the gym a factor? In some older or smaller gyms, the entrances are located near the court area, and wintry winds whip through the doors every time they are opened. In such cases, we want to be shooting at the other end of the court in the second half; let the home team worry about wind gusts and getting cold hands when the game is on the line!

Finally, is the scouted team disciplined in its approach to pregame warmups? You can learn a lot about the coach and his team by watching the way the players warm up. If, for example, their warmup routine is lackadaisical or disorganized, you can expect their game performance to be equally indifferent because that's probably the way they practice, too.

8. Scouting individual players. If any phase of your scouting is likely to be wrong, it's your assessment of individual players. Team patterns and styles of play usually don't change much from game to game—although occasionally you'll see a team play zone defense all night only to find them playing man-to-man against you, or vice versa—but individual players may vary greatly in their productivity due to factors such as sickness, minor injury, or the quality of their opponents.

Shooting ability is likely to be the most difficult aspect of a player's game to assess. All players have hot and cold nights shooting, partly because shooting a basketball is such a finely tuned neuromuscular activity that even minor deviations from normal shooting form can render a player's shot temporarily out of sync, and partly because a particular defender may consistently be able to deny the player his preferred shooting areas or his initial moves to set up his shot.

In scouting individual players, it's important to note, not just where players like to shoot from, but also how they set up their shots and how the defenders take away their preferred shooting options as well. If it works for them, maybe your players can do it, too. (Or maybe not, which is why coaching is such a challenging and exciting profession.)

• *Pregame scouting of individual players.* Where shooting is concerned, there's no sure-fire way to know whether a player is a good shooter just by watching his pregame shooting: We've seen players hit six to eight long jumpers in pregame warmups, only to disappear on the bench never to be seen again once the game starts. On the other hand, you *can* tell if a given player is a poor or inconsistent shooter by watching the backspin he imparts (or fails to impart) to his shots: If you can see the name stamped on the cover while the shot is in the air, he isn't putting enough backspin on the shot to control it adequately. And if the shot has no backspin at all, you might want to note in your scouting report that *that's* the player you want taking the shot for them when the game is on the line, because the odds greatly favor his missing it. Except for slam dunks, shooting accuracy requires fingertip control of the ball; without it, a player isn't likely to shoot the lights out even if he's aiming for them.

Another factor to be considered in watching pregame warmups is *left-handedness*. Southpaws tend to set up their shots or penetrate in exactly the opposite manner from right-handers; that is, they may go to their right initially to move their defender in that direction, but more often than not they'll wind up going to their left via a crossover dribble or reverse pivot when they're ready to shoot. To reduce opponents' ability to dribble-penetrate or shoot from their dominant side against man-to-man defense, some coaches like to cheat their on-the-ball defenders as much as a half-body width toward the dribbler's dominant side, thus forcing the defender to penetrate weak-handed or not at all. To accomplish this (or to enhance their shot-blocking capability), defenders absolutely *must* know whether the player they are covering is left- or right-handed.

We also think it's important to note the presence of knee braces, since such injuries are usually of long duration and may impair the players' mobility. Limping, taped fingers or wrists, and elbow pads are other indications of injuries that may or may not be of long duration, or severe enough to affect the player in question—you'll find *that* out during the course of the game—but you can bet that if *he's* the player they need to beat you he'll be in the lineup when they play you. And he won't be limping then, either.

Finally, because some coaches are devious enough to use different numbers for their players' home and road uniforms—presumably to disrupt game plans based on scouting reports—we recommend noting in your pregame scouting such individual characteristics as approximate height/weight, body build, hair color, glasses, or other identifying features whenever you're unfamiliar with the coach or his team.

• *Scouting individual players during the game.* Identifying a team's best shooters is helpful, but it's more important to know who their *scorers* are—the ones they go to to get the job done offensively. Many good shooters

Figure 10–4 SCOUTING CHECKLIST—INDIVIDUAL SKILLS

I. SHOOTING/SCORING

☐ Who are their best (and worst) perimeter and inside shooters? Who are their best scorers?

☐ Where do their best shooters like to shoot from? What is their effective shooting range?

☐ How do their scorers likes to set up their shots? (Off the dribble, or do they shoot coming off screens?) Do they use shot-fakes against tight one-on-one coverage?

☐ Who are their best (and worst) free-throw shooters?

☐ In last-second game situations, who do we want to keep the ball away from?

II. REBOUNDING

☐ Who are their best rebounders/offensive rebounders? How big are they? (Approximate height/weight)

☐ Do they block out aggressively, or do they rely on vertical jumping ability? How do they compare to our best rebounders?

☐ Can they be trapped after defensive rebounds? Where do they look for the outlet pass receiver in fast-breaking after rebounds? Which big men fill the lanes in fast-break situations?

III. BALLHANDLING

☐ Who are their best ballhandlers? To what extent does the team's success depend on their ballhandling ability? Do they become flustered if denied the ball constantly?

☐ How effective are they at high-speed dribbling, and dribbling and passing under pressure? Do they protect the ball well? (Can they be trapped or do they consistently find the open man?)

☐ How well do they penetrate? (Do they favor one side over the other or can they go either way?) Can we neutralize their driving ability without resorting to double-teaming?

☐ Whom do we want to keep the ball away from when the game is on the line?

☐ Can we press them effectively?

IV. SPEED AND QUICKNESS

☐ Who are their fastest players? How does their quickness compare to that of our players?

☐ Do they play effectively at full speed or do they tend to play out of control offensively or defensively?

☐ Can we neutralize their speed advantage, if any? How?

V. DEFENSE

☐ Who are their best inside defenders? How tall/mobile are they? (Approximate height/weight) Can we get them in foul trouble by isolating them one-on-one? Are they susceptible to shot-fakes to get them airborne to block shots? Do they work hard? Are they in good shape physically?

☐ Can we drive, penetrate, or force double-teams against their guards?

☐ Who are their weakest defenders? How can we take advantage of them?

VI. GENERAL

☐ Who are their key players? (Do they rely heavily on one or two players offensively?) How can we neutralize those players offensively and/or defensively?

☐ Who are their most effective subs off the bench? How, if at all, does the team's performance diminish when they're in? Why?

☐ Which players are most likely to get rattled in pressure situations?

☐ Of the players who receive the most playing time, which ones are the youngest or most inexperienced?

☐ Are any players sick, injured, suspended, or otherwise not in uniform? Will they be back in the lineup when we play them?

can be shut down because the rest of their offensive game isn't complete enough to make them effective scorers. If your kids play tough D, the shooters may bother you occasionally like gnats and mosquitoes, but they won't hurt you as much as the scorers who can shred your defense like lions and tigers.

The same applies to other phases of individual play such as ballhandling, rebounding, and defense. In each area, your mind set as you watch them play and study their individual tendencies, strengths, and weaknesses should be, Who is most likely to hurt us, and how can we control them?

Still, as important as scouting individual traits and tendencies is, the important thing initially is to get a feel for how the scouted team intends to play the game at both ends of the court, and how their opponents intend to counter their offensive and defensive strategy as well. Thus, the first two to three minutes of the game are best spent watching the teams go about the process of implementing their game plans on offense and defense. As patterns and styles of play emerge and are noted, *then* the coach can begin to note how individual tendencies, matchups, and so on, affect the scouted team's ability to control the opponents at either end of the court—always, of course, from the standpoint of how his own players might fare against the team being scouted.

The questions in Figure 10–4 pertain to individual characteristics and playing tendencies that may be noted during the game.

9. *The opening tip.* The first organized play that a team uses is likely to be its opening tip play. While virtually every team keeps at least one player back as a deterrent to fast-breaks off the tip, the location of the other players around the center circle reflects their expectations regarding winning or losing the tip. After diagramming the lineup (using Xs to denote the location of the other team's players), you can use an arrow to show where the ball was tipped—if, that is, the team you're scouting won the tip. Some coaches simply describe the direction of the tip in terms of a clock face.

If the scouted team wins the tip, they will either try to score immediately or else set up in their half-court offense. In noting whichever scenario actually occurs, you should also consider the center jumper's ability relative to that of your own players to help you decide whether—and how—to offense or defense the tip when your team plays them.

The same consideration holds true if the scouted team loses the tip, too—but you should also note how the players react in terms of their ability to stop the fast break or set up their half-court defense quickly.

10. *Scouting the early game.* It does little or no good to start diagramming offensive plays furiously the first time the team runs through its patterns, since what you're seeing may not in fact be a set play at all but a sequence of freelance or passing game movements. If the team is using set plays or a continuity pattern, you'll have ample time during the course of the game to diagram the basic pattern and its automatics. The same holds true for zone offenses and, to a lesser extent, freelance and passing game offenses as well. Offensive patterns emerge as the team settles into its offensive playing style, as well as the opponents' defensive countermeasures designed to nullify those patterns. In the early portion of the game, however, the patterns are less important than getting a feel for the game and how both teams intend to approach it.

11. Scouting the offense. There are seven areas of offensive basketball to be taken into account in scouting—eight, if you count individual offensive skills as an area. They are (1) zone offenses, (2) patterned man-to-man offenses (set plays, continuity patterns), (3) unstructured man-to-man offenses (passing game and freelancing), (4) fast-breaking, (5) slowdown and delay patterns, (6) beating the presses, and (7) situational offense (last-second plays and bring-in plays). Not all areas will be seen in any given game, of course, since their use may depend on factors such as coaching preferences, the opponents' defensive style, and the score (e.g., last-second plays).

While offensive styles of play were considered in greater detail in Section 5, the questions in Figure 10–5 may be helpful in defining the scouted team's offensive strategy, and strengths and weaknesses, especially as they relate to your own team.

12. Scouting the defense. In the old days, all you had to do to scout a team defensively was to note whether they played man-to-man or zone defense, and maybe jot down the alignments they used in their zone coverage. No more, however: With at least four different styles of man-to-man defense being played today, three or more types of combination defense, and a minimum of seven styles of zone defense available—and those numbers refer just to the ways those defenses may be played on a half-court basis, not to different alignments or extended-court (pressing) defenses—a coach needs a great deal more information to adequately prepare his game plans. Modern basketball defenses have grown so complex that in many cases minimal information is no better than having no information at all.

The questions in Figure 10–6 may be helpful in analyzing the scouted team's defensive strategy, strengths, and weaknesses.

Of course, the answers to many of these questions (and those in Figures 10–4 and 10–5 as well) may not be readily apparent as the game progresses, especially the questions regarding possible solutions to problems posed by the scouted team. Those answers will arise later, as you begin to study your scouting notes, organize your initial impressions into a systematic analysis of what you've seen, and critically compare and contrast your team and your players with the scouted team and its players.

13. Scouting the game. As the game progresses, you'll want to note not only the offensive and defensive changes made by both teams but when they

Figure 10–5 SCOUTING CHECKLIST—TEAM OFFENSE

I. ZONE OFFENSES

☐ Are their zone offenses basically perimeter oriented, inside oriented, or do they attack both ways? (If we have to give up something, where are they least likely to hurt us?)

☐ How effective is their perimeter shooting/passing? Do they try to pass over the zone or around it? Can the ball be trapped in the corners?

☐ How effective is their inside game? Do they use one post player or a high–low arrangement? Will their post player require double-teaming?

☐ Do they attack the defense by dribble-penetrating from a balanced alignment and forcing double-teams to free teammates for shots? Or do they use cutter patterns or overloads to create numerical superiority or mismatches on weak side or ball side? (If they operate from overload alignments, do they overload with three or four players on ball side? And will overplaying the rotation passes to weak side upset the timing of their offense?)

☐ How can we reduce whatever advantages their zone offenses afford them? (How successful were their opponents in this regard, and why?)

II. SET PLAYS/CONTINUITY OFFENSES

☐ Are they patient in their shot selection, or do they take the first open shot they get?

☐ Will their play execution cause us trouble defensively? (Can we fight through their screens and overplay passing lanes to disrupt their offense? Or will we be better off using passive sinking and switching techniques to combat screens and protect the lane and post areas?)

☐ Do their automatics permit them to continue attacking the defense, or do automatics merely serve to reestablish the basic pattern?

☐ Do all of their players handle the ball in their plays or patterns, or do they rely on one or two players to run the offense? (Can we match up to reduce those players' offensive effectiveness?)

☐ What are the weakest aspects of their offense? How can we best exploit those areas?

III. UNSTRUCTURED MAN-TO-MAN OFFENSES

☐ How do they initiate their offense? (Do they begin their attack from the middle of the court? If not, which side do they seem to prefer, and why?) Will pressure defense force them farther outside than they prefer to begin their patterns? (Can we match up in such a manner as to create problems for them in the initial stages of their offense?) Do they use backdoor cuts effectively against pressure man-to-man?

© 1992 by Parker Publishing Company

☐ Is their offense basically oriented toward guard, forward, or post? (What do they like to do in their half-court offense? Isolate their best scorer for one-on-one matchups inside or along the perimeter? Drive and shoot or pass to an open teammate? Use inside screens or movement away from the ball to free their big men inside for open shots or one-on-one matchups around the paint? Isolate two-on-two for pick-and-roll, give-and-go, etc.?) How can we play our man-to-man to disrupt their offense and take away their favorite moves and tactics?

☐ Are all five players actively involved in trying to score, or just two or three at a time, with the others setting screens to alter the matchups or simply clearing out and watching the action from weak side? How active are their weak-side players? (Can we take advantage of their inactivity to offer help on ball side?)

☐ Do their big men play better facing the basket or with their backs to it? Do they favor one side over the other in cutting to the ball or establishing position? Do they attack from high post?

IV. FAST BREAKING

☐ How committed to fast-breaking are they? Do they fast-break (1) after turnovers or transitions, (2) after missed shots, (3) after scores, (4) against pressure defense, (5) all of the above, or (6) none of the above? How many players will we need to get back on defense to stop their fast-break?

☐ If their initial offensive thrust is denied, do they tend to press their attack and go for the first open shot or to settle into their half-court offense?

☐ How many ballhandlers can lead the fast-break? How effective is their court vision and ballhandling at high speed? Do they prefer to force the ball upcourt on the dribble or to pass the ball ahead to a teammate?

☐ Do they consistently get as many as three players involved in the break? (If so, who?) Do they use a sideline fast break or bring the ball up the middle of the court? Can we deny the pass to their outlet pass receiver, or pressure the passer into turnovers? (Can we trap him effectively?) Are there other ways we can slow down or stop their fast-break?

V. SLOWDOWNS AND DELAY PATTERNS

☐ Do they generally use the middle of the court or the corners in their spread formation? (Can we trap them in the corners?)

☐ How many players do they feature in their delay patterns? Are all of them good ballhandlers? Are they basically dribble oriented or pass oriented in their delay game?

☐ Who are their best (and worst) free-throw shooters? (Can our matchups force the ball away from their best ballhandlers and/or free-throw shooters? Whom do we want to put on the line if we have to foul to catch up?)

Figure 10–5: Scouting Checklist—Team Offense, continued

VI. BEATING THE PRESSES

☐ Is their inbounds passer's arm good enough to make the full-court pass accurately and consistently?

☐ Can we dictate where they receive the inbounds pass? Which ballhandlers should we try to keep the ball away from or attack? Should we double-team their best dribbler on the inbounds pass?

☐ Do they prefer to beat the press by dribbling through or around it, or to move the ball downcourt by passing?

☐ Do they fast-break when they beat the press? (At what point should we call off the press and retreat to our half-court coverage?)

☐ How well do they react to unexpected pressure in the backcourt? Which players are most likely to respond poorly and commit turnovers?

VII. SPECIAL SITUATIONS

☐ On baseline bring-in plays at their offensive end, which do they try to set up—inside scoring opportunities or shots from the perimeter? Or both? (Or do they just try to inbound the ball safely?) Do they throw lob passes to the big man inside? Where do they set their screens?

☐ Where do they prefer to inbound the ball to on sideline bring-ins? Do they use any trick plays such as rear screens and alley-oop passes for slam dunks, or back door cuts by the inbounds passer?

☐ What plays do they run in last-second-shot situations? Who is their most likely preferred shooter (1) from the perimeter and (2) near the basket? How do they set up his shot?

VIII. OTHER CONSIDERATIONS

☐ How many players do they send to the offensive boards? How effective is their offensive rebounding? Are they susceptible to fast-breaking?

☐ What are the offensive signals they use during the game?

Figure 10–6 SCOUTING CHECKLIST—TEAM DEFENSE

I. PRESSING DEFENSES

☐ What kind of presses do they use? (Full-, three-quarter-, or halfcourt? Zone or man-to-man?) When do they use then? How effective are they?

☐ Do they trap or run-and-jump? (Where do they like to set up the traps and confrontations?)

☐ Do they guard the inbounds passer? (Do they double-team the best ballhandler?) Are they susceptible to courtlength passes for layups?

☐ How can we beat their press—by dribbling or by passing through or around it?

☐ Do they recover quickly when their press is broken? (How susceptible are they to fast-breaking?)

II. ZONE DEFENSES

☐ What alignments do they use? How do they guard the point and high post? Who covers the passes to the wings?

☐ Do they trap? (If so, where?) Match up? Help-and-recover?

☐ With the ball at the wing, do they use three or four defenders on ball side? (If three, can we attack at high post or the corner? If four, are they vulnerable to rapid ball rotation and weak-side mismatches?)

☐ Are they basically aggressive, passive, or lazy in their coverage and movement? What are their most obvious weaknesses, and how can we take advantage of these?

☐ How effective is their inside coverage? Do they ever double-team at low post? Do they tend to overlook the middle during ball and player rotation from one side of the court to the other?

☐ Why are they using zone defense rather than man-to-man?

III. MAN-TO-MAN DEFENSES

☐ How much pressure do they apply to the ball? Do they try to influence the dribbler by overplaying toward the sideline or toward the dribbler's weak hand? Are they susceptible to backdoor cuts?

☐ Do they fight through screens, or switch? (If the latter, are the switches called or automatic?)

☐ How do they guard the posts—by fronting or by overplaying? How effectively do their big men deny the inside passes?

☐ Can we drive on them? How effective is their inside help?

☐ Does their coverage have any weaknesses that we can exploit? How?

Figure 10–6: Scouting Checklist—Team Defense, continued

IV. COMBINATION DEFENSES

☐ Do they use a standard combination defense (i.e., box-and-one, diamond-and-one, or triangle-and-two)? If so, which player of ours will they put the chaser on?

☐ Do they match up with their other players or simply shift with the movement of the ball along the perimeter?

☐ Where is their coverage weakest? At high post? In the corners? On weak side?

☐ Do they use man-to-man principles from a zone alignment or use zone principles in man-to-man coverage?

V. OTHER CONSIDERATIONS

☐ Do they zone inbounds passes on baseline bring-ins in their defensive half-court?

☐ How often (and when) do they change defenses? Are their changes called verbally? (If not, how do they signal their changes?)

occurred and what impact (if any) they had on each team's play. You'll also want to find out, if you can, how the coach signals his changes.

Coaches often make changes in their offensive or defensive strategy and tactics during timeouts (if you sit near the bench you may be able to overhear some of the things the coach is saying to his assistants or players) or at halftime. But they also make changes during the game action, usually by verbal commands or visual signals. By watching the coaches and players you may be able to pick up on their signals—and if you know their signals and what they signify, you'll be ready for the changes when your team plays that opponent.

In addition to diagramming the plays and patterns that a team uses, it's also important to note their basic approach to the game: Are they organized or undisciplined? Do they force the action or wait patiently for the opponents to make mistakes? How do they react to pressure or to changes in the tempo that they prefer? Do they rely heavily on one or two players? The answers to these questions and others in the Scouting Checklists will provide the basis for the game plan that you will prepare later for that team.

You may also want to note the noise level in the gym during the game if it is sufficiently great to be a factor in your coaching or your team's play.

You may, of course, use any format you like to record your notes. (A sample form is shown in Figure 10–7; it also appears in the Appendix in reproducible form.) Scouting forms should contain half- and full-court diagrams, and space for jotting down notes as well. Some coaches use hand-held microcassette recorders; we don't, for a variety of reasons. They are not as precise as written notes and play diagrams in describing areas of the court; they can be lost or left behind; there can be problems with crowd noises, defective tapes, or weak or defective batteries—and if you combine tapes and written notes, taping with one hand and writing with the other can be troublesome, especially in a crowded gym.

14. After the game. If the game is one-sided, you may want to beat the traffic jams and get a head start on the drive home by leaving as early as midway through the fourth quarter if both teams' scrubs appear to be in for the remainder of the game. (We make it a practice never to leave while the scouted team's starters are still in the game, since whether he is winning big or losing by a lopsided score the coach may want to use the remaining time to work on aspects of his team's game that the starters have rehearsed in practice but used only sparingly if at all in games.)

We learned as graduates of good old Hard Knocks U. that *you never ever leave the game at halftime just because the first half was a rout.* First, the losing team may stage a terrific comeback and if you've already left you won't know how they did it; and second, you need to find out what kind of adjustments, if any, the coach made at halftime.

Generally speaking, you stay with close games to their conclusion, noting late-game strategy, tactics, and how the players handle the pressure; and you

Figure 10-7 SCOUTING FORM

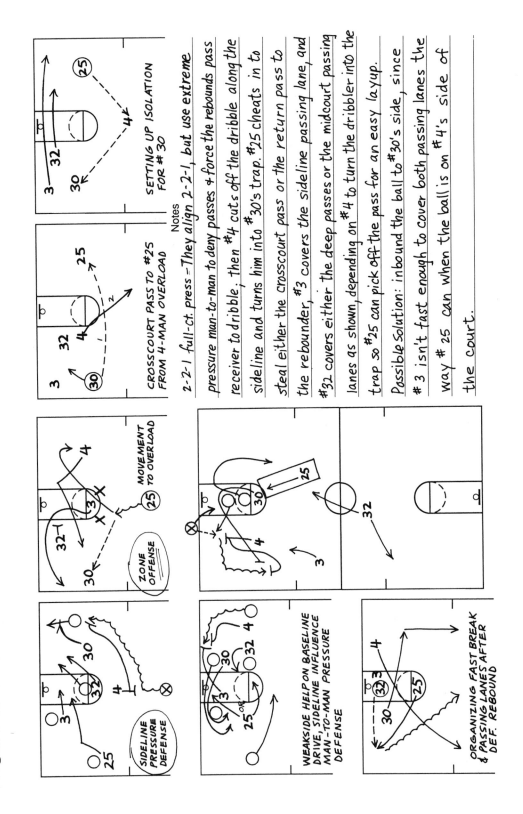

SIDELINE PRESSURE DEFENSE

ZONE OFFENSE — MOVEMENT TO OVERLOAD

CROSSCOURT PASS TO #25 FROM 4-MAN OVERLOAD

SETTING UP ISOLATION FOR #30

WEAKSIDE HELP ON BASELINE DRIVE, SIDELINE INFLUENCE MAN-TO-MAN PRESSURE DEFENSE

ORGANIZING FAST BREAK & PASSING LANES AFTER DEF. REBOUND

Notes

2-2-1 full-ct. press = They align 2-2-1, but use extreme pressure man-to-man to deny passes & force the rebounds pass receiver to dribble; then #4 cuts off the dribble along the sideline and turns him into #30's trap. #25 cheats in to steal either the crosscourt pass or the return pass to the rebounder. #3 covers the sideline passing lane, and #32 covers either the deep passes or the midcourt passing lanes as shown, depending on #4 to turn the dribbler into the trap so #25 can pick off the pass for an easy layup.

Possible Solution: inbound the ball to #30's side, since #3 isn't fast enough to cover both passing lanes the way #25 can when the ball is on #4's side of the court.

stay with blowouts until such time in the second half that you feel reasonably sure that the coach of the scouted team isn't going to show you anything else that you haven't already seen.

Before leaving the gym, you should check one last time to make absolutely sure that you aren't forgetting anything that you might need later, such as your clipboard. Of course, you wouldn't do anything dumb like leaving your scouting notes in the gym, *nobody* would—but the high school gym was locked when we went back for the notes we left behind, and the coach's comments at the next region meeting didn't help any. Actually, he was quite gracious and complimentary about it: said it was the most thorough scouting job he'd ever seen, and if he'd known we were performing that sort of service for area coaches, he wouldn't have paid a scouting service to do the same thing in preseason, because our notes were better than theirs. Said his kids appreciated our constructive criticisms of their individual and collective play, once they got over their initial shock at reading about how lousy they were compared to our players, when they found the photocopies of our scouting notes taped to their lockers the next day.

The next time we went scouting, we practically wiped the place clean of fingerprints before leaving with our scouting notes clutched as firmly in hand as a courier guarding state secrets—and since then we've never left anything in a visitors' gym more incriminating than empty cola cups or popcorn boxes!

15. Preparing the scouting report. The ride home is where you start digesting and assimilating what you've seen. Your notes will be disorganized and in disarray, having been hastily scribbled during the heat of the battle. Later, after you've had time to think over what you saw and study your notes, you'll want to organize the material and prepare the scouting report that you'll present to the players and use in formulating your game plan for that team.

The scouting questionnaires shown in Figures 10–4, 10–5, and 10–6 provide a quick and easy method for organizing and analyzing your scouting notes and preparing your scouting report. To use the checklists effectively, simply (a) place a checkmark in the spaces by those questions you can answer on the basis of your scouting information, (b) answer those questions as fully as possible (including using diagrams wherever applicable), and (c) ignore the rest.

For example, if the scouted team played zone defense all night, your scouting report would address the questions in Section II ("Zone Defenses") of the *Team Defense* questionnaire shown in Figure 10–6—but not the questions in Section III ("Man-to-Man Defenses"). And if they didn't press, you would simply ignore Section I ("Pressing Defenses"), except possibly to hazard a guess as to why they didn't press (e.g., they're too slow).

Using game notes, play diagrams, and the various scouting checklists as our guides, we'll compile a detailed scouting report covering every aspect of the game that our opponents showed us (see Figure 10–8). If possible, we

Figure 10–8 SCOUTING REPORT

Martin Co.H.S. vs. _Trinity H.S._ at _Martinsville_
Scouted Team   Opponent

I. STARTERS _#25, 30, 3, 4, 32_   **Date** _11-20_

II. SCORE BY QTRS.

Team	1st	2nd	3rd	4th	Final
Martin Co.	21	17	24	33	95
Trinity H.S.	19	13	12	24	68

III. OVERALL EVALUATION

They're fast—at guard, anyway—but their up-tempo style of play makes them better than they really are. They press three-quarter-court (2–2–1 zone/man-to-man), and play sideline-influence man-to-man pressure in their half-court defense. They fast break and run constantly, trying to keep up a 98-mph pace to wear you down and tire you out. (They don't call timeouts because they don't want to give you a minute to rest.) *Offensively*, they look for scores off the break, whether layups or shots from three-point range, almost as if they don't care whether they make them or not so long as the pace remains frantic. (But they *can* make them: #25 (point guard) can score from anywhere—he had 38 against Trinity—#30 had 26 pts. on 10/16 shooting, and #3 hit five three-pointers and scored 21 pts.)

Still, they aren't as good as they were last year when they had that big #15 inside. Offensively, they're at their best when a team tries to run with them (as Trinity did)—but they don't rebound well offensively (#10 is *big*, but slow and largely immobile), so they don't get many second shots, and their inside game is *very weak*. (Aside from #25, #30, and #3, the rest of the team scored 10 of their 95 pts. against Trinity.) *Defensively*, their press is good if you try to dribble through or around it—but their team speed drops off drastically if you get past #25, #30, and #4. (#4 is their primary on-the-ball defender in their press, with #25 in position to steal the cross-court pass when #4 turns the dribbler into #30's trap—Diagram 5).

Their press can be beaten by quick passes or inbounding the ball to #30's side of the court, and their half-court defense by backdoor cuts (they overplay the passing lanes) or lob passes inside from the middle of the court (not the sidelines). They front the posts (Diagram 8). And since they aren't a strong rebounding team, you can send three players to the boards at both ends—but you'd better have those other two players back to deal with the break or the scoreboard will register points like donations totals in the final minutes of a Jerry Lewis telethon!

IV. INDIVIDUAL PLAYERS

#25—In a word, *awesome*. Only 5'7", but lightning quick, great vert. jump, excellent ballhandler, penetrates well with either hand, outstanding scorer. (Best bet: play him box-and-one defensively, and post up whoever he guards.)

#30—About 6'1", thin, good speed. White, with freckles. Excellent jump shot going to right, not so hot going to left or stationary from three-point range. Good bh. Pressure him and he'll drive around you (quick first step); lay back and he'll pass and cut. Goes to off. boards better than their center and forwards but doesn't block out well (too thin).

#3—6'2" redhead, very good perimeter shooter. Slow, but will drive if guarded closely; draws a lot of fouls with shot-fakes near the basket. Excellent FT shooter.

#10—About 6'4", 225 lbs. Slow, clumsy. Poor shooter, bh (no moves, just turn and shoot). Doesn't block out well on the boards.

#32—6'3", poor leaper. Plays excellent position defense inside, poorly outside (*very* slow). Doesn't score much: slow-developing shot, poor bh (no moves), doesn't like to dribble. Used primarily on offense to set screens along the baseline for #3's shot (Diagram 2), and as a trailer in the fast-break (Diagram 1).

#4—About 6'2", guard. Very fast, but poor bh and terrible shooter. Good on-the-ball defender (they use him, and not #25 or #30, on the opponents' best bh). Offensively, they use him primarily to inbound the ball after scores, and to relay the ball to #25 or #30 on weakside against zone defense. (Diagrams 3 and 4). Put #4 (or #10) on the line if we need to foul someone at the end of the game.

#55—6'1", heavy. Slow, but works hard, plays physical game. Quick release of jump shot, but slowness and lack of jumping ability reduce opportunities.

#23—5'10", pudgy. A body in uniform, nothing more.

V. BEATING THE PRESS

Trinity didn't press them—and we shouldn't either.

Figure 10-8: Scouting Report, continued

VI. TEAM OFFENSE

1. *Fast-Break.* They lane their fast-break and designate their bh (#25). #3 always fills the rt. lane, #30 the left, and #32 trails to relay the ball to weak side if the primary options break down.

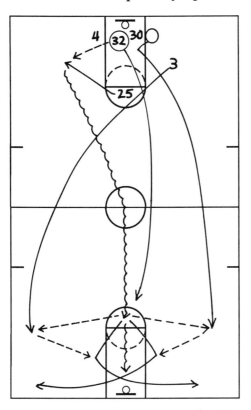

Diagram 1 Martin Co. Fast-Break After Rebound

#25 dribbles upcourt and shoots, drives, or passes to a wing. After passing, #25 cuts to intermediate post for a return pass; if he doesn't get it, he cuts to weak side corner.

#3 or #30, receiving #25's pass, either shoots, drives, passes back to #25 at intermediate post—or passes to #32, the trailer, at the top of the circle. #32 then relays the ball to the weakside wing and cuts to low post away from the ball. (#4, the second trailer, will fill the other low-post position after repeating #32's options at the top of the circle.) Whoever gets the first open shot or chance to drive, takes it. They aren't particular about who shoots or where he shoots from—but their pattern keeps the ball in the hands of their best players—#25, #30, and #3—most of the time.

On transition breakaways, whoever stole the ball takes it all the way to the hole.

On bring-ins after scores, #4 inbounds to #25 while everyone else releases downcourt in their lanes at the speed of light. (Forget trying to trap #25; you might as well stop a tidal wave with a pair of buckets. Anyway, #4 would just throw the baseball pass to #3, #32, or #30.)

2. *Half-Court Offense.* Trinity didn't use any man-to-man defense; they stayed in 2–3 zone all game. To beat it, Martin Co. basically took the lst shooting opportunity that arose, inside or outside. When they were forced to run a pattern, they set up the overload and movements to isolate #25 or #30 with the ball on weak side (Diagrams 2 through 4).

VII. PRESSING DEFENSES

1. *2–2–1 Three-quarter-Court Press.* They line up 2–2–1, with #30 denying the pass to the middle or weak side, but #4 allowing the ball to be

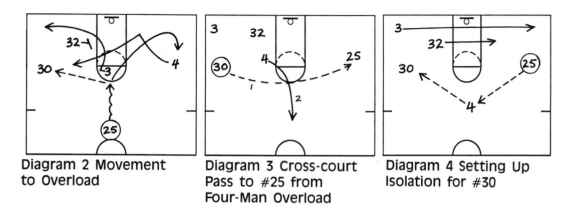

Diagram 2 Movement to Overload

Diagram 3 Cross-court Pass to #25 from Four-Man Overload

Diagram 4 Setting Up Isolation for #30

inbounded in front of him. (That's where they *want* you to throw it.) When the ball is inbounded, #4 quickly bellies up to the receiver while the other players assume man-to-man responsibilities to deny all passes. As soon as the inbounds pass receiver dribbles, #4 pivots sharply and sprints to cut him off and turn him quickly as #30 rushes over to close the trap. By the time the bh picks up his dribble and reverse-pivots away from #4, #30 is in his face

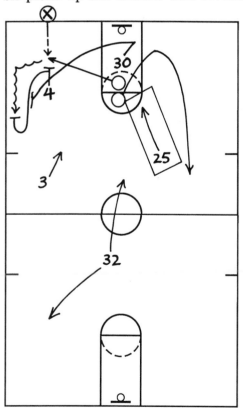

Diagram 5 Martin Co. 2-2-1 Full-Court Press

and #25 has moved into position to pick off the cross-court pass, with #32 moving up to cover the midcourt area vacated by #25. Of course, the whole thing hinges on #4's stopping and turning the dribbler; if he fails, every one simply stays in man-to-man coverage, since #3 is too slow and defensively weak to trap the dribbler along the sideline and #32—who is even slower than 3—can't adequately cover the large zone he's responsible for when the dribbler is controlling the action rather than #4 controlling him.

2. *Other Presses.* When the ball is inbounded to #30's side or the middle, they use straight man-to-man defense without trapping—probably because #3 is too slow to cover both the corner/midcourt areas on his side of the court.

They didn't press three-quarter-court or half-court at all.

Figure 10–8: Scouting Report, continued

VIII. HALF-COURT DEFENSE

They played pressure man-to-man all game, no zone.

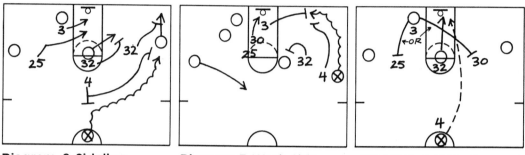

Diagram 6 Sideline
Pressure Defense

Diagram 7 Weak-Side
Help on Baseline Drive

Diagram 8 Fake Screen
and Lob Pass for Layup

#4 picks up the bh at the center circle and influences him toward the sideline with tight pressure defense, trying to cut him off and make him pick up his dribble as far out as possible. If he succeeds, all ball-side passing lanes will be closed off and the only apparently open receiver will be #25's man cross-court (Diagram 6). If he fails and the bh continues to drive the baseline (Diagram 7), #3 (or whoever was covering weak-side low post) cuts off the drive and traps the dribbler with #4, with #25 or someone else on weak side covering #3's man.

Weakness: They're gambling on #4's ability to influence the ball toward the dribbler's strong side without losing defensive control, whether by having the bh dribble past him or reverse-pivot toward the middle to penetrate or pass. #25 could do it—but they want him to steal the cross-court pass rather than waste him on the dribbler. (I'd put #25 on the bh and #30 in #25's place.) A good dribbler can beat #4 most of the time. And the defense is in danger of breaking down any time the ball is in the middle, whether against their press or their half-court defense (Diagram 8).

Other Half-Court Defense. None. They live or die with the half-court sideline-influence pressure man-to-man defense as part of the up-tempo game they want played.

IX. SPECIAL SITUATIONS

1. They defended the opening tip (#32 jumped center), with #3 and #4 back to stop the fast-break.

2. They didn't use any last-second plays or slowdown/delay patterns.

3. *Baseline Bring-in Play.* #25 inbounds to #3 in the corner, who shoots

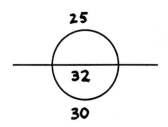

Diagram 9 Martin Co. Center Jump Alignment

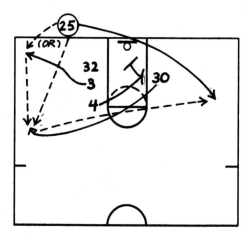

Diagram 10 Baseline Bring-in Play

or passes to #30 (who shoots, penetrates, or passes to #25 on weak side behind #4's screen). Then, when it gets that far, 30 slides to weak-side wing, #4 cuts to the top of the circle to relay #25's pass to #30, and they're back in their zone offense again, looking for the first open shot or penetrating action they can find.

want the written portions of the scouting report to be typed, or at least written in a neat, legible handwriting; whichever is the case, there should be no typing mistakes, strikeovers, messy ink stains, or other flaws in the report. We want our players to know that we care enough to strive for perfection if not attain it in everything we do. We may have to go through a whole bottle of WhiteOut™ with every scouting report or game plan we prepare to achieve our goal, but we think it's worth the effort. To do less is to create a double standard in which we expect our players to give a total effort and do their best while we get by with a sloppy performance that could have been avoided with harder work and greater attention to detail.

Along with that, we like ex-LSU and USC football coach Paul Dietzel's idea of making our presentations to players not just neat and attractive but colorful as well. To that end, we like to use a variety of colored Hi-Liters™ and felt-tip pens to emphasize and underscore important points in our scouting reports and game plans. The finished product is appealing, eye-catching, and easy to read, and the underscoring and highlighting draws the readers' attention to points that we consider important.

16. Going over the scouting report with your players. Some coaches use chalk talks or squad meetings to present the scouting report; others discuss its various aspects in walk-through fashion at appropriate times during daily practices. We use either or both methods, depending on how familiar our players are with the opponent. But we also expect the players to study the scouting report and game plan sometime prior to game day.[4] And if we're playing on the road, we expect the players to study the scouting report and game plan during the bus ride. (We also use that time to discuss individual matchups, goals, strategies, etc., with every player in turn.) In addition to giving them a last in-depth look at the opponents prior to the game, it helps keep them focused on the upcoming game.

17. Scouting a team the second time around. If you've already scouted a team or played them once, you're likely to find a lot of duplication of things you've already seen. Rather than waste time jotting down the same diagrammed plays that we've seen, we prefer to make a few brief notes to the effect that that given phase of the game was covered in a previous report or game plan, and devote our attention to aspects of the game that are new for that team.

In scouting a team for the second time, you'll want to note changes (if any) in the starting lineup and first eight players, variations and adjustments

---

[4]At AUM we also prepare individual profiles of each of the scouted team's top eight players. These profiles, which include individual shot charts and notes regarding each player's strengths, weaknesses, preferences, and tendencies, are posted in the locker room prior to our game with that team or given to the players to study while we're traveling.

in their patterns or playing style, and whether those changes or adjustments are in response to the opponents' style of play, or because the team is improving or going downhill. (Of course, you'll also want to note the relative success or failure of the unscouted opponents' offensive and defensive strategy.) And keeping accurate shot charts and stats this time around, too, will afford a basis for analyzing individual performances in terms of consistency, shooting preferences, and the like.

SECTION 11

Game Plans

If you don't know where you're going, you'll probably wind up somewhere else.

—Dr. Laurence J. Peter

PRELIMINARY QUESTIONS

• ***Is it necessary to have a game plan for every game? Should it be in written form?*** Game plans are important to coaches for the same reason that battle plans are important to generals: While they do not ensure victory, they at least provide direction toward what the coach or general considers to be his or her side's best chances of winning.

Actually, the first question is moot since it's virtually impossible *not* to enter a game without some sort of plan, however simplistic it might be. Even in backyard pickup games or park ball, players will agree on a defensive style and how they will play it before the game begins. So the question is not so much Should we have a game plan? as How complicated should our game plan be, and What should it consist of?

The complexity of a game plan depends on a number of factors, including (among other things) the players' experience, their familiarity with the offensive patterns and defensive styles contained in the game plan, and their ability to absorb information without becoming confused. Game plans should contain only those strategies, tactics, plays, and patterns that have been worked out beforehand in daily practices to the players' complete understanding.

Whereas inexperienced players (or veteran players who are still learning a new coach's system) normally respond best to a simple game plan, players who are familiar with their system should be able to absorb larger amounts of information. At any rate, you should know your players' capabilities well enough to know how much they can absorb. (Your best guide in this regard is the amount of confusion or confidence they display after practicing new plays, patterns, etc.) When in doubt, you're probably better off preparing game plans that give your players a KISS (as in *Keep It Simple, Stupid*) rather than KILL-ing them by *Keeping It Long* and *Laborious*.

As to whether game plans should be in written form—yes, they should be written down so they can be evaluated afterward. Whether they are presented to the players in oral or written form is entirely up to you. It takes a lot of work to prepare *any* game plan; preparing a written game plan for the players to study along with the scouting reports is even more time-consuming. Still, *we* do it because we think it's important—and because we've taught our players that it's important. They *expect* to study the game plan and scouting reports prior to games. It's an accepted part of our preparation for games.

 • *Is it necessary that every game plan be different?* Using the same game plan for every game works best if you don't intend to (or can't) make any changes. For example, Paul Westhead's Loyola–Marymount and Denver Nuggets teams were as predictable as sunrise in their fast-paced, up-tempo style of play. (Coach Westhead doesn't change his basic game plan because any offensive or defensive changes he might make would alter the mile-a-minute tempo that he's trying to achieve.) And at the beginning of our coaching career many years ago we took over a junior high boys' team at midseason. After two days' practice, we played our first game with *one* zone offense (an overload), *one* man-to-man play (a clearout), *no* presses, no man-to-man defense, and a basic 1–2–2 zone defense that was similar to, but even simpler than, the one in the game plan shown in Figure 11–2. And that was it. We didn't even have an opening tip play other than "Tip it to somebody on *our* team," and our baseline bring-in play was called "Stand Still" because our boys kept moving to the open areas even before the referee handed the ball to our inbounds passer.

We added a few new wrinkles to subsequent game plans, of course—but we never strayed far from our basic game plan during that abbreviated first season because the boys were largely unskilled and inexperienced.[1]

In other situations, it may be necessary to modify your game plan to effectively counter opponents' strengths, attack their weaknesses, or hide your own weaknesses. In doing so, however, your actions should be guided by one of basketball coaching's most basic principles, namely:

---

[1]Apparently—and fortunately for us—our opponents were even more unskilled and inexperienced than we were: We finished the season with an 8–2 record, with both losses coming at the hands of high school B teams.

If it works, don't fix it.

If there's a better way to play an upcoming opponent than you're presently using, then by all means go for it—but don't alter your game plan just for the sake of change. Try to keep your changes to a minimum, and within the context of what you're already doing, if possible. Familiarity may breed contempt on a romantic level, at least—but in basketball familiarity breeds confidence and consistency, two important factors in winning.

On the other hand, if what you're presently doing isn't working, your three options consist of: (1) abandoning your original plan and trying something else, (2) staying with the plan until the players learn it well enough to make it work, or (3) devising minor adjustments that allow you to retain the basic plan in modified form. Which method you choose depends on how committed you are to what you've been doing.

• *What should the game plan consist of? Should it duplicate information contained in the scouting reports on that team?* Taking the questions in reverse order, we'll note that repeating information found in the scouting reports is unnecessary, except possibly to underscore the importance of that information.

In their most basic form, game plans describe the way you hope to play the game, both individually and as a team, without reference to what the opponents' strategy might be. For example, knowing absolutely nothing at all about an upcoming opponent, your game plan likely would stress playing to your own team's strengths and hiding your weaknesses rather than strategies for dealing with the opponents' strengths and weaknesses.

If, however, you're familiar with the opponents' personnel and playing style through scouting or previous games with them, you will probably expand your plan to analyze their likely offensive and defensive strategies—and how you intend to counter those strategies, as well. This is, in fact, what most game plans consist of—the strategic moves and countermoves that coaches make to create advantages favoring their team or reduce advantages favoring their opponents. Sometimes these moves and countermoves arise during the course of the game (which is what game coaching is all about), but more often than not they are developed through extensive planning in the course of preparing for upcoming games. As Bear Bryant put it, "I think game coaching is overrated. You develop a game plan that you believe in, and you prepare your players to execute it. But down there on the field, the game belongs to the players. They're the ones who make it work." We echo that sentiment 100 percent.

A third category of game plans involves planning, not merely for what you and the opponents might do, but for what your team might do if your game plan just doesn't work the way it's supposed to. Known as *contingency planning*, this technique can be highly rewarding on those nights when your ballhandlers are all thumbs, your shooters can't find the basket with a road-map and a ladder, and your defense is as leaky as the S.S. Minnow on "Gilligan's Island." On such highly forgettable occasions when, as the poet Yeats put it, "things fall apart," the need for contingency planning becomes apparent.

Put simply, contingency planning involves listing various approaches that might be used in case your original strategy fails to contain the opponents as expected or desired. As we've noted, how much of what you're doing can be changed depends largely on your players' experience and versatility. And you could always wait until adverse situations arise to consider how you might alter your plans, but in the heat of the game you may overlook possibilities that advance planning might have revealed.

Whether you include your contingency plans in the game plan that you present to your players is debatable: On the plus side, it reminds the players of aspects of the game that they've rehearsed in practice and thus should be familiar with; negatively, it hints that your game strategy may not work against that opponent, and as a result, it may introduce an element of doubt in the players' minds that might not have been there otherwise.

Still, we repeat: Contingency planning can be highly rewarding, especially if you're the sort of coach who prefers to anticipate stormy weather regardless of what the weatherman says.

ORGANIZING THE GAME PLAN

Probably the easiest way to organize a game plan is in terms of five sections, as shown in Figure 11–1.

Of course, your game plan should involve only those aspects of team offense, team defense, and special situations that you expect to use or encounter in the upcoming game. Other areas need not be included at all or should be mentioned only in passing, as with the "Slowdowns" section of the sample game plan shown later in this section.

PREPARING THE GAME PLAN

Before considering ways to counter your opponents' strengths or attack their weaknesses, you must have a thorough grasp of your own team's strengths and weaknesses. Assuming that you are sufficiently prepared in that regard, your next step is to gather all of the information you've compiled about your opponent that can aid you in analyzing the two teams' relative strengths, weaknesses, playing styles, strategies, and tactics. Such information includes:

- Scouting reports (including pregame scouting information and shot charts)

Figure 11-1 OUTLINING THE GAME PLAN

I. **OVERALL APPROACH**
   A brief introductory statement describing your plans for the game. (Other sections of the game plan will flesh out the skeleton plan you're revealing here.)

II. **INDIVIDUAL PLAYERS**
   Specific strategies, advice, and techniques for dealing with opposing players or situations your players are likely to encounter.

III. **TEAM OFFENSE**
   A. Zone Offenses
   B. Set Plays/Continuity Patterns
   C. Unstructured Man-to-Man Offenses (Passing Game/Freelancing)
   D. Fast-Breaking
   E. Slowdowns and Delay Patterns
   F. Beating the Presses

IV. **TEAM DEFENSE**
   A. Pressing Defenses
   B. Zone Defenses
   C. Man-to-Man Defenses
   D. Combination Defenses

V. **SPECIAL SITUATIONS**
   A. Tip Plays and Strategy
   B. Bring-in Plays
   C. Late-Game and/or Last-Second Plays and Strategy

- The scouting checklists shown in Figures 10–4, 10–5, and 10–6, which pose questions relevant to comparing your team and individual players with theirs
- Previous game plans (and their evaluations), shot charts, and game statistics, if you've already played that team at least once this season

Armed with such information and data, you will begin to search for ways to control or contain your opponents, whether by establishing your own strengths or exploiting your opponents' weaknesses.[2] Three coaching principles may assist you in this regard:

1. Use Your Strengths

If you're clearly superior to your opponents, don't change what you've been doing. Beat them with your strengths.

2. Don't Beat Them at Their Own Game

If your opponents are clearly superior to your team, don't try to beat them at their own game. Instead, focus on (1) hiding your weaknesses, (2) attacking your opponents' weaknesses, and (3) controlling the tempo of the game.

Hiding your weaknesses. Ways to hide (or reinforce) your weaknesses might include any or all of the following techniques or strategies:

- Using your nonshooters exclusively in nonshooting roles such as screening, pass-and-cut clearouts, and weak-side rebounding
- Matching up your weakest defenders against the opponents' weakest offensive players
- Matching up your highest scorer against the opponents' weakest offensive player to avoid foul difficulty
- Tightening your shot selection requirements (i.e., dictating where shots will be taken from and who will take them)
- Sending more players to the boards than usual to offset height disadvantages in rebounding
- Keeping the ball out of the hands of your unskilled ballhandlers except in potentially high-percentage scoring areas for them
- Playing zone defense to enhance inside coverage or rebounding, to simplify individual responsibilities, and to hide foul-prone players

---

[2]One of the unfortunate side effects of doing a thorough job of scouting is the natural tendency to overestimate their opponents' strength. This tendency should be resisted, lest you find yourself making unnecessary changes in your game plan.

Attacking your opponents' weaknesses. Having already scouted your opponents, you should be aware of the nature and extent of their weaknesses, both as a team and individually.[3] The problem lies in determining how much you can and should deviate from your basic game plan to exploit the weaknesses you've identified but not impair your own team's effectiveness in the process.

To attack or exploit opponents' weaknesses, you might want to consider:

- Using screens to alter matchups and pit your best scorers against weak defenders
- Using pressing or trapping defenses against slower teams or teams with relatively weak ballhandling
- Using combination defense to keep the ball away from a team's high scorer or best ballhandler
- Using a post-oriented offense against smaller but quicker opponents
- Playing off weak perimeter shooters to provide added defensive pressure inside
- Fouling poor free-throw shooters in high-percentage scoring situations or in pressure situations such as near the end of the game if fouling is necessary as a catch-up tactic

Controlling the tempo of the game. Every team plays best at a certain rhythm and tempo; taking them out of it by playing at a different pace than they are used to can upset their timing and render them at least temporarily vulnerable.

Perhaps no better example of this concept exists anywhere in basketball than that of Pete Carril's Princeton Tiger teams, who routinely milk the forty-five-second clock down to its final seconds in their controlled offense before seriously pursuing any shots other than uncontested layups. (That's why Coach Carril has so much trouble scheduling big-name opponents outside the Ivy League conference.)

At the other end of the spectrum, tempowise, stands Loyola–Marymount's 1989–90 squad, which scored a whopping 122.4 ppg. for the entire season—and averaged shooting *every eight seconds* in the process—by controlling the tempo with relentless fast-breaking, unorthodox shot selection, and full-court pressure defense that usually yielded slam dunks at one end of the court or the other.

Either of two problems may hinder your team's ability to control the tempo of the game: First, the opponents may be so highly skilled that they can play effectively at any tempo (as has been the case with most of Dean Smith's UNC teams); and second, your own personnel shortcomings may se-

---

[3]If you haven't scouted them, you won't know their weaknesses until you play them.

verely limit your ability to use your playing style to control or alter the game tempo, to attack opponents' weaknesses, or even to hide your own weaknesses.

At any rate, controlling the tempo may be achieved in any of the following ways:

- Fast-breaking and using full-court man-to-man pressure defense against slow or deliberate teams[4]
- Using a continuity offensive pattern and restricted shot selection to slow down the pace and yield high-percentage shots against running teams
- Using a spread alignment and delaying tactics to hold the ball (and run the clock) until high-percentage shots such as layups are achieved
- Holding the ball for the last shot every quarter. If this strategy does not appear to have much impact on the game, it's because many high school coaches have not fully considered its potential. Consider two best-case scenarios:

    If your team holds the ball throughout the final minute of every quarter and makes all four shots, you not only have outscored the opponents 8–0 during that span, but also (and more important) you have held the opponents scoreless for one eighth of the game. And if you expand that concept to include the final *two* minutes of every quarter and make the shots, you have, in effect, outscored them by 8–0 *in one full quarter of the game!*[5]

Of course, you cannot realistically expect to make all four of those shots—and the opponents aren't likely to sit back and let you hold the ball unopposed for two minutes at a time—but you can hide your intentions to a certain extent by using a continuity pattern such as a shuffle or wheel with wider spreads and longer cuts than usual, rather than announcing your intentions by aligning your players in a four-corner spread or three-man weave alignment. And if you're successful even half of the time, you've kept that portion of the game even against a superior opponent who might otherwise be adding points to the scoreboard like a checkout clerk at the supermarket.

3. Keep from Losing the Game

If your team and the opponents are roughly equal, don't try to win the game. Try to keep from losing it. As more than one coach has acknowledged, before you can win a game you have to keep from losing it. Among teams of equal

---

[4]If you can't press them and they're a possession-oriented team, you may have to consider using a deliberate style of play yourself.

[5]This strategy does not apply to college basketball, of course, with its forty-five-second clock and twenty-minute halves.

ability, this usually means adopting a conservative playing style that emphasizes high-percentage shot selection, careful passing, patience on offense, and low-risk, inside-oriented defense that waits for the opponents to make mistakes rather than trying to force them into errors.

As a rule, games among equals are won or lost in the fourth quarter.

A SAMPLE GAME PLAN

When you're finished preparing your game plan (see Figure 11–2), you should be confident that the information and strategy it contains affords your team its very best chances of winning the game, however slim those chances realistically might be. Your attitude toward the completed game plan should be the same as your players' attitude after games in which they've given a maximum effort, namely, that they gave it their best shot, win or lose.

Unless you feel that way about the game plan that you've devised, you're not really finished with it, after all.

About preparing your game plans: To save time—and space in the game plan, as well—rather than listing every player on your team in every conceivable position he might play, you can number your offensive positions from 1 to 5 and your defensive positions from X1 to X5, and note in the "Individual Players" section which numbers correspond to which players on your team, as we have done in the sample game plan. Using such a system, your players can study the diagrams and know instantly which aspects of a given play or pattern concerns them and which aspects they will not be held responsible for. (*Note:* We refer to our players by name—using the starters' names, not the subs—in the text because opponents' numbers sometimes are the same as our positions, e.g., #3 and #4 for Martin County.)

Alternatively, you can place the opposing players' numbers in the spaces provided and use the "Individual Players" section to describe your strategy for dealing with them on an individual basis.

Either approach is acceptable—provided, of course, that your players understand it fully.

EVALUATING YOUR GAME PLAN

After the game is over and you've had time to sit down and study the stat sheets and maybe watch the game on videotape, you should be able to objectively evaluate the game plan's effectiveness in terms of what worked, what didn't work, and why. (At the same time, of course, you're also evaluating the team's performance, your own as well as your players'.)

Your goal in evaluating the game plan is to decide what to retain and what to change against either (1) that team the next time you play them or

Figure 11-2 GAME PLAN

Martin Co. _____ Home _____ 11-30 _____
Opponent   Location   Date

I. OVERALL APPROACH Our #1 priority is to keep our composure on offense and not let their full-court pressure defense get us rattled. We want to attack them offensively from the center of the court and not let them beat us at the side lines. We can get high-percentage shots if we're patient, especially by passing to high post and looking for back door cuts or reverse pivoting on the dribble and driving down the middle in our half-court offense when they try to force us to the sidelines. Defensively, we have to get back quickly to stop their fast break, and we'll half-court press them when #25 is out of the game. We'll align Bob wider than usual toward #30's side in our 1-2-2 zone defense since they don't go to #4's side much or look to high post, and we'll keep Mike and Wayne back to cover the cross-court pass to #25 when 30 has the ball.

II. INDIVIDUAL PLAYERS

O1, X1 Butch /Donell) Inbound the ball quickly after scores. Penetrate or drive the middle whenever you get a chance to in our half-court offense --- but don't force it. Don't forget: It's your responsibility, along with Stan, to get back on defense stop their fast break when transitions occur. BE ALERT! Don't foul #25 at the point; remember, Wayne & Bob are behind you to help out in the 1-2-2.

O2, X2 (Wayne /Vernard Watch for #25 passing to #3 at high post: They didn't do it against Trinity, but they may against us. (#3 will fake, drive, and fake again before shooting; he'll turn to your left (his right) to drive. Offensively, use the weakside screen: make good cuts, look for the ball, and take it inside whenever you can (Their big men are slow!)

O3, X3 BoB /ARTHUR) Give #30 the stationary 3-pt. shot, but not shots off the dribble - (He'll make his move to your left as you approach him) In beating the press, look for the pass before you dribble. Offensively run the pattern (but drive the middle -- not the baseline, except on your back door cuts -- if they don't overplay you enough. Take all open shots inside.

© 1992 by Parker Publishing Company

Figure 11–2: Game Plan, continued

O4,X4 (Mike/Clarence) Give #4 any perimeter shot he wants, since he can't make them. If anyone passes to you in beating the press, look for Bob and Wayne heading up the sidelines before you start dribbling. Offensively look for open shots from 12 in—and follow your shot (No fallaways, Clarence.)

O5,X5 (Stan/John) Be PHYSICAL on the boards: #32 is a finesse rebounder, but #10 and #55 are earthmovers. Give #10 and #55 any shot from 10' out or more. You and Butch are responsible for getting back to stop their fastbreaks when turnovers occur in our half-court offense: Don't Forget IT! Don't give #3 the corner shot: approach him low and play him close.

III. TEAM OFFENSE BEATING THE PRESS— Butch will look for Wayne cutting wide (they'll probably deny this pass), or for Bob. If Wayne, Butch will cut through the middle to the midcourt corner to occupy #25, and their traps won't hurt us; if Bob, he'll pass back to Butch in the middle and move up court opposite Wayne (Diag.3) or drive around #4, looking for Mike if #3 comes up to trap. Wayne and Butch: Before you dribble, look to both sidelines and to Mike in the middle; if they're all covered, dribble toward #4 and look for Bob and Mike if #3 comes up. And if you go to your left, look for Mike in the middle or Wayne or Stan along the sideline. We Can Beat Their Press By Passing From The Middle or Forcing Double-Teams When & Where We Want Them. HALF-COURT OFFENSE: Our weakside screening offense should work against their pressure man-to-man (Diags. 1, 2, 4), since we use backdoor cuts and a wide alignment anyway. They'll try to deny the outlet pass to Mike, in which case we'll look for the backdoor cut to Mike or reverse the ball to weakside by interchanging Stan and Wayne and sending Mike to the ball-side corner (Diag. 5). Of course, that won't be necessary if Butch can reverse to the middle on the dribble: If he does, he can penetrate (with Stan clearing to screen for Mike's backdoor cut) or pass to Wayne cutting outside (Diag 6). If we go to high post (Diag. 15, 17) we'll play it either as a clearout for Stan or as a post interchange and backdoor cut

IV. TEAM DEFENSE We'll align our 1-2-2 zone (Both will be called, set plays.)

Figure 11–2: Game Plan, continued

defense as shown in Diag. 7, with Bob cheating toward #30. They operate from a 1-3-1 alignment that changes to a 4-man overload with #25 on weak side-- they LOVE to make the cross court pass to #25 or #30 isolated--with #3 operating from the corners for good measure. (See the Scouting Report, Diags. 2-4) When #30 has the ball we'll have Stan, Bob & Butch on ballside (Diag. 9); on the other side it'll be Mike, Wayne, & Butch. When #3 has the ball in the corner (Diag. 10), Stan will cover him and Bob will drop back to cover low post with Mike, leaving Wayne temporarily as the only one back to cover #25 on weak side. (In other words, we'll single-guard low post when #25 or #30 has the ball at the wing, and double-team the low post when #3 has the ball in the corner.) If they pass to #3 at high post, we'll cheat Wayne into cover him with Mike responsible for #4 at the wing.--Which shouldn't be difficult since #4 is a terrible outside shooter and poor dribbler as well.

1. WEAKSIDE SCREENING OFFENSE

2. BACKDOOR CUT WITH ROTATION

3. BEATING THE PRESS

4. ROTATING THE OTHER WAY

5. COUNTERING THE BALLSIDE OVERPLAY

(Diag 11). HALF-COURT PRESS- When #25 is out of the game, #30 is their only good ball handler. Butch & Wayne will trap him, with Bob cutting off the cross-court passing lane, Mike covering the sideline, & Stan covering the middle when the trap contains #30. Otherwise, Stan will cover the deep sideline lane. (Diag 8). If #30 brings the ball down the middle, Butch will overguard him to #30's left, steering him toward Bob as Wayne covers the crosscourt lane, Stan covers the sideline, and Mike covers the middle (Diag 14).

Figure 11–2: Game Plan, continued

V. SPECIAL SITUATIONS Martin Co. zones baseline bringins, so we'll run our regular in bounds play. (Diag.12). They man-to-man sideline bringins, but since they overplay everything they may be susceptible to

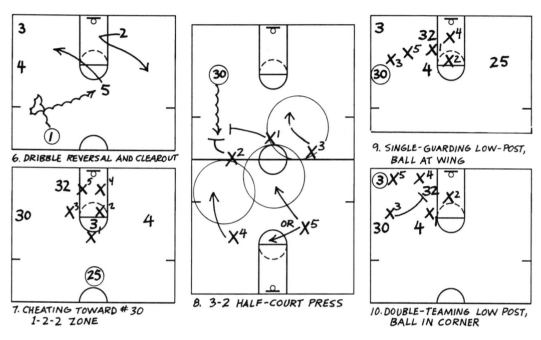

6. DRIBBLE REVERSAL AND CLEAROUT

7. CHEATING TOWARD # 30 1-2-2 ZONE

8. 3-2 HALF-COURT PRESS

9. SINGLE-GUARDING LOW-POST, BALL AT WING

10. DOUBLE-TEAMING LOW POST, BALL IN CORNER

backdoor cuts and Stan may get his first alley-oop slam dunk of the season. OPENING TIP- We'll offense it but not fastbreak off it. They keep 2 players back; so will we, just in case. (Diag 16). SLOW DOWNS- Martin Co. doesn't even slow down for red lights or railroad crossings; our weakside screening pattern will be both our regular offense and our delay game. WE WANT TO PLAY THEM AT A CONTROLLED PACE, NOT RACE WITH THEM!...

Figure 11-2: Game Plan, continued

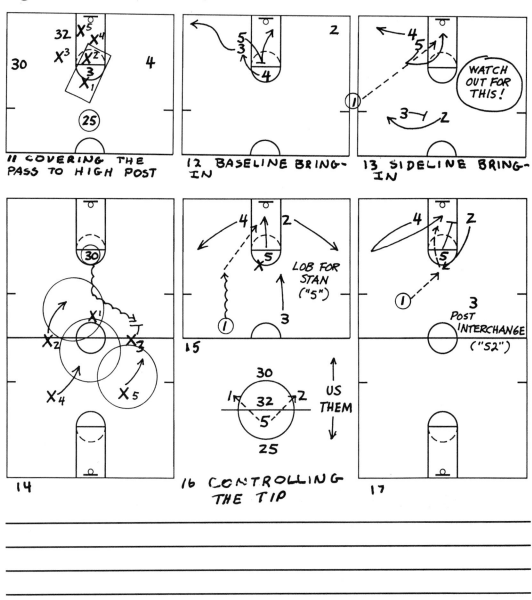

11 COVERING THE
PASS TO HIGH POST

12 BASELINE BRING-
IN

13 SIDELINE BRING-
IN

WATCH
OUT FOR
THIS!

LOB FOR
STAN
("5")

3
POST
INTERCHANGE
("52")

14

15

16 CONTROLLING
THE TIP

17

US
THEM

Figure 11–3 GAME PLAN EVALUATION

Martin Co.
Opponent

home
Location

Nov. 30
Date

1. What Worked Best for Us. Our 1-2-2 zone defense shut off the inside passing lanes and reduced the effectiveness of their cross-court passes to weak side. (After we picked off 3 cross-court passes they quit trying it and used #4 to relay the ball to weak side from the top of the circle). Their press didn't hurt us much, either: forcing the double-teams took away the element of surprise and nullified #25. Butch & Stan did a GREAT job of getting back on defense when transitions occurred. We hit 62% of our FG's for the game.

2. What They Did That We Didn't Expect—and How We Reacted to It. In the 2nd. Qtr, they switched around #25, #4, and #30 in their press (Diag.3), but we kept our cool, forced the double-team by going to Butch or Wayne, & found the seams in the midcourt area to pass beyond their quick guards.

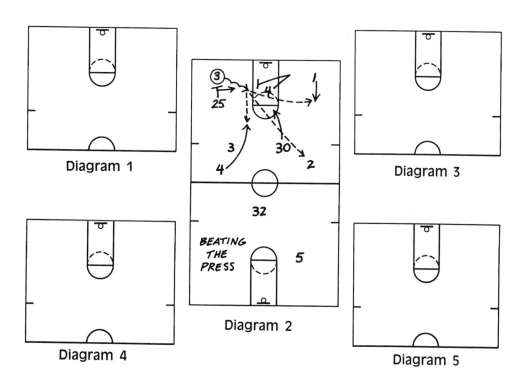

Diagram 1

Diagram 2
BEATING THE PRESS

Diagram 3

Diagram 4

Diagram 5

Figure 11-3: Game Plan Evaluation, continued

3. What Didn't Work for Us and Why. We committed too many turnovers in our half-court offense (usually, when their pressure forced Butch or Wayne wide & their overplaying forced us out of our pattern. We shot well, but we didn't consistently hit the open backdoor cutters & we couldn't get the ball to Stan at high post. Butch did a great job when he was able to reverse to the middle & penetrate, but he didn't do it enough. Defensively Stan had trouble reaching #3 in the corner in time to apply defensive pressure.

4. Possible Changes Next Time. Switch Wayne & Stan in our half court offense & use the post interchange to get the ball to Stan at high post. (Diag. 6). Or, keep the original alignment & use Wayne's screen-to alley oop to Stan cutting to the basket. (Diag. 7). To counter the over play on Mike's cut, we could have Mike screen for Wayne's outside cut & interchange them. (Diag. 9). And instead of overplaying low post from the inside, have Stan or Mike cover #32 from the baseline side to shorten the distance between him and #3 (Diag. 8).

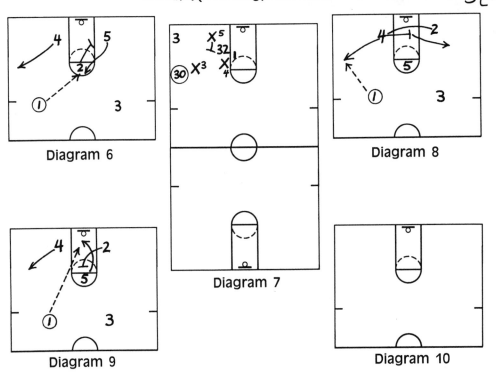

Diagram 6

Diagram 8

Diagram 7

Diagram 9

Diagram 10

(2) the next team on your schedule. Before considering any changes, however, you should be satisfied that the reason a given aspect of the game plan failed had nothing to do with the effort made by your players to make it work. After all, game plans are always based on assumptions of maximum effort by the players, and if your players gave a halfhearted effort you shouldn't be surprised that the game plan failed to achieve the desired results.

Anyway, there are two ways to organize your evaluation. The simplest and least detailed method is to use a colored felt-tip pen to jot down notes on the game plan itself (e.g., "This worked," "This didn't work because they beat our traps," "They didn't run this at all," "Next time maybe we should try this:," etc.). The other method is to use an evaluation form such as the one shown in Figure 11–3.

Game Strategy and Tactics

Do what you can, with what you have, where you are.

—*Theodore Roosevelt*

GAME STRATEGY

The First Half

Games begin with both teams searching for ways to control the opponents and dominate the action and flow at both ends of the court. To do this, they attempt to establish their basic offensive and defensive game plan as early as possible, emphasizing those aspects that are successful initially and gradually expanding or modifying the rest as the opponents make adjustments to the basic patterns and techniques.

As a coach, your first concern is stopping the opponents from doing what they do best; if you don't, they'll hammer you with it for thirty-two minutes and walk away laughing. And if you didn't already know how they prefer to play the game via scouting, you'll see it early as they set about the task of executing their basic game plan. Teams always begin by working toward their strengths, not their weaknesses.

Your second concern is establishing what your team does best—the basic offensive and defensive techniques in your game plan. Certain aspects will work better than you'd expected, and others will work poorly or not at all. Successful game management consists of finding what works best and playing to it until the opponents' adjustments render it ineffective, then either going to other options or making minor adjustments to restore the effectiveness of your original strategy. In either case, it's not wise to show too much, too soon, lest you tip off the opponents to strategies you may want to use later in the game.

Even when things go poorly for your team early on, you shouldn't be too hasty in abandoning your original game plan and adopting desperation tactics; after all, if you believe in your game plan and you believe in your kids, then you've *got* to believe that they can come back from early adversity.[1] Sometimes things go wrong simply because they go wrong, and later they correct themselves naturally with no more rhyme or reason than before. Sometimes it's just a matter of the players attuning themselves to the flow of the game; sometimes it's a matter of fine-tuning the offense or defense through small adjustments that turn the game around.

Having established your style of play, your goal is to keep the game flow and action to your liking throughout the rest of the first half, including inserting first-line substitutes in the latter stages of the first quarter and giving them enough playing time to warm up and contribute in a meaningful way. How deeply you substitute beyond your first-line reserves will depend on your personal philosophy, the score, and possibly other factors as well. (Except in blowouts, Adolph Rupp never used more than eight players in games; we try to get as many players as possible into games, if not in the first half then in the second—but only within the context of playing time earned through hard work in practice.[2]

Halftime

Halftime is a time for rest and regrouping. It's fifteen minutes long in college, ten minutes in high school. When you're on a roll, you don't want to stop for halftime at all—and when things aren't going so well, three hours isn't long enough. (When a manager came to the door and announced that there were three minutes left in halftime, an assistant coach grumbled, "We're busy. Tell 'em to go ahead and start without us.")

We believe that pregame talks to the team should be mainly technical in nature; that is, going over the scouting reports and game plan and outlining individual responsibilities. In addition to the fact that players shouldn't have to be externally motivated to play hard when they aren't tired, you can save a lot of mental wear and tear by preparing only *one* motivational talk per game and using it at halftime—and if things are going well, you can save it

---

[1]Or, as a coach whose team was winless after ten games grumbled, "Our philosophy is, the sooner we get behind in games, the sooner we can start trying to catch up."

[2]We like to tell our kids, "Basketball is *hard*: You can practice *hard*, and play *hard* in games, or you'll do *hard* time on the *hard* pine."

for next time. As Lou Carnesecca put it, "It's tough to give 118 halftime talks. After a while, the players start giving them back to you."[3]

Before exhorting your players to go out there in the second half and win one for the Gipper, there are three important things you *must* do, one of which is to prepare your team for the first five minutes of the third quarter. With the exception of the last three minutes of the game, more games are won or lost in the first five minutes of the third quarter than any other time. Coming off halftime, players are often sluggish and stiff, or otherwise slow in regaining their first-half tempo. If yours is an up-tempo team, you should take advantage of the halftime break by pressing, fast-breaking, and forcing transition advantages; and if it's the opponents who were born to run, you need to have your players limber, loose, and ready to deal with their speed from the very first second of the last half.

Beyond that, you also need to be prepared to deal with possible changes in your opponents' strategy. They are well aware of which scorers are hurting them, and you can bet they'll try something different in the second half to shut off that particular threat. At the same time, if you were clever enough not to reveal every ace up your sleeve in the first half you may want to unveil certain new offensive or defensive tactics in the third quarter, because it's always harder to adjust to new tactics after halftime.

The Second Half

Assuming that everything else is more or less under control, it's important to keep close tabs on the foul situation (yours and the opponents) throughout the last half, and to consider the fatigue factor as well. Your goal is to have your five best players on the court at crunch time when the game is in the balance, and if a player picks up his third or fourth foul too early—or if he shows signs of early fatigue—you may have to rest him either periodically or for long stretches. Whichever is the case, you'll want him ready to go full speed for the last five minutes of the game—and if he's had to sit for a long time you might extend it to six or seven minutes, since it normally takes a couple of minutes for players to regain their game legs after prolonged bench duty.

Late-Game Strategy

A statistically minded veteran high school boys coach told us that, over the past ten seasons, his teams played 216 regular season games (including holiday tournaments), of which 147 games, 68 percent, were won or lost by nine points or less and 64 games—30 percent—were decided by five points or less.

[3]*Atlanta Journal* (March 24, 1991), p. E2.

We think those percentages are roughly accurate for most teams. If so, it means that about two thirds of your games will be decided by the equivalent of three three-point field goals or less, and about a third of your games by a margin of less than two three-point goals. How many of those games you win will be determined at least in part by the way you prepare your team for games that could go either way.

Nowhere is the old coaching adage that "Games are won or lost in practice" more applicable than in close games. Players learn how to function effectively under game pressure by being placed in pressure situations in daily practice. If the drills you use are both game-related and more demanding than your players will face under actual game conditions, they will learn to respond quickly and automatically without having to think about their movements. And if you carefully rehearse the specific kinds of late-game situations and strategies that they will be involved with in the latter stages of close games, their familiarity with the techniques involved will tend to offset much of the pressure that normally accompanies win-or-lose situations.

Catch-Up Tactics

When you're behind and need several scores in a hurry, pressing and trapping defensively are only part of the answer. The rest lies in getting the ball upcourt and developing high-percentage shots quickly, whether by fast-breaking or using offensive options that feature your best scorers. Since you have nothing to lose by gambling that probably won't be lost anyway by *not* gambling, you may want to send all five players to the boards to rebound offensively. If you have fouls to give, do so early—but not "intentionally" and not the jump shooters. When the other team is in the bonus situation, foul the poorest free-throw shooters. Use situational substitutions after scores to stop the clock and get your best offensive or defensive players into the game—especially on defense, since if you can't stop them from scoring you'll never catch them. It doesn't matter if it's your leading scorer, a player should be replaced at the defensive end if his or her presence hurts your overall defensive effort; after all, you can always return the player to the lineup when your team gets the ball back. And to paraphrase Karl Malden's credit card commercial, "Timeouts. Don't enter the last three minutes of the game without them."

Protecting the Lead

When is a lead safe enough for you to abandon your regular offense and go to a freeze or delay game? Since the players know better than we do what they feel most comfortable doing, we've occasionally asked them during timeouts what they'd rather do—but only when we've had effective leadership and dependable guard play. If you make the decision yourself, you should maintain an air of complete confidence as you outline your strategy and tactics to the team. Your strategy should be familiar to the players, and your explanation brief and clear.

At any rate, in protecting a lead you want to keep the ball in the hands of your best ballhandlers and scorers as much as possible, and to stress even higher-percentage shot selection than usual, since every score makes it more difficult for the opponents to catch up. And because gambles have an uncanny way of backfiring at critical moments, you'll probably either abandon your presses altogether or play them loosely to slow the opponents' advance. Many coaches use zone defense to protect late leads (especially at home, where visitors are less familiar with the baskets), playing the percentages and keeping their rebounders inside.

Other considerations: Be prepared for the opponents' presses (tell your players to inbound the ball quickly after scores), direct play offensively toward opponents who are in foul trouble, and remind your players to maintain court balance offensively so the opponents won't get cheap baskets after defensive rebounds or turnovers.

Finishing the Close Games

If you're trailing by three points going into the final minute of play, you're probably better off going for a high-percentage two-point field goal than taking the first three-pointer that comes along: If you make the deuce, you're only down one and you can force the opponents to beat you with pressure free throws down the stretch. If you miss the three, you may find yourself down five next time you get the ball.

If you're down by one or two points in the final minute, careful shot selection is a *must*, since if you miss it the other guys are going to spread and hold the ball until you foul them. If you miss the shot, you'll need to apply pressure defense and foul a nonshooter immediately. If you make it, you're probably better off going man-to-man than dropping back into a zone defense, since *any* last-second shot can beat you.

If you're tied going into the final minute, you'll probably put the ball on ice, accepting nothing but open layups until you decide to call a timeout with, say, twelve to twenty seconds left to discuss your last-shot options. If the opponents have the ball with the score tied late, however, while you want to avoid giving up an easy basket you also want to avoid fouling anyone, especially the shooter. It's better to give them a last-second shot opportunity than to risk giving them a lead that puts the pressure squarely in your court to catch them.

If you're ahead with the ball during the final minute, the clock is your ally only when it's moving. To keep it moving, players should whenever possible pass the ball to open teammates before their defenders get close enough to foul them. And in shooting free throws, you'll want to have two players at the defensive end to deal with possible fast-break situations.

Last-Shot Situations

Defensively, it doesn't get any tougher than playing the opponents' last-second shot. On the ball, you've got to stop the penetration and get a hand in the jump shooter's face without fouling; off the ball, it's even tougher because you've got to play denial without giving up the lob pass or backdoor cut and alley-oop pass over you (especially on the inbounds pass), and you also have to be ready to switch off to deal with the dribbler if he gets by his man.

If your team has the ball for the last shot, your players will need to know how the intended shot will be set up, who's going to take it, when the scoring play should be initiated (e.g., with seven, ten, or twelve seconds left on the clock), how many timeouts your team has left, what they should do if the play doesn't develop as expected—and, if you're allowing time to rebound offensively, they should know how the defense should be organized if the opponents rebound the missed shot. USC's George Raveling suggests taking the ball inside for your last shot if you're playing at home and taking the outside jumper if you're playing on the road, presumably because referees tend to give the benefit of the doubt to the home team on close contact/noncontact calls; however, while we agree with his strategy we should note that the opposite strategy also may produce favorable results, since most teams shoot better at home than on the road.

At any rate, part of every regular-season daily practice session should be devoted to practicing the various late-game situations, pressure free-throw shooting, and last-shot strategies with the ball in play and out of bounds. (You need a full-court bring-in play, a backcourt sideline bring-in play, a frontcourt sideline bring-in play, and a different frontcourt baseline bring-in play from the ones you've used earlier in the game.)

Some coaches practice late-game tactics and other special situations at the end of practice; others intersperse late-game situations among their other drills throughout practice. Either method is acceptable as long as the players practice the situations often enough to become thoroughly familiar with the techniques associated with each. All you do is put the desired time remaining on the clock, describe the situation (game score, who has the ball) and the strategy (what offenses, defenses, plays, or patterns both teams will use), and monitor the play.

We've known coaches who prided themselves on being able to draw up improvised last-second plays on the spot during timeouts; still, we think it's unfair to the players to place the burden of responsibility on them for executing a play, however cleverly designed it may be, that they haven't rehearsed in daily practice. If up to one third of your games are going to be won or lost in the last three to five minutes of games, you owe it to yourself and your players to prepare them as thoroughly as possible to deal with those situations.

After all, it doesn't make much sense to spend all of your daily practice time preparing your team to play twenty-seven to twenty-nine minutes of a thirty-two-minute game.

USING TIMEOUTS WISELY

Timeouts rank among the coach's most valuable game-management tools. Although other, narrower reasons for their usage exist, timeouts generally are used to discuss team strategy or tactics, to adjust or modify patterns that aren't working, to upset the flow when opponents have seized control of the game, to ice opposing free-throw shooters late in games, or to control the action in one way or another during the last few minutes of games.

Alternatives to Calling Timeouts

Because timeouts are both valuable and limited in number, they should be reserved for occasions when their need is clearly indicated. In other situations, a coach should look for alternatives that can serve his purposes and conserve his timeouts.

1. Try to avoid calling timeouts early in games. Young coaches often have a tendency to overcoach their teams by trying to control every minute of the game from the opening tip to the final buzzer. As they mature as coaches, however, they gain a feel for the game that allows them to distinguish between the normal ebb and flow of miniruns by both teams that characterize most game action and the times when opponents' scoring runs are likely to become scoring *runaways*; as a result, they no longer feel compelled to call timeouts every time the opponents score six unanswered points. It's important to control game flow and tempo whenever possible—but it's even *more* important to be able to do so through timeouts when the clock is winding down, the game is on the line, and winning strategy is of critical importance.

Of course, this strategy does not apply universally, since if the opponents are methodically dismantling your offense and defense *right now* it won't matter how many timeouts you have left when you're down forty-seven points with three minutes left in the game. Still, you'll conserve a lot of first-half timeouts over the course of the season if you'll save them for the sort of major changes that potential early blowouts require, and use substitutions to make your minor adjustments. You can also use signals from the bench and huddles before free throws to alert players to offensive or defensive charges.

2. Don't let players call timeouts on their own. It's hard enough for the coach to keep up with the timeout situation; for the players, it's virtually impossible. Players who are tired should signal to the bench that they need to rest, not call a timeout. (We like George Raveling's idea here: He tells his players, "If *I* take you out, you'll go back in when I decide to send you in; but if you signal that you need a break, you can go back in whenever you're ready to.")

The single exception to this rule of thumb concerning players calling timeouts on their own is when, in the latter stages of a close game, a player is able to retain ball possession for his team by calling a timeout to avoid a held ball or turnover. When every shot is a potential game-winner, retaining possession is important at all costs.

On the other hand, we've seen kids call timeouts as early as the first minute of a game to avoid a turnover or because they were upset about something. Our feeling is that, over the course of the game, we'll get the ball back many times, but we'll never get back timeouts that were wasted early in the game. Even when the opponents' full-court pressing defense is creating obvious confusion, we feel that calling timeouts should be the coach's decision. And when a coach decides to let his players call timeouts to avoid turnovers, he should tell them to do so only after he has made sure that the team does indeed have timeouts to call. (We once won a game to qualify us for the state playoffs by converting a four-point play with seconds remaining when the other team's center called a timeout that exceeded their limit. They got the timeout—but we got the win.)

3. Before calling for a timeout, see if the other coach is trying to call one.

Timeout Behavior

Assuming that the clock operator is going to give you an honest minute—which unfortunately isn't always the case when you're playing on the road; and assuming further that your players hustle over to the bench as they should when timeout is called—you still have only about fifty seconds to confer with your assistants about such things as team strategy, who will do the talking to the team, and which players need to be addressed individually, while the managers pass out towels and water.

While it is neither necessary nor desirable to say nothing but positive things to players during timeouts—for example, a player may not be aware that he isn't playing up to his capabilities, or else he may be the kind of athlete who responds better to prodding and challenges than to compliments—the coach should *always* be positive when discussing or describing team strategy, since players' attitudes tend to mirror those of their coaches. (And yes, we've occasionally asked our players what they would rather do in a certain situation[4]—but always in the context that *either of their choices is going to work.* We haven't asked them, "Which do you think

---

[4]*Rarely* is probably a more accurate assessment. Our basketball teams aren't democratic; they're more like benevolent dictatorships. We love our players, but they know who's the boss.

will work?" but rather, "Which would you feel more comfortable doing?" The difference between the two approaches is, we feel, more than subtle: It's obvious.)

Since every second of timeouts is valuable and must be used wisely, it follows that the head coach must be organized and focused so that everything that needs to be done and said in the brief time allotted can be accomplished. Once the coaches are ready to address the team, no one else should speak except to ask or answer questions. Although all coaches may discuss techniques, and the like, with individual players simultaneously, only one should speak when the team is being addressed. For best results, the coach should confine his comments to the team to one or two points, and repeat them if necessary.

To emphasize your statements to individual players, call them by name and look at them when you're talking to them—and if it's necessary to underscore the importance of what you're saying, touch the player and maintain the contact while you're speaking to him.

Finally, it's well to remember that not every timeout is an urgent concern. Sometimes, when things are going well and it's the opponents who are having all the problems, you may not want to say anything at all. If that's the case, keep quiet, let the players rest and get water, and save your motivational minispeeches for other occasions when things aren't going so well.

Other Considerations

1. Don't waste timeouts to argue with referees about judgment calls. (You aren't likely to win the arguments, anyway, since referees reverse their calls about as often as the Supreme Court reverses its decisions.) If it's a matter of rules interpretation, consult your rule book before calling timeout. And if you need to talk to your team during the timeout, send a player or assistant coach to discuss the problem with the referees.

2. Don't call timeouts during the final minute of the first, second, or third quarter; instead, wait for the automatic timeout that you're given between quarters, or the ten or fifteen minutes at halftime.

3. Don't make more than one major change in your strategy or playing style per timeout. In addition to the time factor, there's also the fact that multiple changes may confuse the players or otherwise cause them to become passive or reactive when you need them to be actively involved in the game.

4. Be careful if you're using timeouts rather than substitutions to stop the clock and organize your pressing defense after scores. A timeout cannot be reduced in length unless both teams are ready to play before the timeout is over.

5. If your state association adopts a 10:00 weeknight curfew on games, you can either schedule games to begin earlier—which probably will require

scheduling B-team or jayvee games on different days from your varsity games, since most states presently frown on the practice of letting athletes out of class while school is in session to travel to away games—or you can take your chances on beating the curfew by keeping the 4:00–5:30–7:00–8:30 starting-time format for girls and boys jayvee/varsity games. If you decide to go with your regular starting times on weeknights, be aware that delays in any of the earlier games can greatly affect the outcome of the last game. (In Georgia, where we had the weeknight curfew rule briefly until our legislators, educators, and high school association came to their collective senses, we witnessed numerous bizarre instances in which coaches were saving their timeouts so that, if they were leading the game at, say, 9:57, they would call three consecutive timeouts and win the game via the curfew rule.)

———————————————— ROAD GAMES ————————————————

> You cannot go on the road and be flip and frivolous and count on winning. You've got to be more focused and more precise on the road. You cannot play the same way on the road that you do at home and win. And if you think you're going to, you're wrong.
>
> —*Pat Riley*[5]

Everything is working against you when your team hits the road. The fans are hostile; the court, backboards, goals, and shooting background are different; and there's the commonly held perception among players and coaches that referees tend to favor the home team in their calls—all of these factors must be taken into account in preparing your team for road games.

Preparing for Road Games

The following suggestions can help you to get your team ready for road games:

1. Since game plans are always based on assumptions of total effort by the players, it's imperative to have your players in the proper frame of mind to play on the road. Your game plan should reflect your confidence that it represents the very best way of approaching the game. Your behavior should reflect your confidence that the players will execute the game plan to the best of their ability.

---

[5]*Atlanta Constitution* (Feb. 6, 1991), p. F1.

2. Most coaches want their players to be confident and loose before games; others prefer that players' confidence be sustained within an atmosphere of growing tension and intensity. In either case, however, the players can focus on the upcoming game by studying the game plan and scouting reports and discussing them quietly among themselves on the way to the game.

3. If possible, you should try to arrive early enough to get in twenty to thirty minutes of extra shooting practice. And while that's not always possible due to preliminary games, even a few shots taken at halftime of the earlier game can help players familiarize themselves with the court, baskets, and so on. (If you're going to shoot at halftime, have the players dressed out in warmups and uniforms, since street clothes will restrict their shooting form—and thus possibly their confidence as well.)

4. "You've got to play defense on the road. That's the difference. It's not offense; it's defense."—Dominique Wilkins.[6] The problems and pressures associated with road games should not affect players' ability to play effective defense; after all, defense is based on stance, footwork, anticipation, and hard work, not on handling the ball with cold hands or jittery fingers. Without exception, teams that win consistently on the road are those that consistently give the proverbial 110 percent effort defensively regardless of where they're playing, at home or away.

To be a championship team, you must either learn to win on the road or find a way to arrange for the championships to be played in your gym. And since the latter is clearly unattainable beyond the league level in most cases, the surest road to championships is through playing tough D at home *and* on the road. It's a habit and an attitude that players should assume every time they put on their uniforms—but it's even more important in away games than at home.

5. Offensively, stress rebounding, free-throw accuracy, and good shot selection. Nowhere do Coach Riley's comments about being focused apply more strongly than to road shooting: If players are not hitting their open shots, perhaps they should narrow their shot selection or concentrate harder. Since they likely will not be shooting as many free throws as the home team, they need to hit a high percentage to make up the difference. Hitting the offensive boards with a vengeance can help offset poor field-goal percentages by providing second and third shots.

6. If crowd noise is likely to affect your team, whether by increasing the pressure on them or disrupting communication between you and your players, you can prepare for it by playing loud tapes during practice scrimmages and using hand signals or colored cards to signal plays, options, or changes in

---

[6]*Atlanta Constitution*, (Feb. 6, 1991), p. F1.

defenses. You can also move your timeout huddles away from the sideline and onto the court if you don't mind the players standing during the timeouts, or you could simply have them sit on the floor while you take a knee to talk to them.

At any rate, if the crowd noise or pep band is uncomfortably loud you might want to have a manager stand near the clock, listening for the buzzer and watching the referees for signs that they're ready for play to resume. You *don't* want to lose a game because no one heard the horns or whistles that called the players back onto the court.

If the home crowd *isn't* a factor, treat the fans as you'd treat a sleeping lion: Don't wake them up or incite them to action by exhibiting poor sportsmanship or allowing a slam dunk.

7. When in unfriendly territory, urge your players to stay together before, during, and after the game, and to avoid responding to any kind of negative comments or actions by the fans. Play the game, and if any sort of problems arise that could potentially impair the safety of anyone associated with your team, immediately request the assistance of the home team's principal. If that doesn't work, get your team out as quickly as possible after the game, and ask your own principal to file written complaints with the state office, with copies to the other school's principal and superintendent.

— SHOULD YOU RUN UP SCORES AGAINST INFERIOR TEAMS? —

It's not an easy question to answer—but because the practice is becoming more widespread with each passing year, it merits our attention.

At one end of the spectrum, there's the unflinchingly hard-line sentiments expressed by a coaching acquaintance:

> You'd better believe I'll run it up in a heartbeat if I get a chance. When I first came here, we were getting pounded regularly by every school for fifty miles around. One coach criticized me in the press for sitting on the ball and holding his team to 84 points, although they won the game by 28. They'd scored 120 against us the year before. And now that I've built a good basketball program, there's no way I'm gonna sit back and let these guys off easy. Hey, I'm not being paid to coach their teams for them.
>
> Anyway, we're a rural school, smaller than most of our opponents, and scoring big is the best way I know of keeping the kids motivated and getting new ones to come out for the team. We never got any big-city press coverage until we started posting big scores, and the recruiters weren't exactly breaking down our doors, either. They know who we are now, though. We feel like we're forcing the other teams in our area to get better now instead of the other way around, because they know if they don't come to play with everything they've got, we'll beat 'em like Custer's Last Stand.

In other situations, the reason most often cited by coaches for running up lopsided victories is the desire to improve state rankings. And while in most states rankings are unofficial and have no bearing on entry into, or placement within, postseason tournament play, college coaches *do* pay attention to the newspapers and their polls. They wouldn't be human if they didn't. (And if you disagree with that statement, you tell us: If Team A is 18–0 and winning by 33 ppg. and Team B is 14–4 and winning by 10 ppg., *which team deserves to be ranked higher in the polls?* Team B may in fact be the better team—but the weekly polls won't reflect that viewpoint, will they?)

At the other end of the spectrum are the comments from another coach:

> A few years ago, I watched our girls team get beat by 98–10 or something like that, and the leading scorer got 68 points—24 of them *in the fourth quarter alone!* My boys wanted me to let them avenge the loss by doing the same thing to their boys in our game, but I wouldn't let them do it because two wrongs don't make a right. I just don't think anybody wins a game like that. It's simply a question of who's the bigger loser, the team that's behind on the scoreboard or a coach who would subject young kids to that kind of humiliation.

– KEEPING THE SCORE RESPECTABLE AGAINST INFERIOR TEAMS –

For starters, there's Warren's First Law of Bench Coaching; namely, *Do what is necessary to win the game.*[7] Don't pitty-pat around trying to keep the score respectable while there's the slightest chance that the opponents can come back and beat you. So yes, we *do* believe in running up scores, at least, until you're satisfied that winning is no longer in doubt. At that point—which may occur as early as the second quarter, depending on the disparity of skills between your squad and the opponents—in addition to any humane reasons for calling off the dogs there are two practical considerations that merit liberal substitution: the possibility of injury to your regulars and rewarding the hard work exhibited in practice by your substitutes.

When substitutes are playing, you have every right to expect the same effort if not level of achievement from them that you get from your starters. If that effort continues to expand your team's lead, you can either (1) dig deeper into your bench or (2) use the game as a modified daily practice session in which you rehearse new patterns, strategies, and so forth, that have not as yet received enough attention to merit inclusion in your game plans. Or (3) you could practice your delay game to run time off the clock.

If you have only seven or eight players on your team, you can move the guards inside and let your center and forwards take turns manning the guard slots. They'll enjoy the experience—especially your center, who, like most big

---

[7]William E. Warren, *Coaching and Winning* (Prentice Hall, 1988), p. 129.

men, probably envisions himself as an undiscovered Magic Johnson—and at the same time you may actually be helping your team by diversifying individual players' skills.

– KEEPING THE SCORE RESPECTABLE AGAINST SUPERIOR TEAMS –

When facing a team that is clearly superior to yours, your first responsibility is to prepare the best possible game plan under the circumstances. If your team has one chance in ten thousand of beating the opponents, your game plan should be built around that chance (unless it involves hiding snipers in the stands or booby-trapping the visitors' locker room).

In playing a superior team, you're actually working at a five-on-six disadvantage: the five players *and the scoreboard clock*. If games were three minutes long, you could play them any way you like and probably not be beaten too badly. But since by definition a superior team is one that is consistently capable of creating and taking advantage of more scoring opportunities than their opponents, your problem is to keep the game close long enough to win in the last three minutes, or at least to avoid the kind of humiliation that accompanies lopsided defeats. In either case, the obvious solution is to reduce the opponents' scoring opportunities by slowdown or delay tactics to keep the ball away from them.

There are two kinds of slowdown tactics: *deep freezes* and *delays*. In deep freezes, players either ignore shooting altogether or take only wide-open, unmolested layups. In delaying, they run their pattern (and the clock) until whatever high-percentage shots the coach deems appropriate arise. Which strategy you use depends on several factors, including the quality of the opponents, your players' ability to handle the pressure, and your own preferences. However, most coaches tend to shy away from the sort of deep freezes that produce such final scores as 4–1, 7–3, and so on, because even home fans dislike such tactics: Feeling cheated out of their admission fees to watch players who aren't even trying to score, they tend to switch allegiance to the better team, and their vocal displeasure intensifies the pressure on the underdogs. Players seldom function at their best when the fans are solidly against them. That's one reason why most teams do poorly on the road.

Thus, if deep-freeze tactics are the only path to victory or respectability in defeat, we suggest using the tactics outlined in Section 11, namely, running a continuity pattern in delay form and taking only high-percentage shots for the first six minutes of every quarter, and then going deep freeze for the last two minutes by ignoring *all* scoring options in the pattern except unmolested layups and the last-second shot. The advantages to this tactic are that (1) in running the same pattern throughout the game, your opponents will be less likely to recognize the subtle differences in shot selection that would be more apparent if you switched to a four-corner stall or three-man weave late in every quarter, and any adjustments they make will thus be directed toward your continuity pattern rather than your deep freeze tactics; and (2) as long as you remain in your pattern, the opponents are limited in the ways they can effectively alter their man-to-man coverage, since they still have to protect the posts and basket area.

Of course, no tactics are infallible or foolproof because players are, as Nietzsche put it, "human, all too human." We once saw a high school boys team hold the ball—or try to, at least—throughout the first half against a vastly superior team. They trailed by 27–0 at the intermission, went back to their conventional offense in the second half, and eventually lost the game, 85–19. All the befuddled coach who had tried it both ways could say after the game was, "Did somebody call for a steamroller?"

——————— HOW TO HANDLE BLOWOUTS AGAINST YOU ———————

The universal signal for admitting that you're beaten and you want the opponents to call off the dogs is to pull your starting lineup and send in the scrubs. (And if that doesn't work, another less savory but equally obvious signal that we've occasionally seen coaches use is to call a timeout and instruct their players to go out and start fights to have themselves and opposing players thrown out of games.) We reject both strategies: In the first place, while giving up is easier than continuing to pursue team goals when the going gets tough, it sets an unhealthy precedent for future efforts in difficult situations; and regarding the latter, in addition to being a blatant violation of sportsmanship standards there's always the very real possibility of injuries, suspensions, or crowd intervention to make a bad situation even worse.

But if you don't want to give up and you refuse to let your players fight back with their fists, what's left? You can't just walk off the court and go home—at least, not unless you're willing to accept a healthy fine and suspension from your state association for violating a game contract.

No, you can't quit—but you *can* use timeouts to calm down your players and direct their attention away from the score and toward other goals such as running their patterns more precisely, concentrating on proper execution of fundamentals (especially passing and dribbling), and defining the limits of their shot selection more precisely. You can substitute liberally to give more players a chance to gain game experience—but within the context of working to improve their play, not merely throwing them to the wolves.

Even in the worst of blowouts, all is not lost if you can keep your head and focus on positive steps that can improve individual and team play. A coach told us he believes that, because they're so much like nightmares, blowouts aren't real. And because they aren't real, such games should be treated as open scrimmages with fans watching.

"Look at the scoreboard," we overheard the coach telling his players during a timeout. The players did so, gloomily and with great reluctance. It wasn't a pretty sight. "Take a good look at it, because it's the last time you'll look at that clock tonight—if you want any more playing time this season, that is," (We suspected he was exaggerating a bit here—but if we had been playing for him, we would not have made that assumption.)

"Now we're going to forget the score," the coach went on. "The score no longer exists, because *this game* doesn't exist. Neither do the fans, the other team, or anyone else except you, me, and [the assistant coach]. We're going to practice the same things we work on every day."

Then the coach applied his carefully prearranged zinger, a gimmick he borrowed from Ohio State's fabled football coach Woody Hayes. He calmly took off his wristwatch, held it up for the players to see, and then dropped it on the floor and stepped on it.

"See?" he said, smiling as the players gaped in amazement at the shattered watch, "we don't need a clock. All we need to do is forget everything else and concentrate on running our patterns with precision, the way we do at practice."

Later, we asked the coach about the watch, and about what he said to his team after the game.

"Aw, it was just an old watch I had at home. It never kept good time anyway." He paused. "In the locker room, I shook each player's hand and told all of them how proud I was to be a part of their team. They never quit, you know"—he gave us a crooked little half-smile—"and after my little performance we hung tough, executed better, and we only got beat by three points the rest of the way. I went over each player's performance with him, stressing the good things I saw, the improvement. I'll talk to them about the negatives tomorrow at practice, but only in terms of how we can improve as a team."

He started to walk away, and then stopped and said, "As I was leaving the dressing room, one of the players offered to give me his watch. I thanked him but said I'd get another one. That kind of attitude doesn't show up in the game stats, but it's what every coach tries to build on. I hope we can put this one behind us, because if we can't, I told [his assistant coach] that next time we were going to use *his* watch!"

GAME STATISTICS

"There are three kinds of lies," declared British Prime Minister Benjamin Disraeli, "lies, damned lies, and statistics."

"Statistics are like a bikini," said Aaron Levenstein. "What they reveal is suggestive, but what they conceal is vital."

Statistics have always gotten a bad rap, from Scotty Bowman's assertion that "Statistics are for losers" to W.I.E. Gate's sarcastic comment about "the man who drowned while crossing a stream with an average depth of six inches."

In fact, statistics are nothing more sinister than performance figures that have been grouped and averaged. And because averages always paint a broader picture than individual performances, they are open to broader interpretation. If a basketball player scores 30, 1, and 2 points in three games, his 11-ppg. average bears little resemblance to any of his actual game performances—but few coaches would question the use of individual or team scoring averages as an indicator of performance or progress.

Statistics aren't for losers, they're for players and teams who are learning how to win. Of *course* coaches use statistics selectively to reveal or conceal certain truths; we could hardly expect players to keep on working hard to improve, whether individually or as a team, unless we offer them concrete evidence that their hard work is paying off.

How extensive your stats are will depend on which ones you consider important enough to collect, and on the number and quality of your team managers as well. Consider the following list of statistical categories:

1. Shot charts (both teams)
2. Field goals attempted/made/percentage (both teams)
   a. Three-point
   b. Two-point
   c. Combined
3. Free throws attempted/made/percentage (both teams)
4. Total points (both teams)
5. Assists (our team)
6. Offensive/defensive rebounds (our team)
7. Total rebounds (both teams)
8. Offensive violations (lane, traveling) (our team)
9. Offensive turnovers (our team)
10. Offensive held balls (our team)
11. Fouls (both teams)
12. Defensive steals (our team)
13. Defensive forced turnovers/charging fouls drawn (our team)
14. Minutes played (our team)
15. Offensive/defensive pattern charts (i.e., how many possessions/shots taken/shots made/pct. from each offensive pattern and defensive style used) (our team)
16. Offensive/defensive lineup charts (i.e., how many possessions/shots taken/shots made/pct. from each lineup appeared in the game) (our team)

Four managers (and someone keeping the scorebook) could compile statistics in the preceding sixteen categories, using simple division of labor: three managers and the scorer could keep either 1 through 15 or 1 through 14 and 16; two managers and the scorer could keep 1 through 13 (with the scorer recording 3, 4, and 11, one manager keeping 1 and 2, and the other manager keeping 5 through 10 and 12 through 13); and one manager and the scorer could conceivably record categories 1 through 4 and possibly a few others as well, if the manager is not otherwise involved in bench responsibilities.

Reproducible forms for keeping stats in all sixteen categories are provided in the Appendix.

Referees from A to Zebra

The refs called fouls like they were getting a commission.

—Peter Salzburg

Every basketball coach has horror stories to tell about referees who epitomize everything that referees should not be. Our personal favorite concerns a referee who showed up twenty minutes late for a 7:00 P.M. high school girls' game (his partner never showed up at all) and asked in a slow drawl, "When do y'all start your games around here, anyway?" Then he proceeded to ask in all seriousness if there were any rules changes since last year that he ought to know about because, as he explained, "I been sick. I didn't make it to the rules clinic." The coaches stared at each other in disbelief. Well, yes, as a matter of fact there *were* a couple of changes in the girls' game that he should have been aware of, since the state had just switched over from six-player girls' basketball to the five-player format used by the boys.

The referee frowned and shook his head. "That ain't good, 'cause now I gotta do *two* full-court games a night. Are there any other new rules that I oughta know about?" Without missing a beat one of the coaches spoke up, straight-faced. The state high school association executive director owned a sporting goods store, the coach said, and it was now legal for girls to wear high heel sneakers in games. The ref looked startled, but nodded and glanced around. "I guess I won't have no trouble with that," he said, looking relieved, " 'cause none of these girls are wearing 'em tonight."

Fortunately, referees of such colossal ineptitude are rare, and seldom last long. Still, there never seems to be a shortage of referees who are either unwilling or incapable of executing their roles with any degree of precision or skill. There are lazy referees, just as there are lazy coaches and insurance

219

salesmen and store clerks—and there are also highly competent officials who take considerable pride in their work, night after night, with genuine affection for the game and those who play and coach it. You can expect to encounter approximately the same percentage of under- and overachievers in officiating as you'd find in any classroom or corporation in America. Although we coaches sometimes like to think differently, referees don't have a corner on incompetence, any more than we are always right when we question their calls.

THE PROBLEM WITH REFEREES

An important part of the problem with referees is that, because their goals differ so markedly from ours, they are natural adversaries of coaches—or at least potential impediments that stand between the coach and winning. Of course, we still try to influence the refs, but it never works, because the vast majority of referees don't care whether we win or lose. It is simply a matter of different perspectives.

The coach wants to win; the referees want the game to proceed in an orderly manner. The coach tends to view the game from a biased viewpoint, approving calls made in his team's favor and overlooking bad calls made against the opposing team; the referees, facing no pressure to win, simply call the game as they see it. The coach wants to control every aspect of the game—his players, the opponents, the tempo of the game—but he cannot control the refs. The result is, as we said, an adversarial relationship and friction that is always present even when not in evidence.

A common cliché regarding our profession is that you're only as good as your last win. And in the eyes of most coaches, a referee is only as good as his last call.

A second part of the problem with referees is that modern basketball has become such a high-speed game—not just in fast-breaking styles of play but even more so in terms of player quickness—that it is virtually impossible to see much of the split-second contact that occurs. For example, in the same sense that hitters cannot actually see the bat making contact with the ball in baseball, referees often cannot see whether a defender's hand contacts the ball, the shooter's hand, or his wrist in deflecting a shot—except, of course, when the defender blocks the shot with his hand *above* the ball. The action is simply too fast, except when viewed in slow-motion replays, which are not available to the refs. And to compound the problem, if the referee is watching the shooter's hands, he cannot see whatever bodily contact occurred unless it is so blatant that the shooter is knocked down by it. Just last night on television we saw a player go down as he drove around a screen. A foul was called on the defender. It looked like a good call, too, until the slo-mo replay revealed that the dribbler had fallen because he stepped on his teammate's foot.

Other problem areas for referees involving quickness include charging fouls as opposed to blocking fouls, stealing the ball, and traveling violations. All of these situations can be extremely difficult to evaluate because they occur with such unexpected suddenness that, by the time the brain makes the connection with what the eye has seen, the game action has proceeded beyond that point, leaving the viewer unsure of what she just saw. (We coaches know what *we* saw, though: We saw that it was the other kid's fault, not ours. And the ref would see it that way, too, if he weren't as blind as a bat!)

We once had an angry referee tell us, "You do your job, and I'll do mine!" His next act was to pop a T on us when we replied, "Okay, when do you want to start?" But the ref was wrong in this case, because we had been on the job since 7:30 that morning. His "job" began that evening when he arrived at the gym.

There are good referees, and there are bad referees, and countless varieties in between. All of them have good nights and bad nights, just as players and coaches do. The best referees work hard, are fair, and generally enjoy their work because they love the sport of basketball. But with the exception of pro basketball, *all* referees share a common shortcoming, namely, that while officiating is *work* it's not a *full-time job*. At best, it's a second job that, over a year of working the various sports in their respective seasons, can bring in several thousand dollars in supplemental income. And like teachers who remain in the classroom to keep the monthly paychecks rolling in, although their passion for teaching has cooled, some referees continue to tread the courts long after their original enthusiasm and love for the game have faded to a memory, for the very same reason.

Still, the fact remains: *No referee expends as much time or effort working at his craft and improving her court skills as any basketball coach does in preparing his teams to play.* The result, which quite possibly defines the roots of the problem at hand, is that we find amateur athletes having their on-court actions evaluated by semiprofessional referees under the watchful eyes of professional coaches.[1] And of the three, only the coach is likely to lose his job when things fall apart on the basketball court.

The solution, of course, is to pay referees enough to make their part-time jobs full-time. That won't happen, though, because the schools—even colleges and universities—cannot afford such hefty cash outlays. The states aren't likely to pick up the tab, either: We'll see cows dancing on the moon before we see taxpayers voting in the revenue necessary to make officiating a full-time job with fringe benefits such as retirement systems and health plans.

So we as coaches are stuck. We're caught between the proverbial rock and hard place, with immature teenage players on the one hand and gener-

---

[1]While some coaches' game conduct can be decidedly unprofessional at times, we're using the word in its larger sense, namely, that coaches are college-trained, state-certified educators whose area of specialization is coaching.

ally well-meaning but often ill-prepared referees on the other, both groups of whom are directly related to our success and survival as basketball coaches.[2] We hope we can at least partly control our players' actions on the court—but there is precious little that we can do to control the refs. . . . Or is there?

Maybe we're not as helpless as we thought. If not, the first step toward learning to live with referees is to understand them.

TRAITS TO LOOK FOR IN GOOD REFEREES

These are the traits that define and describe the very best basketball officials:

1. They know the rules, but they don't flaunt their knowledge. We once saw a referee call *three* false double fouls in one game. Since the odds against such an occurrence are about the same as being dealt back-to-back royal flushes in poker, we guessed that he was using the game to show off his newfound understanding of one of basketball's least understood rules.

While every good official at least occasionally consults his rule book during games, the best referees do so only rarely because they already know the rules. And because understanding breeds confidence, they have no need to display their rules savvy by looking for opportunities to apply the fine print between the rules.

2. They understand the game. Basketball is more than a set of rules; it is a constantly unfolding sequence of highly sophisticated, integrated movement patterns that are intended to create scoring opportunities on the one hand, and to minimize the opponents' scoring via effective defense on the other hand. Referees who understand what teams are trying to accomplish offensively and defensively are able to anticipate problem situations and thus to evaluate problems from generally favorable vantage points when they occur. They also have a firm grasp of the difference between incidental and illegal contact, which in turn considerably increases their consistency.

3. They are consistent. Actually, consistency refers to two things, namely, applying the rules equally to both teams and making the same call (or noncall) every time the situation arises. Granted, it is difficult to call a traveling violation on the home team when it trails by a point or two with seconds remaining in the game and several thousand fans screaming in the stands—but the best refs always make the call anyway, if the violation occurred. That's why they're the best.

Referees generally try to establish their consistency early in every game;

---

[2]Except for the pros, the only qualification necessary to become a referee is to pass a written exam in the sport you want to officiate.

that is, by the pattern of their calls and noncalls they indicate how they expect the game to be played. Coaches and players alike understand that referees differ greatly in their interpretation of the rules governing contact, and so on. Some refs call games tightly, enforcing the rules rigidly for the sake of game control; others take a looser approach, giving the players a certain amount of leeway where minor violations and contact are concerned. Both methods are acceptable, as long as the coaches and players know what to expect, and as long as the referees are consistent in their calls at both ends of the court.

Incidentally, the previous paragraph explains why we see so many games in which one referee seems to be making all of the calls while the other one seems to have misplaced his whistle: They haven't established internal consistency as a pair of referees working together. One is calling the game consistently *tight*, while the other is calling it consistently *loose*. They aren't cheating when they call this way, although the effect is the same as if they *were* calling dishonestly since their areas of responsibility are not the same at both ends of the court.

The solution—which should have been done before the game began—is for them to sit down at halftime and work out the level of consistency they want to establish so that both of them will make the same calls during the second half.

4. *They are fair, honest, and willing to admit to making mistakes at least occasionally.* If during this section we seem to be harping on the subject of referees' mistakes, it's because we've known so many refs over the years who have acted as if putting on the zebra-striped shirt somehow conferred on them divine infallibility to error. Yes, most referees are honest, and yes, most of them try to be fair. But only occasionally have we seen a ref overrule another ref's call—and rarer still are those occasions when we've seen referees change their own calls. (At least in football they have the inadvertent whistle; if there's a basketball equivalent, it's rarer than a politician who keeps his campaign promises.) And that's why relatively few referees rate among the Very Best in the game.

5. *They know when and where to move to see the action—and they do it.* The first part of this statement repeats point 2: They understand the game of basketball. The last part refers to the referee's willingness and ability to move around as much—and as quickly—as necessary to retain clear view of player contact when it occurs. In this regard, the best referee we've ever seen probably does more running during the games he calls than any of the players. Fans often laugh at him because he's like the Tasmanian devil in the Bugs Bunny cartoons, a whirling dervish of perpetual motion who sprints downcourt with fast-breaks, runs or slide-steps along the baseline to one side or the other to maintain his view, pausing only to lean this way or that or even hop into the air to see over or around someone who is blocking his view. The fans think he's just about the funniest thing they've seen since "America's

Funniest Home Videos"—which shows exactly how different he is from his peers. He works hard at being the best referee he can be, which isn't perfect but is literally miles ahead of most of the refs he works with.

One more point: Good referees are already in shape when the season starts. They don't use the games they call during the first two or three weeks of the season to get them in shape for the rest of the season.

6. They seldom if ever lose control of themselves or the game. While more will be said about this later, we'll point out here that, if a referee rates high on the five points already listed, he'll also rate high in terms of controlling games.

The converse is also true, of course.

7. They have a sense of humor and enjoy their association with the game. Bad things usually happen when a referee—or a coach, for that matter—starts taking the game too seriously. The best referees are almost never so wrapped up in the game that they cannot enjoy it. And while the ref's role as a spectator is far removed from that of the fan in the stands, when the time comes that he cannot silently admire the awesome skills of great teams and great players, it is time for him to hang up his whistle and leave the game to younger, more enthusiastic minds.

Great referees never die; they just report to a higher Scorer's table.

——————— REFEREES TO BEWARE OF ———————

In the heat of battle, coaches sometimes make the mistake of expecting referees *not* to make mistakes—an impossible task—or of considering a "good" official to be one who makes his calls in *our* favor, not the opponents'. The absurdity of both positions should be obvious. Less obvious (but of infinitely more importance) are the sometimes subtle clues to officiating incompetence that you as a coach should be aware of.

1. Referees who count the fouls in the scorebook at halftime or after the game is over. While competent officials do not need to know the ratio of fouls called against the two teams, some inept officials like to see balanced totals in the fouls columns of the scorebook as proof that they didn't call the game to one team's advantage. Yet that is precisely what they did if they selectively called—or ignored—fouls in order to balance the ledger. And you can bet that that's exactly what they intend to do in the second half if you see them counting the team fouls in the scorebook at halftime.

Closely allied to this problem (but harder to identify) are cases in which referees overlook fouls or minor violations by one team when it is hopelessly behind by a lopsided score, or by both teams to keep the clock running and get the game over with. And while the latter situation will be considered at length in a later part of this section regarding its implications for using referees to your team's advantage, we'll point out here that any referee who attempts to influence a team's score or scoring ability in any manner other than by calling the game objectively for both sides is cheating, just as surely as the coach who knowingly plays ineligible players. It is not the referees' responsibility to keep scores close or speed up long games by ignoring fouls or violations any more than it is to balance the foul totals between the two teams.

2. Referees who consistently fail to achieve or maintain favorable visual angles in watching the action as it unfolds on the court. There's nothing wrong with a referee's being obese, as long as it doesn't hinder his ability to move and to *see* the game. And there's nothing wrong with a referee's standing still on the court, either, as long as he has full view of the action in his area of responsibility. Still, we've all seen officials who, having headed downcourt and set themselves in position, behave as if their feet have grown roots to the floor. There might be four or five players between them and the contact when it occurs, but nothing short of an earthquake will induce them to move to a better viewing angle—yet they still make the calls, based on what they hear or what they *think* might have happened.

In fact, the presence of ten players who are constantly moving around and shifting positions in a rather confined court space makes it virtually impossible for two—or even three—officials to properly evaluate court action without moving almost constantly in live-ball situations to improve their viewing angles. Referees who are willing to make calls based on what they hear or what they imagine happened rather than what they actually see are both lazy and incompetent. With the possible exception of *homers* (see point 3), they are the worst officials you're likely to encounter.

3. Referees who allow their calls to be influenced by the home crowd. In a sense, every foul or violation is a judgment call, since the official has to decide whether to make the call or let it go. But it's not that easy, because every violation that is whistled or ignored is applauded by one team and its supporters and objected to by the other team and its fans. And because the home team's supporters are usually more numerous—and thus more vocal—than those of the visitors, visiting coaches often accuse referees of letting the home crowd influence their calls. (The term for such referees is *homers*.)

Frankly, we believe that, on the high school level, at least there are far fewer outright homers than most coaches think. Oh, they exist, all right: We once saw a male referee and a female coach embrace before a high school girls' game, and we later learned from someone who had taught at the school that the ref was a town commissioner who ate lunch every day in the school cafeteria. (Any bets on who won that game? The visitors, who were 13–0 going into the game, lost by 18 points.) Still, most referee associations, sensitive to such criticisms, carefully avoid assigning officials to games in which they have obvious ties to one team, such as the preceding example or calling games at their alma mater.

You're most likely to find homers at the college level, where travel considerations often dictate the use of referees from the home team's area—or else at the lowest levels of play that do not require certified officials. In some instances, especially at the lower levels of play, homers can serve as an extension of the home team itself, acting virtually as another player on the floor. We recall a junior high game a number of years ago in which the first fourteen fouls called in the game were directed against the visiting team's three highest scorers. The game officials were a manager and a player from the local high school team.

Sometimes weak-willed referees who are not really homers are guilty of giving in to the temptation to make the "popular" call, that is, the call that evokes thunderous crowd approval. Almost invariably, such calls are made at critical times in close games, since other situations would not elicit much in the way of crowd response. The payoff regarding whether the ref is using the situation to his own advantage may be seen, if at all, in the amount of time he takes to explain his call after he blows his whistle to end the play. If he's playing to the crowd, he'll wait for the noise to gradually fade away to a hushed whisper as tension builds and all eyes turn his way before he gestures emphatically that, say, a traveling violation has occurred . . . *and the ball goes over to . . . THE HOME TEAM!!!*

4. Referees who hold grudges. It's only a game—or at least it's supposed to be. Sometimes, though, it's more than that to the coaches, players, and fans involved. If coaching is a pressure cooker for coaches, basketball games are all that and more for referees.

Like teachers in the classroom, referees are the most visible targets for criticism and abuse on the basketball court when things go wrong. Fans display their displeasure with refs by booing, heckling, and sometimes unfortunately, by throwing ice or other objects onto the floor. Sometimes they throw things at the officials.

Coaches do their part to make life miserable for referees by needling them incessantly—and loudly—questioning their calls and their integrity, and inciting the fans to action. Referees are supposed to overlook crowd behavior and the antics of unruly coaches and players whenever possible, and to assess technical fouls and disqualifications whenever players or coaches overstep the bounds of acceptable behavior. And having assessed their penalties, they are supposed to continue to call the game objectively, with malice toward none. But it doesn't always work out that way.

As might be expected, some officials tolerate more verbal abuse than others, and coaches usually learn rather quickly where the limits lie for the referees who regularly call their games. Unfortunately, some coaches are experts at applying the needle to sensitive areas of a given referee's psyche— for example, by asking an overweight referee when the baby is due. And also, unfortunately, some referees tend to hold grudges against coaches or players who have embarrassed them. One coach told us:

> I had been getting on one of the refs pretty good—you know, giving him a [verbal] shot every time he passed us heading downcourt, because he had swallowed his whistle. The other guy was having to make all the calls. So I yelled out to him, 'Hey, Mr. Ref, I've got an extra whistle in my office if you need it!' 'No thanks, I'll use mine,' he says, blowing his whistle and hitting me with a T. Came to find out that the *other* ref had called one on me too, for the same thing. They were gonna give the other team four free throws. "Wait a minute," my assistant coach says, "do you mean that if both of you call the same foul on a player, it counts as two fouls and the shooter gets four free throws?" So they popped a T on him, too, and threw *me* out of the game for having three techs on me.[3] Later, they admitted that they were wrong and apologized to the principal after the game was over. But at the time they were so hot to get back at me that they'd have hit me with a T if the lights had gone out in the gym.

Commonly referred to by the derisive term *rabbit-ears*, officials who hold grudges can often be identified by their tendency to stand near the offending coach's huddle during timeouts with an ear cocked to hear what is being said about them, or else by positioning themselves near the hash marks at the offending coach's end of the court during play for the same purpose. They tend to whistle technicals while their backs are turned to the offending coach or his bench, or at least while they are not looking in that direction—presumably to show that the offense was so flagrant that they could hear it without even listening for it. And their T's are always called in the white-hot grip of anger.

The reader will note that we aren't saying coaches and players don't lose control from time to time, or that referees should not call technicals; they do, and they should. Some coaches are notorious referee baiters. But again, like the teacher in the classroom, the referee's job is to ensure that the game progresses in an orderly manner. When problems arise, they should be resolved quickly and forcefully—and then they should be promptly forgotten. Don't count on it, though: At a referee's meeting we attended one ref called out across the room to another, "Hey, John, how many technicals did you have to call on that [expletive deleted] last Friday night?"

Where some referees are concerned, grudges, like diamonds, are forever. If you ever embarrass them, they'll never forget it—or forgive it. And they have ways of ensuring that *you* never forget it, either.

5. Referees who abuse the power of their position. The referee walked over to the bench, poked an assistant coach in the chest three times

---

[3]Technical fouls against the bench are counted against the head coach.

with an index finger, and told him, "You'd better sit down and shut up right now, or you'll be outside listening to the rest of the game on the radio!" The incident was reported to the state high school association because it involved physical contact, but nothing was done about it. But if the situations had been reversed—if the coach had poked the referee with his finger—the school might have been fined and the coach probably would have been suspended from coaching by the state high school association.

An ancient Greek writer, Pittacus, stated that the measure of a man is what he does with power. Thus it is with referees. Those who are most concerned with power are most likely to look for opportunities to exercise it, or at least to have it challenged. Such officials dislike having their calls questioned simply because they do not make mistakes—and for the same reason they see no sense in debating the issue with ignorant coaches whose judgment is clouded by the fact that they are wrong. Such officials tend to quick-whistle plays before they are completed, and to take criticism or questioning as a personal challenge to their authority, integrity, or ability. Like Rodney Dangerfield, they feel that they "don't get no respect"; thus, they are prepared to dispense T's like candies on Halloween if necessary to preserve their self-image of infallibility.

Contrast, if you will, such an arrogant and dogmatic approach to the game with that of a high school referee we once encountered. Having made an absolutely outrageous call that went against our team, the ref slowly walked over to where we were standing and blowing off steam at 140 decibels. "Coach," he said quietly, "I make mistakes from time to time. And this time you're right, I blew the call. It was my mistake. There's nothing I can do about it now. All I can say is, I'm sorry, and I'll try to do better next time. But for now I'd like for you to sit down so we can get back to the game." We did, without another word, because there was nothing else to say.

– WHAT YOU CAN (AND CANNOT) DO ABOUT POOR OFFICIATING –

First, the "cannot": *You cannot change a referee's basic nature*. If, for example, a referee is lazy or incompetent, nothing you can say or do will alter that fact or his behavior.

Except . . .

We feel impelled to briefly relate the story of a coach who, for one brief moment in time, beat the odds and elevated the level of two officials' performances for a single game. We offer it here, not in the hope that other coaches will try it, but because to our knowledge it is unique in the annals of basketball coaching history. We call this amazing tale:

"THE NIGHT THAT THE REFEREES CALLED A NEARLY PERFECT GAME."

THE COACH, who shall remain nameless, although he is long gone from coaching, knew that he was in trouble. His team, a region title contender, was scheduled to play its next game in a notorious snake pit where referees were often intimidated by the vocal, unruly home fans.

On game night, the first thing the coach did when his team took the court for warmups was to draw the referees aside for a brief chat. He pointed to a man standing beside a camera and tripod near the top of the bleachers.

"See that man? He's from the high school association office," the coach lied—the gentleman was a member of his booster club. "They called me last week and said they were making a new film to show at the referees' clinics, and they wanted to use clips from tonight's game to illustrate the rules. I told them I didn't think you'd mind." The coach paused to let his words sink in before adding, "Is it okay with you if he films the game?"

The refs glanced at each other in wide-eyed amazement . . . looked up at the camera in the stands . . . and turned back to the coach. "No, no, it's fine with us," one of the refs said eagerly, withdrawing a comb from his back pocket to run through his hair.

Throughout the game (which the visitors won, incidentally), the refs applied themselves with unusual vigor and flair, moving with the dexterity of jungle cats and signaling their calls with the precision of a drum major leading a band. And they never let the home crowd influence their calls even once.

Having heard the story from the coach whose team lost the game, we looked up the coach in question and asked him about it. Yes, it was true, he said with a laugh. "The other coach thought I was cheating when he found out about it later, but that wasn't it at all. All I was trying to do was to get them to call the game impartially at both ends of the court, which was pretty near impossible to do back in those days in that gym."

Let's face it—as coaches, we're pretty much at the mercy of the refs. They call what they want to call, ignore the rest, and generally control such things as acceptable contact between players and verbal outbursts from the bench and fans within the limits of their patience and tolerance. As we have seen, some officials are woefully inept or unprepared for the rigors and responsibilities of their position. And while it may not seem like much, there *are* at least three things you can do about poor officiating. Taking them in reverse order of their likely effectiveness, they are:

1. When referees overstep the boundaries of their authority (as with the official who prodded a coach in the chest with his finger repeatedly to underscore his verbal warning to the coach); or when they display ignorance of the rules (e.g., the refs who assessed *two* technical fouls on a coach for one remark that he made)—their behavior should be reported in a letter to the state high school association office, regardless of whether they apologize later for their conduct. Little or nothing is likely to be done about the incident (depending on its severity, of course), since as ex-coaches themselves association officers generally tend to side with referees in disputes with coaches. Still, many coaches feel obligated to report referees' offenses in the same manner that referees are required to report all technical fouls to the state office. Despite the unlikelihood of decisive action being taken against the referee(s) in question, the state association cannot act at all unless offenses are reported.

2. If certain referees are unsatisfactory to you, you can notify the head of the officials' association you're using and have those referees crossed off your list of acceptable officials for your home games. Most officials' associations permit coaches to eliminate one or two of their referees from calling that coach's home games. It doesn't exactly solve the problem, since (a) you're likely to encounter them at away games (and woe be unto you if those officials are the sort who hold grudges!) and (b) there may be more than one or two refs in that association whose performances are unacceptable to you. But at least you're taking positive action that can offer you some relief in your home games, and that thought should console you somewhat.

If you're coaching in an area that is new to you, it wouldn't hurt to keep a file on the refs until you get to know them. Such a file should include detailed information about each referee's court behavior, temperament, accessibility to coaches, game control, mobility, consistency, fairness to visiting teams, limits of incidental player contact, and anything else that would help you evaluate his overall ability. You should not confine those evaluations to your own games, either: Scouting trips offer excellent opportunities to see how the refs respond to other coaches and other situations—and such information is far more likely to be objective and accurate than evaluations based on your own games.

3. If your unhappy experiences indicate that a high percentage of officials from a given association are unsatisfactory, you may want to find another association to supply officials for your home games next year. It will probably cost more in terms of travel allowance, but if you think you've been getting a raw deal from one association, you're perfectly within your rights to switch to another group. You can also urge coaches at other schools to do likewise. We've seen instances in which all of the basketball coaches in a region or subregion agreed at their spring meeting not to use a certain association next year—and in one extreme case the coaches agreed not to schedule teams who used that association!

– UNDERSTANDING AND USING REFEREES TO YOUR ADVANTAGE –

Several years ago, UNLV's Jerry Tarkanian made a startling discovery regarding the psychology of referee behavior, one that has drastically altered the game of basketball—but it had no such effect at the time because Tark wisely kept his discovery largely to himself. Only now, more than a century after James A. Naismith nailed a peach basket to the wall at Springfield College and invented basketball, can we see Tark's unique theory taking root and gaining widespread acceptance. His discovery, which goes far deeper than its apparent simplicity would indicate, is this:

> When faced with a team whose defensive style is intensely aggressive and physical (e.g., hand-checking, bodychecking, overplaying, pushing, holding, fighting through screens, and diving after loose balls), referees initially will call fouls against that team as expected—*but as the game progresses, they tend to stop making those calls except in flagrant situations.*

Of course, there's an important corollary to this rule, namely, that *your players must be skilled defensively*. Still, if your players are fundamentally unskilled you probably shouldn't be using an aggressive defensive style that exaggerates and underscores their shortcomings anyway, so that's not a factor in our present analysis.

With the exception of homers, every referee is concerned with establishing *consistency*. When confronted with a hard-nosed defensive team that claws, scratches, pushes, holds, and wears floor burns with the pride of a master sergeant's stripes, the refs must choose between two options: They can call the contact as usual, in which case marching back and forth to the foul lines may extend the game to as much as twice its normal length and the foul discrepancy between the two teams will make the refs look like homers; or they can revise their original concept of what sort of contact constitutes a foul. In Tark's experience—and ours as well—most officials will opt for the second choice as being more expedient and consistent.

At the college level, three-and-a-half-hour televised games do not sit well with network programmers—and thus with the sport's governing bodies, who enjoy rich television contracts; at the high school level, there's the 10:00 P.M. curfew for week night games in some states for officials to consider. (We once saw a Tuesday night high school girls' game in which the referees stuck to their guns and whistled a total of 87 fouls. The game, which began at 7:00 P.M., ended at 9:30 P.M. The boys' teams took three minutes to warm up and played slightly more than a quarter before their game was called due to the curfew rule.)

In terms of its effect on officiating, a nonstop, high-speed, racehorse brand of offense combined with an ultraphysical, contact-oriented defensive style is likely to be highly effective in either of two situations: When the referees are overweight, elderly, or out of shape; or when they are concerned with balancing the foul totals in the scorebook. Regarding the former, high school girls' teams may stand to benefit from this reckless, wild-and-woolly style of play even more than the boys, since the refs may have to drastically curtail their range of movement and court coverage to avoid becoming totally exhausted even before the boys' game begins. And regarding the latter, it takes an unusual amount of confidence—and courage—for officials to go into an arena and call forty-seven fouls on the home team and only twelve on the visitors. (We saw that happen once—and we also saw an officiating crew setting land speed records getting to their cars and out of the parking lot after the games, too!)

If you harbor any doubts as to whether such a defensive playing style is really effective, you haven't watched UNLV, Oklahoma, or the Detroit Pistons lately. They do it with defense that's almost as physical as the NFL's bump-and-run coverage. And their players don't foul out any more often than those of other teams—probably less, in fact, due to the factor that we'll consider next.

Jerry Tarkanian is not the only coach who has studied referee behavior and tendencies: We've done a bit of research ourselves. And after years of sometimes-painful observation here's what we've learned: *Referee expectations tend to govern what referees call.*

In the example previously cited, referees who anticipate a three-hour girls' game will usually take steps to shorten the game by cutting down on the number of fouls and minor violations called. But there are other familiar examples at hand. All are based, not necessarily on facts, but on commonly held beliefs.

• ***Tall teams tend to outrebound smaller teams.*** Such a notion is hardly surprising, since a six-feet-four-inch player normally has to jump at least eight inches merely to equal the *standing* reach of a seven-foot player. But what this means to you as a coach is that, no matter how much you emphasize positioning and blocking out under the boards with your small players, referees will tend to let the opponents' taller players reach over your players' backs to take away rebounds.

If your team is small and must constantly battle for inside rebounding positions against taller foes, you should try to secure mobile, hard-working officials for your home games who will move constantly to see who initiates the illegal contact that goes on around the boards while (and after) positioning is established. You should also work the refs during pregame warmups, telling them how hard your players work on blocking out in practice and hope that the refs give your players a fair chance. Don't count on it, though: We've had refs tell us that there's no such thing as "over-the-back" fouls. (What they mean is that there's no signal for fouls involving reaching over a player's back: The signal consists of extending two hands outward for *pushing*. Still, the fact that some refs don't know the difference between the foul and the signal speaks volumes about their lack of understanding of the game.)

If, on the other hand, you're blessed with tall players and leapers who can jump into orbit, you want to teach them to crowd the basket area when shots are taken, since over the long haul refs tend to expect the tallest players to get most of the rebounds anyway. As a result, they usually give taller players considerable leeway when contact occurs in rebounding, especially when they—the refs—do not take pains to see who initiated the contact. (There's an old saying that applies here: "Possession is nine-tenths of the law.")

With a tall lineup, you'd like to have referees whose mobility along the baseline resembles that of a parked car; after all, the less mobile the ref is, the less likely he is to whistle the contact that occurs when your skyscrapers are late moving into the lane to rebound missed shots. If a ref's vision is even partly obscured by the bodies moving around in the lane area, he is far more likely to see the smaller player's reaction to being pushed from behind than to see the push itself—if, indeed, he is able to see anything at all.

Perhaps we should point out here that many coaches believe that adding a third official to the college game has not appreciably improved the officiating at that level—probably because, while vision is improved, interpretation of the action is just as error-prone as ever among those referees who do not really understand the game. As Bobby Knight put it, adding a third referee just increases the chances of refereeing mistakes by 50 percent.

• *Basketball has become more physical at all levels of play.* Tark's "secret" is not really a secret anymore. Oklahoma coach Billy Tubbs was in a complaining mood recently: "The game at this point is becoming block and tackle, push and shove, and if that's the way everybody wants the game to be played, I'm not being critical of [the referees]."[4] It's a strange remark coming

---

[4]"College Game Getting Too Physical, Tubbs Says," *Atlanta Journal–Constitution* (Jan. 26, 1991), p. D6.

from Tubbs, whose OU teams have used precisely that intimidating style of play with great success for many years—but it serves to focus on the problem: from hand-checking to push-and-shove, block-and-tackle defense, everybody's doing it nowadays, it seems, even junior high and middle-school teams whose best defenders couldn't guard a tackling dummy.

Powerless to stem the rising tide of contact-oriented defenses for reasons that have already been cited, officials have in many instances expanded their concept of unacceptable bodily contact literally from "no harm, no foul" to "no blood, no foul." Where will it stop? Who knows? Perhaps someday in the future basketball uniforms will include helmets, shoulder pads, and cleats. Until then, though, we're reminded that, in the words of one grizzled old coach, "It ain't a foul unless they call it." And if they aren't calling it, the prudent coach will either take advantage of it or enter every game at a marked disadvantage. Stress defensive fundamentals such as stance footwork and positioning in your daily practices—but don't overlook the physical aspects of defensive play, if for no other reason than to be prepared to deal with teams who play that way. You may not like the block-and-tackle, push-and-shove style of play any more than the referees do, but it's probably here to stay. Whether you use it or not, you'd better have your teams ready to deal with it.

• *Good defensive teams don't commit as many fouls as poor defensive teams.* While this statement may or may not be true—for example, we always want our teams to play aggressively enough to commit more fouls than our opponents do—you'd better believe that the *referees* believe it! Referees know a good defensive team when they see it, and they likely will give your players the benefit of the doubt in many contact situations if they know that your defense is fundamentally sound. It doesn't matter whether your team plays man-to-man or zone defense, or aggressively or passively; the key here is to *stress defense constantly in your daily practices to build a team defense that does not make fundamental mistakes more often than occasionally.* (*Note:* The fundamental mistakes that are most easily spotted by the refs include reaching around or over the pass receiver or dribbler to deflect a pass or steal the ball; using the hands to push a post player in the back or move his outstretched arms out of the way; and standing erect while guarding the dribbler, then stepping into his path or reaching across his body from in front or behind to swat at the ball as he drives past the defender.)

At any rate, the point is important enough to bear repeating: Whether due to your team's defensive reputation or past experiences calling your games, if the refs believe that your team seldom makes fundamental defensive mistakes, they are likely to interpret a certain amount of your players' fouls as incidental contact or fouls committed by the other team.

Other ways of using referees to your advantage exist, but they are situational in the sense that their chances of succeeding relate to the types of referees or players involved. For example, if the referees are overweight or poorly conditioned, you would want to exaggerate your normal offensive style, whether by running relentlessly with your fast-breaking squad (thus challenging the refs to keep up with the pace or miss the calls) or playing more deliberately than normal with a slow, pattern-oriented team (to give the refs time to catch up and better observe the opponents' half-court defense). And if the referees are lazy and prefer not to move around to improve their view, you might instruct your players to play a more physical game defensively, including bellying up to post players and doing a lot of pushing (but not with the hands), trying to draw charging fouls, and combating screens by falling down when they can't fight their way through. Sure, there's a rule against faking a charging foul collision, but when's the last time you saw it called?

Are such tactics feasible? Maybe. Are they unethical? No more so than it is to play to an opposing team's weaknesses. After all, it's not your fault that the referees are out of shape or lazy. It's *their* fault, the zebras', and they—and the opponents—should suffer the consequences of their shortcomings, not you and your team.

— FINAL THOUGHTS (ABOUT THE RULES, REFS, AND COACHES) —

According to the rules (on the high school level, at least) teams are given one minute for timeouts. They can be assessed a technical foul for failing to return to the court promptly at the end of the timeout. On the surface it appears to be a good rule, since some coaches would keep their teams on the sideline indefinitely if there were no such rule.[5] But there's a down side to it, too: Clock operators don't always give the teams a full minute, especially when the visitors called the timeout.

The worst abuse we've ever experienced in this regard was a *ten-second timeout* we received in an important road game. (Our scorebook keeper, suspicious of several abbreviated timeouts that occurred earlier in the game, did the timing.) Later, at a rules clinic the next fall, we asked a representative from the state high school association what could be done about the problem. He thought about it briefly. "You need to tell your clock operators to be sure to give the full minute," was his reply. But that was no answer, since the *honest* coaches always do that anyway.

The *real* answer would be for the rule book to require the *referees* to time the timeouts.

One of the biggest problems that referees have with coaches—and a major reason why referees don't always have a great deal of respect for coaches—is that *a surprisingly large number of basketball coaches don't know*

---

[5]"If you don't throw it, they can't hit it."—Lefty Gomez

the rules. (Years ago, we saw a high school coach screaming at the refs that backcourt fouls were two-shot fouls, which was true at the time—*in the NBA!*)

If you're starting out in basketball coaching, you need to read the entire rule book and casebook as slowly as necessary for you to gain a thorough understanding of the rules. Plowing through that vast sea of rules and interpretations will give you a new awareness of the difficulties facing referees— but more important, it should serve to reduce the friction between you and the refs (and enhance their respect for you as well) by reducing the number of times when your complaints and criticisms of their calls are dead wrong.

If you're looking for the Perfect Referee, you'd better hope that your fans and boosters aren't looking for the Perfect Coach, because neither of them exists. But if you're looking for a referee who will give you a total effort night in and night out, try a woman referee. As in coaching, women referees feel they have to work twice as hard to be considered half as good as their male counterparts.

Finally, if you really have your team's best interests at heart, there's one more thing you should consider about referees—and that's your own self-control and bench conduct.

Sure, it feels good to let off steam every now and then by screaming at the refs, especially when they richly deserve it—but you also need to remember that *the referees always get in the last word when they want to in arguments with players and coaches.* And if they hold grudges, you'll be at their mercy every time they call your games if you ever antagonize them.

The best thing you can do for your team where the refs are concerned is to control your temper and not say things that will come back to haunt you in the future, no matter how badly you think they're crucifying you.

SECTION 14

The Postseason Blues and Blahs

There are so many things we wish we had done yesterday, so few that we feel like doing today.

—*Mignon McLaughlin*

If a man takes no thought about what is distant, he will find sorrow near at hand.

—*Confucius (c. 551–479 B.C.)*

WHO SAYS THE OFF-SEASON IS "OFF"?

First, of course, there's the fact that, for many basketball coaches, the end of basketball season simply marks the beginning of another sport season. After taking a day off from coaching to inventory equipment and uniforms and box them up for the summer, they begin holding tryouts in whichever spring sport they're coaching. Whether the additional coaching is part of the requirement for the head basketball coaching position or is undertaken for its supplemental income or experiential value, coaching sports back-to-back makes for a long and tiring school year.

If you're coaching a spring sport, because you'll be involved with it on a daily basis you need to be even more organized than if you weren't coaching after basketball season. Do as much of your postseason work *during the season* as possible, so you won't have to worry about it later. You can:

- Determine letter winners early. Try to arrange to order your jackets and letters during the Christmas holidays, if possible.

237

- Begin scheduling opponents for next year in January, or early February at the latest, to complete the task by the end of the season.

- If your basketball awards dinner or banquet is held separately from those for spring sports and football, start making arrangements early, including date, location, invitation list, program, meal, preparers, servers, speaker, awards (order trophies at least three to four weeks in advance), and whatever else you can think of to ease your last-minute preparations.

- Write thank-you notes to everyone who helped out during the season, and be sure to invite them to the banquet.[1]

- Restock your mimeograped forms before the school runs out of paper.

- Begin budgeting for next year, including making arrangements for ordering uniforms six to nine months in advance and equipment three to five months in advance. (The current trend among athletic suppliers seems to be toward slower service than ever before.)

- Set up off-season strength and conditioning programs for those basketball players who are not otherwise involved in spring sports. Their workouts should include weight training; jumping (bench and rope); running; and juggling and playing tennis, badminton, handball, racquetball, and/or table tennis, all of which are excellent activities for hand–eye coordination and quickness. You can set up shooting schedules and encourage your players to record their spot-shooting practice results in notebooks. You can also provide them with ballhandling improvement drills. (One excellent source is the Pete Maravich "Homework Basketball" series from ESPN; it's expensive—about $100 for the four videotapes—but the ballhandling tape alone is worth the price. The other tapes cover shooting, passing, and defense.)

Regardless of whether or not you're coaching a spring sport, you need to continue monitoring your basketball players' grades, academic progress, and classroom conduct after the season is over. In our experience, at least, kids are most likely to get in trouble, whether in terms of declining grades or improper conduct, when they are not involved in athletics on a daily basis. Playing a team sport requires a certain amount of self-discipline that carries over into other aspects of an athlete's life—and because *not* playing requires no such self-monitoring, it's easy for a youngster to grow lax and develop lazy

---

[1] And if their contribution was truly worthwhile, recognize it with a certificate, plaque, or small gift of some kind. When we gave our scorebook keeper a gold Cross™ pen and pencil set she told us later that she hadn't missed a home or away game in seven years, and that we were the first coaches during that span who had even thanked her for helping out.

study habits or poor personal habits, especially if most of his closest friends are not athletes.

We feel that it's important to keep your athletes together as much as possible in the off-season, whether by encouraging them to participate in spring sports or by setting up training programs for them. (Most coaches like weight training because it increases players' strength; we like it for that reason, too—but even more because it keeps the players involved during the off-season in working together toward team goals.) In our age of easy temptation to crime, drugs, alcohol, sex, and other negative solutions to life's problems, it's important for youngsters to be exposed to as many positive influences as possible—and few better sources exist than having teammates who are their best friends.

If you're not coaching a spring sport, the extent of your legal coaching contact with your players is spelled out in your high school association by-laws. It will tell you whether you can have spring or summer leagues open to all students in the school, or run one-on-one, two-on-two, three-on-three, or free-throw shooting tournaments, hot shot competitions, and so on. You may even be able to coach your players in basketball fundamentals during the off-season—and if so, by all means do so. It's a luxury that some coaches in other places don't have.

If you're otherwise uninvolved during the spring, you can also have individual meetings with your returning players to discuss the team's (and their) prospects and goals for next year, including outlining individual strengths and devising programs to shore up areas of individual weakness. You can compile your season statistics and file them away. You can prepare highlight films. And you can start working on any or all of the tasks outlined below.

———— SUMMERTIME: THE CALM BEFORE THE STORM ————

Get a Job, Sha-na-na-na

Here's the way a member of the local school board in a small south Georgia town called it at the monthly board of education meeting when discussion arose concerning coaching supplements for the upcoming school year:

> The way I see it, them coaches are already overpaid as it is. They're gettin' twelve months worth of teacher salaries for just nine months of work—and how much work does it take to roll out a ball, anyway? We're givin' 'em these huge supplements every year for coachin' a kids' game when there's poverty, malnutrition, and unemployment all around us. They should be willing to coach for free out of a love for the game so we can use that supplement money to get good math and science teachers.

We'd bet that, when the old gentleman sleeps on his side at night, he always wonders why he finds sawdust on his pillow the next morning.

In reality, most coaches have to find summer jobs to help make ends meet. We've known coaches to take such disparate and diverse summer jobs as lifeguarding, carpentry, house painting, road construction, bartending, lawn maintenance, and summer camp coaching.

A warning, though: Don't expect the gravy train of $ummer job megabuck$ to keep rolling in if your state is moving toward longer school hours. For instance, we're heading toward *year-round school* in Georgia, which will replace the eight weeks of summer break with shorter breaks interspersed at intervals throughout the school year—and also, incidentally, will produce at least three unfortunate side effects:

1. We won't have to worry about finding summer jobs any more: There won't be any available, since three-week jobs are as scarce as tap-dancing rhinos

2. We won't be fulfilling residency requirements for advanced degrees by taking full course-loads during the colleges' eight-week summer quarters

3. Sports seasons will be disrupted by the intermittent breaks—although doubtless we as coaches will adapt to the changes with the same vigor that we've responded to other supposedly well-intentioned but misguided educational innovations and challenges such as *no-pass, no-play.*

Taking Summer Courses for Fun and Credit

Perhaps it's just our paranoia showing through, but whatever happened to the good old summertime? The addition of pre- and postplanning weeks have pared the ten weeks of summer vacation down to eight weeks for teachers, and the accreditation agencies and state boards of education have done their best to waste the rest of our summers by requiring us to go back to school to take courses. (Naturally, those courses have nothing to do with coaching, since we already took the basketball coaching course as undergraduates.) Presidents, congressmen, doctors, lawyers, Indian chiefs: None of them are required to take additional college courses to to remain certified in their jobs—but we are, even though as teachers we're still going to be blamed for everything short of the breakup of the Soviet Union.

Part of the problem is that many educational leaders find it difficult, tedious, and embarrassing to explain to their nonteaching professional friends at cocktail parties why teachers are paid during the eight weeks of summer when they aren't teaching: The rest of the problem is financial.[2]

The colleges and universities desperately need the money, and requiring teachers to take courses is a quick and easy way of at least partially satisfying that need. (That's why you don't receive credit toward recertification for attending coaching clinics, although you'll get more useful information out of one clinic session than you'll get from the next ten education courses you take. Coaching clinics don't make money for colleges and universities.)

A-Camping We Shall Go . . .

It's always entertaining—albeit more than a bit depressing—to find out what new avenues the NFSHSAA and our state high school associations are exploring in their never-ending quest to protect and control the games we play.

NFSHSAA Greatest Hits, Vol. 1: During the late 1960s and early 1970s, when athletics was paving the way for widespread racial integration in our society, the NFSHSAA basketball rules committee showed great sensitivity to the problem in its rules changes. Three examples will suffice:

- Players could wear sweatbands, but only of one color. No patriotic red, white, and blue wrist- or headbands were permitted—but more important, no patriotic red, green, and black sweatbands symbolizing African-American unity and heritage could be worn. The penalty: A technical foul was assessed against the wearer. (The rule was rescinded after one year.)

- Fouls were no longer committed by players; instead, they were now committed by the floor. (That's where the refs pointed to indicate the fouler.) This technique lingered for more than a decade; in fact, many older referees still use it for its nonconfrontational value.

- When players were called for fouls, they were required to identify themselves by raising one hand—not two—above their heads with *all five fingers* (certainly not one—nor two, three, or four fingers) fully extended. The penalty for violations (including raising a closed fist, which was a gesture symbolic of black power) was a technical foul. The rule was changed the following year to what it should have been in the first place: players no longer had to raise their hands or otherwise signify to the scorer that they had been called for a foul.

---

[2]These same guilt feelings explain the reason why teachers don't have "free" periods anymore, but *planning periods*: Heaven forbid that any educator should consider time spent away from the students as *free* time!

State associations have been concerned in recent years with perceptions of high school athletes as illiterate cretins who don't "spel verry gud" and couldn't add water to an empty bucket. That the same applies to an equal or greater number of nonathletic students doesn't seem to matter much. The result has been a crazy quilt of rules in many states governing: (1) the opening date of basketball practice, (2) limits of total number of games played, (3) travel distance for weeknight games preceeding school days, (4) the presence and/or length of spring practice, and (5) limitations on other out-of-season coaching, especially summertime. In many cases, these rules change so much from year to year that one wonders if they aren't actually being rewritten annually by the IRS.

Way back in the Dark Ages of the mid-1960s, when there were no limits on out-of-season practice, we began working on our players' shooting form and ballhandling skills immediately after the season ended. We were practicing basketball during the school day, too—another current no-no—and for seven years at least half of our varsity basketball players were in the Beta Club, including the president, vice-president, and either secretary or treasurer. We did it by setting expected GPAs for each player and then penalizing players in the form of daily miles running for Ds, Fs, or GPAs that fell below our stated expectations. The players made studying a habit because they had to, the same way that players make a habit of working hard on defense.

But then, due at least in part to the influence of coaches in our state who resented the idea that boys or girls might practice a sport other than football if given a choice, strict limits were placed on out-of-season coaching in the various sports.[3] Then spring practice was eliminated so our state's basketball players could devote themselves to studying full-time away from school, in the same manner as monks devoting their lives to meditation and prayer. Then the state said that players could attend one week of summer camp. Currently in Georgia (although this could change by the next time you glance at your wristwatch), players can play for any team(s) they want to during the summer as long as their coach(es) are not coaching them; and coaches are confined to *one coach working with one player per day on basketball skills* at any time during the off-season, or working with groups in indirectly related basketball activities such as conditioning, weight training,

---

[3]In Georgia, the state Department of Education will take away a coach's teaching certificate for violating out-of-season practice rules. If this "get-tough" trend continues, we envision a day when, dragged kicking and screaming past cells filled with murderers, rapists, child molesters, drug pushers, kidnappers, thieves, Congressmen, and televangelists, Coach X is hauled away to meet his maker—given "thirty days in the electric chair," as Abe Lemons put it—for the unpardonable crime of playing three-on-three with a few of his players and other students in mid-May.

Who'd ever of thunk that shooting up basketballs would ever be considered as dangerous and subversive an activity as shooting up heroin or crack cocaine?

and so on, as long as participation is not required as a condition for team membership.

What You Can Do

The rules in your state probably are different from ours. For your own protection, you need to know precisely what rules you're playing by. You should study the bylaws section of your high school association handbook very carefully every year. (Ours carefully points out that *ignorance of the rules is no defense against violations*.)

At any rate, although you may or may not be permitted by your state to practice during the off-season and summertime, depending on how much heat your state legislators are feeling to produce a scapegoat to blame for declining SAT scores, there *are* things you can do to improve or advance your program during the summertime. You can:

- Attend coaching clinics and renew your subscriptions to various coaching magazines
- Acquaint yourself with rules changes in the basketball rule book and the bylaws of your state association
- Evaluate your program, practice plans, and playbook
- Prepare or update your basketball media guides
- Prepare motivational signs, posters, and the like, for next year
- Oversee gym maintenance, repair, and improvement (e.g., sealing the gym floor, painting the dressing room areas, etc.)
- Prepare or update school/region/state performance signs, charts, and so on
- Send out letters to players outlining your expectations for the upcoming year, including what they should do to get ready for tryouts and practice
- Supervise summer weight-training programs, jumping (jumprope, bench jumping), and whatever other strength and conditioning regimen you set up for your players. And if your state association hasn't yet banned summer practice, then by all means take advantage of it before your legislature decides that it's better for kids to be out on the street with the drug dealers than to be participating in supervised basketball practice.

SECTION 15

The World Beyond Coaching

Retirement is the time when you never do all the things you'd intended to do when you have the time.

— *Dr. Laurence J. Peter*

The time of my departure is at hand. I have fought a good fight, I have finished my course, I have kept the faith.

— *The Apostle Paul (II Timothy 4:7)*

WHY PEOPLE GO INTO COACHING

There are probably as many reasons why people decide to become basketball coaches as there are basketball coaches themselves. The desire to remain associated with the sport once one's playing days are over is certainly a major impetus toward coaching. Another is that, because basketball is a high-profile activity in our society, coaching is often viewed as a glamorous occupation—"glamorous" in the sense that, in any given week between November and March, you as a basketball coach are far more likely to receive media attention than, say, an auto mechanic, secretary, dentist, or bank president. Some people become basketball coaches to satisfy their competitive nature through athletics rather than competing in the dog-eat-dog bu$ine$$ world; others enjoy teaching young people to play basketball, or believe strongly in values such as commitment, dedication, and self-sacrifice that are inherent in the pursuit of team goals. Some may want to emulate coaches who served as their own role models—and some feel that they owe a debt of gratitude to the sport

245

for the positive influence that playing the game had on their lives. We also like the answer given by Del Harris, former coach of the Milwaukee Bucks, when asked if he enjoyed coaching basketball:

> Enjoy coaching? No, I don't think that's the word to describe my relationship to my job. But what other job is there where you can have this kind of excitement every day? About the most you can say is it's like robbing a bank, holding up a stagecoach. I think basketball coaches are the last of the old cowboys. You know, you live on the edge every day, and the posse is just around the corner. By posse I mean the owners, the media, and here we are strategizing our attack like cops and robbers.[1]

WHY PEOPLE GET OUT OF COACHING

Living on the edge can be exciting—but it can also be traumatic. The highs afforded by victories and the lows that accompany losses can be intense—and the pressures can take their toll on the best of coaches. Sometimes, even winning games is not enough: Fans or boosters, who are not always logical, patient, or well informed, may expect you to win championships every season, or to use the same style of play as the previous coach, or to adopt a more exciting, wide-open (or conservative) style of play than you're presently using, or to keep scores close because they enjoy watching tight games, or to play their kid because Daddy is the booster club president. And while it's easy to say that a coach should be able to take the heat, it's something else entirely to live with that kind of pressure on a daily basis. Ask any UCLA basketball coach or Notre Dame football coach.

Because—on the high school level and below, at least—coaching pay is supplemental to teaching salary, states consider coaches to be teachers first and coaches second. As a result, most basketball coaches are seriously over-worked. Many noncoaching classroom teachers scoff at the "huge" supplements that basketball coaches receive, blissfully unaware that coaching is the equivalent of having a second full-time job at greatly reduced pay. On a per-hour wage basis, we'd probably be better off selling ice water to Eskimos than coaching basketball.

Overwork can create a state of mental and physical fatigue that drags a coach down like a case of walking pneumonia. As we've said, coaching basketball is never easy. There are always problems to be solved, with no time off for good behavior, not even in the off-season.[2] Whenever players have

---

[1]*Atlanta Journal–Constitution* (Dec. 23, 1990), p. C2.

[2]After more than a decade of basketball coaching in the mid-1970s, Jerry Tarkanian reluctantly let his UNLV boosters talk him into accepting a two-week summer vacation in Hawaii with his wife, Lois. While they were gone, one of Jerry's returning starters signed a pro contract and another transferred to another school.

problems—which is most of the time—the coach has problems to solve, or at least to deal with, in addition to his other responsibilities and concerns. Family and social life often must take a backseat to these problems, which is why a married coach desperately needs an understanding, supportive spouse.

When a coach can no longer find ways to keep a fresh perspective in his coaching—when he is no longer interested in facing the daily challenges of coaching—he is said to be suffering from *coaching burnout*. He is also a prime candidate for voluntary withdrawal from the coaching profession. And while coaching burnout is not an inevitable end to the coaching process—indeed, there are thousands of basketball coaches across the nation whose careers have spanned decades without their ever having seriously considered quitting coaching—for some coaches it is a very real aspect of their daily existence.

It's not always just a matter of losing more often than a coach or the fans finds acceptable, either. Not every burnout candidate believes, as the late George Allen did, that every time you lose, you die a little. Burnout is far more complex than that, because the coaching task encompasses so much more than winning or losing games. It is the coaching process itself—the long hours on the job, the overwork, the travel, the struggle to make ends meet on a coach's pay, that sometimes grinds up coaches and spits them out in scattered disarray. The end results—frustration, disappointment, ulcers, and high blood pressure—are merely evidence of having taken one's job too seriously.

How do you know if you're taking coaching too seriously? We offer, only half facetiously, the following list of symptoms that suggest that you're overdoing your coaching.

YOU KNOW THAT YOU'RE TAKING COACHING TOO SERIOUSLY WHEN . . .

- Your resting pulse rate never drops below 120 between November and March.
- You try to call your spouse at home, only to find that the phone was disconnected a month ago.
- You find Os, Xs, and play diagrams scribbled all over the last check in your checkbook.
- For your anniversary dinner, you take your spouse to the pregame meal, followed later by a movie (watching the game film).
- You have to order milk on the rocks at your favorite watering hole.
- You wake up in the morning and find yourself talking on the telephone, with absolutely no idea whom you're talking to or why.
- You can remember your daughter's wedding date because it was the day that Dean Smith won his 700th game at UNC.
- Other than game films, the last ten movies you've seen . . . was *Hoosiers*.

The burnout factor aside, there are probably three main reasons why basketball coaches leave the profession. First, of course, there's the possibility of a noncoaching job offer that promises greater financial security and more stable working hours. Second, there's retirement at the end of a long career in coaching. And third, at the other end of the timeline from retirement there are the young men and women fresh out of college who, used to viewing their sport from a player's perspective, either have overestimated the "glamour" and underestimated the hard work associated with coaching, or else they have failed to grasp the fundamental difference between players and coaches, namely, that the players are merely playing a game while the coach is a working professional in his field. In both cases, if they fail to make the transition in mind set from amateur to professional, they soon find themselves overwhelmed and disillusioned by the enormity of the coaching task.

———————— THE EIGHT DON'TS OF LEAVING COACHING ————————

1. Don't get out of coaching if you can't live without it. This advice serves as a useful bookend to some other sage advice given to us years ago by a veteran basketball coach. When asked if he thought we should consider pursuing a career in coaching, the coach replied, "Don't go into coaching if you can live without it."

What you'll miss *least* about coaching are

- The pressures to win at all costs.
- Unprincipled recruiters who promise young athletes the sun, moon, and stars in exchange for their names on a letter of intent, and the unspeakably vile subhumans who introduce young athletes to the dead-end street called *drugs*.
- Parents and other fans who loudly direct verbal abuse at you from the stands when your spouse is sitting a few seats away within earshot.[3]
- State-mandated changes regarding athletic eligibility and limits on practice time. Increasingly states are adopting no-pass, no-play policies for athletes and cutting back on pre- and postseason practice time.[4] On the surface, at least, such changes reflect a deep and abiding interest in the student athletes; in reality, no-pass, no-play encourages cheating and deprives marginal student athletes of their main reason for staying in school when athletics is taken away from them. And regarding the

---

[3]Now, there's an apt phrase: "within earshot." Some of the fans we've encountered over the years have acted like they've been shot between the ears.

[4]Georgia already has adopted no-pass, no-play, and has rolled back the start of preseason basketball practice to Oct. 29 and eliminated spring practice altogether.

latter, UGA women's basketball coach Andy Landers complained, "There is the mistaken idea kids were spending too much time in sports, but what's happening now is they're spending less in supervised situations. . . . That's bad for the sports but potentially worse for the kids. There are plenty of bad alternatives out there."[5] No, you won't miss the hypocrisy in high places *at all*.

- You won't miss the paperwork, long hours on the job, hassles over budgeting and finances, or traveling, either.

What you *will* miss is the kids. They're what coaching is all about, anyway—and because you probably spend more quality time with most of them than their parents do, you'll miss watching them grow as athletes and individuals.

On the other hand, if you're married with children, the demands of coaching probably have deprived you of quality time with your own children and spouse, and *that* time can never be made up via an incoming freshman class.

2. Don't expect life out of coaching to be anything more or less than it is. It's remarkable how your view changes when you move from the folding chair on the sideline to a permanent seat a few rows higher in the stands. Gone are the pressures, responsibilities, problems, and frustrations that always accompany the task of teaching kids how to bounce a ball and throw it through a hoop—but also gone are the coaching supplement, coaching passes, complimentary cars, free coffee every morning at Stella's Dunk 'n Dine, and whatever other fringe benefits you've managed to accrue via your status as a COACH.

As an ex-coach, you may still be regarded with respect and admiration by those people who appreciate what you did for the community and the kids you coached, but it's not the same anymore. In their hearts, people know that now you're just like them: Just another pair of eyes in the stands watching someone else's team find ways to lose games. And also like them, you're now an unqualified basketball "expert" whose second-guesses are never wrong, except in the sense that (as we were once reminded) as *ex* is a has-been and a *spurt* is a drip that fizzled.

3. A Timely Tip from Tarzan of the Apes: Don't let go of one vine until you've got hold of the next one. In troubled times like these, it doesn't pay to make a hasty career decision based on a gut feeling[6] that you ought to change jobs—at least, not until your next employment is signed, sealed, and delivered.

---

[5]*Atlanta Journal–Constitution* (Aug. 25, 1991), p. E11.

[6]Ulcers, usually.

An experienced coach told us about the time he had his personal moment of truth concerning job changes. Shortly after basketball season was over, he said, he received a telephone call from a representative of a prestigious basketball school in another part of the state. The caller identified himself as the school superintendent and said that he was looking for a boys basketball coach to replace the incumbent, who had built a highly successful program at the school but was leaving to accept a college coaching position.

"Your name came up several times in conversations we've had with coaches in our area concerning possible replacements for [Coach X]," the superintendent said, "and because the comments about you were so positive we've taken the liberty of adding your name to our list of candidates, if that's all right with you."

The coach hastened to assure his caller that it was indeed all right to consider him a candidate for the vacant head coaching position. (The boys team had won the state championship twice in the last three years, and made it to the final four that season.)

"I'll be in your area sometime during the early part of next week," the superintendent went on, "and I'll call you when I arrive so we can set up an interview." He paused briefly, and then added, "Maybe I shouldn't be saying this, but if you're even half as good as the coaches around here say you are, well, you sound like exactly the kind of person we're looking for."

By now, the coach told us, he could hardly hear the man over the pounding of his heart. He had done extremely well with his teams, but he recognized that his present coaching situation was not exactly conducive to advancement up the coaching ladder. This sounded like exactly the break he was looking for.

Later, still elated about the unexpected phone call, the coach called the other school to talk to the incumbent coach, but it was Friday afternoon and he couldn't be reached at the school and no one answered at home. However, the school secretary verified that the boys head coaching position for next year was indeed vacant. The coach spent the weekend updating his résumé and worrying about the upcoming interview.

Monday morning, he went to his principal and announced that he was resigning effective when his current employment ended in June. The principal suggested that he hold off tendering his letter of resignation until after the interview. The coach agreed—and waited impatiently as Monday and Tuesday crept by with no telephone call from the superintendent. Finally, on Wednesday afternoon, the coach called the board of education to find out when the superintendent would be in his area. He was told that, due to an unfortunate set of circumstances, their school system had been without a superintendent for the past three months. There was no one working in the system whose name was even remotely similar to the one he had been given. Shamefacedly, the coach had to admit to himself that the call had been a hoax. He asked the principal if it was too late for him to keep his job and was told that his decision to resign was not official because he had not submitted a letter of resignation.

Of course, this sort of problem probably won't concern you if you're retiring from teaching with the requisite number of years in to receive your full retirement benefits. In other situations, though, for instance, if you're considering getting out of education to pursue another line of work—the proper procedure is to *get the job—and then resign.* Your board of education members wouldn't agree with that statement, of course, but it's *your* gluteus maximus on the line, not theirs. Where employment and other business decisions are concerned, your first loyalty should always be to yourself and your family.

It's nothing personal, just a matter of economic survival.

4. If you've already decided to get out of education altogether—or if you're moving to another state—don't forget to take your money out of the teacher retirement system. In Georgia, you can withdraw your retirement savings once without penalty prior to age sixty-five; your state may have a different policy. Check it out—and then take it out.

5. If you're a tenured physical education teacher who is giving up coaching but not your physical education position, don't expect your decision to be greeted warmly by the athletic director or school administration. After all, your decision means that they must either open up a new p.e. teaching slot or find a coach who is certified in a classroom teaching field. They may not go so far as to give you office space that formerly served as the janitor's restroom—but they won't welcome your decision with open arms either.

6. If you're moving into administration from coaching, please don't treat physical education and athletics as ugly stepchildren in the educational process. We've seen so many ex-coaches-turned-principals who treat p.e. (and, to a lesser extent, athletics) as if they were a form of venereal disease, and we've wondered: How can people turn their backs on the very thing that brought them into education in the first place? (Probably, they're the educational equivalent of fathers who don't trust their teenage daughters because they remember how wild they were themselves when they were kids.)

Sure, there are plenty of "roll-out-a-ball-and-let-'em-go" types of coaches out there—but there are also a lot of dedicated physical educators who work just as hard in their p.e. classes to give every child a valuable and worthwhile p.e. experience as they do to build a successful program in basketball or other sports.

7. Don't go back. The author Thomas Wolfe was right: You can't go home again. As coaches, we teach our players that Winners Never Quit, And Quitters Never Win. Having discovered how easy quitting actually is once you've wrestled with the problem and made the decision to quit coaching, though, the process itself is quite simple: Just announce your intention to quit and send in a letter of resignation. That's all there is to it. But having once quit, the mind set against quitting as an undesirable alternative is more easily overcome the second time around. An ex-college basketball player explained:

> I'd never been a quitter before, but when, near the end of my sophomore season as a little-used reserve on a lousy team, a teammate who was also a benchwarmer told the coach that he'd forgotten his jersey on a road trip, the coach suggested that we share my jersey for a half each, with the other one keeping stats on the bench in street clothes. I was stunned. I told him that the boy could have my whole uniform, because I wouldn't be needing it anymore. I quit the team right then and there. But what shocked me most of all was how *easy* it was to quit. All those years I played basketball, I'd thought of quitters as losers who didn't really love the game, and there I was doing the very same thing.

Of course, your case may be entirely different. But if you stop to think of the people in sports who have quit playing or coaching and tried to come back, you'll find that most of them don't make it. Most of those who fail the second time around do so for the very same reasons that caused them to hang it up the first time. The reasons to quit will still be there when you go back into coaching: They've *always* been there, and always will be. The difference is, it's harder to overlook them the second time around.

8. Don't forget to turn out the gym lights and lock up before you leave. Turn in your keys at the office.

——————— **YES VIRGINIA, THERE *IS* LIFE AFTER COACHING** ———————

Basically, there are four alternatives to coaching: retirement, giving up your coaching but not your teaching position, going into educational administration, and leaving education for another line of work.

Retirement

Best advice here is, *plan early*. Assuming that you've been a teacher long enough to be eligible for full retirement benefits, you've had twenty-five to thirty years to prepare for the day when you pack up your whistle and your Converse® high-tops for the last time. Unless you're financially independent or you already have another job lined up, don't wait until the last two weeks before your retirement becomes official to start considering your postteaching options. If you do, you may find to your dismay that it takes up to six months for the paperwork to be processed that qualifies you for monthly teacher retirement, social security, Medicare/Medicaid, and other possible benefits.

(And if you began teaching at age twenty-two or twenty-three, there can be as much as a twelve- to eighteen-year gap between retirement age and eligibility to begin receiving social security, unless you're willing to accept about half of what you'd get if you waited until age sixty-five.) Meanwhile, as the philosopher says, "Time, tide, and bills to be paid wait for no man."

The end of labor is to gain leisure.
—*Aristotle.*

Of course, that was easy for Aristotle to say, since he didn't have a job. But if you've been a workaholic throughout your coaching career, you'd better have some pretty definite plans for how you'll be spending your newfound leisure time, or else you may find yourself literally becoming bored to death. Actuarial studies have consistently shown that workaholics who suddenly become nonworkaholics are far more likely to suffer heart attacks than either workaholics who keep on working or nonworkaholics who keep on not working.

Leisure planning is not always as easy as it appears to be. Golf is a great leisure-time activity—but it can be expensive. Clubs, shoes, balls, and a golf bag constitute the initial cash outlay; after that, it's a matter of scraping up $22 or more ($12 for a round of golf, and $10 for the golf cart rental—that is, if you can find somewhere to play that cheaply) every time you want to punish yourself for eighteen holes.[7] Tennis is cheaper, but it requires a partner, which may or may not be a problem. Bowling a couple of evenings a week may be within the acceptable limits of fixed-income retirees; hunting requires a gun, hunting license, a continuous supply of shells or bullets, and passing a hunter safety course; and fishing can cost whatever you want it to, but although the license is cheap, the exercise involved is minimal.

Whatever the case, daily exercise is a *must*. Until you retire, you never really understand how much exercise you get in coaching even if you don't scrimmage with the kids anymore. And therein lies the greatest danger you'll face in retirement: In adopting a sedentary life style, your cardiopulmonary system tends to lose much of its former efficiency with startling rapidity, especially after age fifty.

---

[7] "It took me seventeen years to get 3,000 hits in baseball. I did it in one afternoon on the golf course."—Henry Aaron

Giving Up Your Coaching, but Not Your Teaching, Position

We've said enough about this already, except to point out that, as a practicing coach, you *might* have been able to get away with, let us say, relaxed teaching methods in your p.e. classes; the same may or may not hold true for your status as a noncoaching p.e. teacher, since the athletic director and/or principal may have preferred to see you retire gracefully or accept a Peace Corps post in Timbuktu, so that they could fill your teaching slot with another coach. And if you're the athletic director, they may ask you to vacate the post so that they can package it with the head coaching position as an added financial inducement to attract the best candidates for the job. Again, it's nothing personal, purely a business decision. (If you aren't going to make it easy for them, why should they go out of their way to make it easy for you?)

Going Into Educational Administration

There are two reasons why coaches become principals, assistant principals, and so on: The pay is better and the work is easier. In becoming an educational administrator, you'll be abandoning the tedious, uneventful, always-predictable life of a basketball coach for such breathtakingly exciting administrative duties as attending committee meetings; preparing recommendations, reports, and policy and procedural statements; exchanging memos with other administrators; finding ways to increase the school budget for next year; and most important of all, creating work for yourself, your peers, and your subordinates.[8]

Still, one does what one must, and if going into administration is the necessary next step in your professional evolution, then by all means go for it by taking the courses necessary to become certified in your state.

Leaving Education for Another Line of Work

In deciding to give up coaching and find a job outside of education, you're liable to discover rather quickly that, of the roughly half a million different occupations in the U.S., your training in the field of education doesn't prepare you for many of them that you'd want to have. (Of course, you might switch to a career in, say, sanitation engineering—and probably at an *enormous* leap in salary, by the way—although you might have trouble explaining such a career move to your spouse or your golfing buddies. But the fact is, teacher training doesn't prepare students to do much else besides teaching.)

As an ex-coach, however, you have two things going for you that other teachers may not have.

---

[8]"The function of administrators is to make work for each other."—C. Northcote Parkinson

First, there's *salesmanship*. As a coach, you motivated players to dedicate themselves to team goals and work hard; salespersons motivate customers to buy cars, televisions, and such. At heart they're one and the same thing. The bottom line for both lies in getting people to do things that they might not want to do otherwise. Many ex-coaches have found new careers in sales, whether in education-related areas such as selling senior rings, sports-related areas such as selling athletic supplies or equipment or sports club memberships, or general areas such as selling insurance.

Second, there are *business contacts* that may be found among your basketball boosters or parents of players you've coached or result from the high-visibility factor associated with coaching. Any or all of those can be instrumental in landing you a job outside of education.

Other sports-related avenues of employment might include operating a summer basketball camp, which can be *very* lucrative (but difficult to establish unless you operate under the sponsorship of an organization with built-in contacts such as the Fellowship of Christian Athletes); working at a fitness/ aerobics center or health club (which generally doesn't pay much unless you're at management level or higher); community recreation program management or working with local organizations such as the scouts, YMCA, or YWCA (which usually require a major in recreation); or, if you're looking for a lucrative second job or healthy supplement to your retirement income, refereeing or scouting. Regarding the former, you can easily add $7,000 to $10,000 thousand or more to your annual income by becoming certified in the various seasonal sports and officiating year round; and as for the latter, you might either join an established scouting service such as Bill Bertka's, or start your own.

Beyond sports, your avenues and options are limited only by your contacts and your occupational preferences. Happy hunting—and remember that if, like us, your cheeks no longer sport the rosy bloom of youth, job discrimination on the basis of age—or race or sex, for that matter—is illegal.

Appendix

Forms for Section 7

Basketball Players' Classroom Progress Report
Home-Game Workers—Master List
Insurance Coverage Form
Basketball Inventory
Player Information Sheet
Basketball Workers' Sign-up Sheet

Forms for Section 8

Aspects of Team Preparation to Be Covered Prior to First Game
Strength and Conditioning Program—Men's Basketball
Coaching Tasks and Preparation—Preseason
Managers' Game Duties Checklist
Player Evaluation Form—Preseason Tryouts

Forms for Section 9

Daily Practice Schedule
Weekly Practice Schedule

Forms for Section 10

Pregame Scouting Form

Scouting Checklist—Individual Skills
Scouting Checklist—Team Defense
Scouting Checklist—Team Offense
Scouting Form
Scouting Report
Scouting Schedule
Shot Chart

Forms for Section 11

Game Plan
Game Plan Evaluation

Forms for Section 12

Defensive Stat Sheet
Game Pattern Chart
Lineup Efficiency Chart
Offensive Stat Sheet
Stat Summary Sheet

BASKETBALL PLAYERS' CLASSROOM PROGRESS REPORT

for

_____   _____
Student Athlete's Name   Date

Period	Subject	Attendance	Class Progress (Grades, Behavior, etc.)	Teacher

COMMENTS: _____

_____

_____

_____

_____

_____

_____

_____

_____

_____

_____

_____

_____

_____

HOME-GAME WORKERS—MASTER LIST

(CS = Concession Stand; T/A = Tickets/Admission)

Team	Date	Team	Date	Team	Date	Team	Date
	/		/		/		/
1.	( )	1.	( )	1.	( )	1.	( )
2.	( )	2.	( )	2.	( )	2.	( )
3.	( )	3.	( )	3.	( )	3.	( )
4.	( )	4.	( )	4.	( )	4.	( )
5.	( )	5.	( )	5.	( )	5.	( )
6.	( )	6.	( )	6.	( )	6.	( )
	/		/		/		/
1.	( )	1.	( )	1.	( )	1.	( )
2.	( )	2.	( )	2.	( )	2.	( )
3.	( )	3.	( )	3.	( )	3.	( )
4.	( )	4.	( )	4.	( )	4.	( )
5.	( )	5.	( )	5.	( )	5.	( )
6.	( )	6.	( )	6.	( )	6.	( )
	/		/		/		/
1.	( )	1.	( )	1.	( )	1.	( )
2.	( )	2.	( )	2.	( )	2.	( )
3.	( )	3.	( )	3.	( )	3.	( )
4.	( )	4.	( )	4.	( )	4.	( )
5.	( )	5.	( )	5.	( )	5.	( )
6.	( )	6.	( )	6.	( )	6.	( )

INSURANCE COVERAGE FORM

DIRECTIONS: Place a check mark in the appropriate space below indicating your son/daughter/ward's insurance coverage, and add your signature and the date of signing at the bottom.

☐ This is to certify that _____ has adequate in-
　　　　　　　　　　　　　　Pupil's Name
surance coverage and does not wish to participate in the school insurance program provided through the school. I assume full responsibility for any expenses incurred as a result of injuries he/she may receive while participating in interscholastic athletics at

_____.
　　Name of School

☐ This is to certify that _____ is covered by
　　　　　　　　　　　　　　Pupil's Name
school insurance for the present school year.

_____
　　Parent/Guardian's Signature

_____
　　Date

BASKETBALL INVENTORY

School _____   Date _____   Inventory Conducted by _____

Item	Previous Inventory Total	Total Units Added	Total Units Lost or Destroyed	Present Total Units

NOTE: Use separate listings for items that are *usable* and items that *need repair*.

PLAYER INFORMATION SHEET—BASKETBALL (_____)
Year

Name _____

Home Address _____

City _____ State _____ Zip Code _____

Church _____

Parents'/Guardians' names _____

Brothers'/Sisters' names and ages _____

_____

Phone No.	Age	Birthday
Height	Weight	Class

CLASS SCHEDULE

Period	Subject	Teacher
HR		
1st		
2nd		
3rd		
4th		
5th		
6th		
7th		

Varsity Experience (all sports) _____

_____

_____

Clubs/Activities _____

_____

_____

Honors _____

_____

_____

Hobbies/Interests _____

_____

_____

Coach's Comments _____

_____

_____

BASKETBALL WORKERS' SIGN-UP SHEET

Name _____   Address _____   Tel. No. _____

	Game	Date	Nature of Work
___	___	___	_____
___	___	___	_____
___	___	___	_____
___	___	___	_____
___	___	___	_____
___	___	___	_____
___	___	___	_____
___	___	___	_____
___	___	___	_____
___	___	___	_____
___	___	___	_____
___	___	___	_____
___	___	___	_____
___	___	___	_____
___	___	___	_____
___	___	___	_____
___	___	___	_____
___	___	___	_____
___	___	___	_____
___	___	___	_____

© 1992 by Parker Publishing Company

DIRECTIONS: Place a checkmark in the left-hand column beside the home games you're willing to work at, and indicate the type of work you prefer (concession stand, tickets).

ASPECTS OF TEAM PREPARATION TO BE COVERED PRIOR TO FIRST GAME

☐ I. INDIVIDUAL

    ☐ A. Conditioning (pretryout)

        ☐ 1. Running

            ☐ a. Sprints (60s and 220s)

            ☐ b. Mile run (alternate days from sprints)

            ☐ c. Timed once in each event, on last day before tryouts begin

        ☐ 2. Weight training (leg work only during preseason/season)

    ☐ B. Defense

        ☐ 1. Stance/footwork

        ☐ 2. On-the-ball defense

        ☐ 3. Post coverage

        ☐ 4. Ball-side defense

        ☐ 5. Help-side defense

        ☐ 6. Taking the charge

    ☐ C. Rebounding (offensive and defensive)

        ☐ 1. Anticipation/timing/positioning

        ☐ 2. Outlet pass

    ☐ D. Offense

        ☐ 1. Without the ball

            ☐ a. Screening and using screens

            ☐ b. Creating a lead

            ☐ c. Balancing the court

            ☐ d. Post play

        ☐ 2. With the ball

            ☐ a. Triple-threat stance

            ☐ b. Creating space

Aspects of Team Preparation to be Covered Prior to First Game, continued

☐ c. High-speed/protective dribbling
☐ d. Moves to strong side
☐ e. Moves to weak side (crossover dribble/reverse pivot)
☐ f. Power moves
☐ g. Post play

☐ 3. Shooting (layups/jump shot/hook shot/free throw/ power shot)

☐ a. Form
☐ b. Stationary/off the dribble
☐ c. Shot selection

☐ II. TEAM

☐ A. Offense

☐ 1. Man-to-man
☐ 2. Zone
☐ 3. Beating the press
☐ 4. Fast-break

☐ a. Against pressing defense
☐ b. From transitions or loose balls
☐ c. From missed shots/free throws

☐ 5. Rebounding (missed shots/free throws)
☐ 6. Slowdown/delay techniques and tactics

☐ B. Defense

☐ 1. Man-to-man
☐ 2. Zone
☐ 3. Combination
☐ 4. Pressing

☐ a. Man-to-man/zone
☐ b. Full-, three-quarter-, half-court

☐ 5. Transition from offense

☐ C. Special situations

    ☐ 1. Jump balls (offensing/defensing tips)

    ☐ 2. Out-of-bounds situations

        ☐ a. Offensive plays (baseline/sideline)

        ☐ b. Defensive techniques

    ☐ 3. Late game/last-shot situations

AUBURN UNIVERSITY AT MONTGOMERY
Strength and Conditioning Program—Men's Basketball

Note: The following is a detailed ten-week summer strength and conditioning program designed for the athletes who participate in the AUM men's basketball program. For purposes of this book, the program has been expanded and modified for use by high school and junior high school athletes. Included in the program are a series of stretching exercises, muscle strengthening exercises, and a running program designed to promote improvements in aerobic and anaerobic endurance. It is used with the permission of Shelby Searcy, AUM Head Athletic Trainer.

As far as weight training for fourteen- and fifteen-year olds is concerned, it's all right as long as the workouts are closely monitored by the coach or an athletic trainer. Young boys should start out with light weights and progress slowly, both in terms of poundage and repetitions. Primary emphasis should be on form and technique.

The program is easy to follow with the following information included in this material.

1. Percent maximum heart rate: This chart will help you determine the intensity at which you are to exercise when performing the endurance activities.

2. Stretching exercises: To be performed each day before each workout.

3. Workout phases: A listing of exercises to be performed in the weight room for each phase of the strength training program. Also, includes the number of sets and repetitions to be completed during each phase.

4. Daily training program: This list is designed to help guide you through your exercise program. The list tells you what activities you should do each day of the week. You must follow this list closely to receive any benefits from the training program.

5. Workout record: This chart is provided so you can record your daily workouts and chart the progress you make over the summer.

When you run it is important to exercise at an intensity that will promote physiological changes within your body. The intensity of exercise can be measured by monitoring your heart rate as you exercise. The percent maximum heart rate (% MHR) chart will help you judge the intensity at which you are exercising. Keep your heart rate within five to ten heartbeats of your %MHR while you exercise. You can check your intensity of exercise by counting your heart rate (pulse) at the carotid artery of the neck or radial artery of the wrist. Count your pulse for 10 seconds and multiply by 6. This will give you an approximate count of your heart rate and enable you to determine your exercising heart rate. If your heart rate is below your %MHR, then you need to increase your pace. If your heart rate is above your %MHR then you need to decrease your exercise pace.

Remember to run during the cooler parts of the day, such as the early morning or evening. Drink lots of water before and after you exercise. Wear a good pair of running shoes and socks when you run. Also, remember to stretch and warm up before you exercise and cool down after you exercise with an easy jog or walk.

Note: If you have not had a physical examination in the past year or if you are having any type of physical illnesses at the present time, then you MUST obtain a physical examination before starting this exercise program.

PERCENTAGE MAXIMUM HEART RATE

%MHR

AGE	.60	.65	.70	.75	.80
14	124	134	144	155	165
15	123	133	144	154	164
16	122	133	143	153	163
17	122	132	142	152	162
18	121	131	141	152	162
19	121	131	141	151	161

STRETCHING EXERCISES

Stand and Reach

Stand straight with feet together and knees slightly bent. Bend at waist with hands reaching toward the floor. Hold. Repeat 5 times.

Cross-over

Stand straight with one foot crossed in front of the other and knees slightly bent. Bend at the waist with hands reaching toward the floor. Hold. Repeat 5 times. Repeat on other leg.

Auburn University at Montgomery
Strength and Conditioning Program—Men's Basketball, continued

Forward Lunge

Kneel on left leg, with right leg forward at a right angle. Lunge forward, keeping back straight. Stretch should be felt in left groin. Repeat 5 times. Repeat on other leg.

Side Lunge

Stand with legs apart, bending the left knee, lean toward the left, keeping the back straight and the right leg straight. Hold. Repeat 5 times. Repeat on other leg.

Seat Side Straddle

Sit with legs spread, placing both hands on the same ankle. Bring chin to the knee, keeping the leg straight. Hold. Repeat 5 times. Repeat with other leg.

Seat Forward Straddle

Sit with legs spread, placing one hand on each ankle. Lean forward, bringing chest toward ground. Hold. Repeat 5 times.

Seat Stretch

Sit with legs together, toes pointed up, hands reaching toward the ankles. Bring chin to knees. Hold. Repeat 5 times.

Leg Cross-over

Lie on back, legs spread and arms out to the side. Bring right toe to left hand, keeping leg straight. Hold for 20 seconds. Repeat with left leg to right hand.

Knees to Chest

Lie on back with knees bent. Grasp tops of both knees and bring to the chest. Hold for 20 seconds. Repeat 5 times. DO NOT ROCK.

Overhead Shoulder Stretch

Both arms are raised overhead; left elbow is bent and grasped by right hand. Pull left upper arm toward body. Hold. Repeat 5 times. Repeat on other side.

Double Anterior Shoulder Stretch

Both hands grasped behind the back with elbows straight. Both arms are slowly raised until the stretch is felt in front of shoulder. Stay in upright position. Hold. Repeat 5 times.

Achilles Tendon Stretch

Face wall with one leg positioned back while leaning toward the wall. Keep heel of foot on floor. Hold for 30 seconds. Repeat 5 times. Repeat on other leg.

WORKOUT PHASES

Phase I

Intensity: Moderate weight. You should be able to complete 2 sets of 10 repetitions the first day.

Duration: Start with 2 sets of 10 repetitions and work up to 3 sets of 10 repetitions.

Exercises:

Bench press	Leg press
Squats	Forearm curls
Leg extensions	Upright rows
Leg curls	Arm pulldowns
Bent rowing	Jump rope (5–8 minutes)
Triceps press	

Phase II

Intensity: Increase weight 10 to 15 pounds.

Duration: 3 sets of 7 repetitions.

Exercises:

Bench press	Forearm curls
Squats	Arm pulldowns
Leg extensions	Triceps press
Leg curls	Behind neck press
Leg press	Bent rowing
Upright rowing	Jump rope (10–12 minutes)
Heel raises	

Phase III

Intensity: Increase weight 5 to 10 pounds.

Duration: 3 sets of 5 repetitions.

Exercises:

Bench press	Behind-neck press*
Leg extensions	Arm pulldowns
Leg curls	Triceps press*
Leg press	Dumbbell flys**
Heel raises*	Dumbbell press**

© 1992 by Parker Publishing Company

Forearm curls*   Jump rope (2–8 minutes)
Bent rowing*
*Increase weight. Continue with 3 sets of 7 repetitions.
**Start with moderate weight. Continue with 3 sets of 10 repetitions.

Phase IV

Intensity: Try to keep weight equal to amount used in Phase III.
Duration: 3 sets of 10 to 12 repetitions.
Exercises: Bench press   Arm pulldowns
                Leg extensions   Triceps press
                Leg curls   Dumbbell flys*
                Leg press   Dumbbell press**
                Heel raises   Forearm curls
                Behind-neck press   Bent rowing
*Increase weight 5 to 10 pounds. Continue 3 sets of 10 repetitions.

DAILY TRAINING PROGRAM

Warmup exercises (to be performed daily)

    a. Stretching exercises: 10 min.
    b. Push-ups: 25
    c. Bent-knee sit-ups: 50

Week One (July 15–19)

    M: Weight room (phase I)
    T: Run 1.5 mi. (65% MHR)
    W: Weight room (phase I)
  TH: Run 1.5 mi. (65% MHR)
    F: Weight room (phase I)

Week Two (July 22–26)

    M: Weight room (phase I)
    T: Run 1.5 mi. (65% MHR)
    W: Weight room (phase I: increase to 3 sets of 10 repetitions)
  TH: Run 1.5 mi. (65% MHR)
    F: weight room (phase I)

Week Three (July 29–Aug. 2)

    M: Weight room (phase I)
    T: Run 2.0 mi. (65% MHR)
    W: Weight room (phase I)
  TH: Run 2.0 mi. (65% MHR)
    F: Weight room (phase I: increase weight 5–10 lbs.)

Week Four (Aug. 5–9)

    M: Weight room (phase II: use same weight used at end of phase I)
    T: Run 2.0 mi. (65% MHR)
    W: Weight room (phase II)
  TH: Run 2.0 mi. (65% MHR)
    F: Weight room (phase II)

Week Five (Aug. 12–16)

    M: Weight room (phase II: increase weight 5–10 lbs.)

T: Run 2.0 mi. (65% MHR)
W: Weight room (phase II)
TH: Run 2.0 mi. (65% MHR)
F: Weight room (phase II)

Week Six (Aug. 19–23)

M: Weight room (phase II)
T: Run 2.0 mi. (65% MHR)
W: Weight room (phase II)
TH: Run 2.0 mi. (65% MHR)
F: Weight room (phase III)

Week Seven (Aug. 26–30)

M: Weight room (phase III)
T: Jog 1.0 mi.
   4—30 yd. sprints (1 min. rest between sprints)
   2—50 yd. sprints
   4—20 yd. sprints
W: Weight room (phase III)
TH: Same as Tuesday
F: Weight room (phase III)

Week Eight (Sept. 2–6)

M: Weight room (phase III: increase weight 5–10 lbs.)
T: Jog 1.0 mi.
   5—30 yd. sprints (1 min. rest between sprints)
   3—50 yd. sprints
   5—20 yd. sprints
W: Weight room (phase III)
TH: Same as Tuesday
F: Weight room (phase IV: use same weight used at end of phase III)

Week Nine (Sept. 9–13)

M: Jog 1.0 mi.
   6—30 yd. sprints (1½ mins. rest between sprints)
   4—50 yd. sprints
   6—20 yd. sprints
T: Weight room (phase IV)
W: Same as Monday

Daily Training Program, continued

TH: Weight room (phase IV)
  F: Same as Monday

Week Ten (Sept. 16–20)

  M: Jog 1.0 mi.
      8—30 yd. sprints (1 ½ mins. rest between sprints)
      4—50 yd. sprints
      8—20 yd. sprints
   T: Weight room (phase IV)
  W: Same as Monday
TH: Weight room (phase IV)
  F: Same as Monday

Name ——————— Sport ———————

Exercise

NOTE: The date goes in the empty squares at the top of the page. Pounds lifted goes in the upper diagonal of the other squares, reps in the lower diagonal.

COACHING TASKS AND PREPARATION—PRESEASON

Before Practice Begins

- [ ] Order uniforms and equipment
- [ ] Prepare dressing rooms, refinish gym floor
- [ ] Schedule gym use
- [ ] Prepare/update player handbook
- [ ] Verify team physician
- [ ] Estimate expenses
- [ ] Schedule Physical exams/insurance/flu shots
- [ ] Order basketball shoes
- [ ] Check player eligibility (school records)
- [ ] Make travel plans (bus driver/ overnight trips)
- [ ] Contract with officials' assn. (send schedule)
- [ ] Paint rims/clean backboards/ put up new nets
- [ ] Check gym lighting
- [ ] Check scoreboard clock/control panel, replace burnt-out bulbs
- [ ] Fill out Managers' responsibilities checklist
- [ ] Fill out Trainers' responsibilities checklist
- [ ] Order scorebooks/rule books
- [ ] Prepare scouting schedule

Before Your First Game

- [ ] Send in eligibility reports well in advance
- [ ] Player information sheets
- [ ] Recheck clock/controls/bulbs
- [ ] Timer/scorer/ticket takers/concession-stand workers
- [ ] Security arrangements
- [ ] Officials to discuss rules changes, referee scrimmages
- [ ] Plan filming of games
- [ ] Mimeograph forms that will be used

MANAGERS' GAME DUTIES CHECKLIST

Home Games

Before/During Game	After Game	
☐	☐	1. Clean coach's office, home and visitors' dressing rooms
☐	☐	2. Sweep gym floor
☐	☐	3. Prepare scoreboard clock
☐	☐	4. Give visitors' locker room key to/from visiting coach
☐	☐	5. Prepare shot charts/stat sheets/pencils/clipboards (give to coach after game, along with scorebook)
☐	☐	6. Take scorebook to scorer's table
☐	☐	7. Fill water-containers early and at halftime
☐	☐	8. Prepare towels, medicine kit for home bench
☐	☐	9. Transport basketballs (incl. game ball) to midcourt area
☐	☐	10. Collect warmups
☐	☐	11. Unlock home dressing room and referees' room before halftime
☐	☐	12. Take soft drinks to refs, scorers, visiting team, and home team at halftime
☐	☐	13. Carry halftime statistics to coach

Away Games*

Before/During Game	After Game	
☐	☐	1. Gather ball bag and five basketballs
☐	☐	2. Have shot charts/stat sheets/pencils/clipboards
☐	☐	3. Take scorebook
☐	☐	4. Prepare water containers, towels
☐	☐	5. Prepare medicine kit
☐	☐	6. Collect valuables for valuables bag (DON'T LET IT OUT OF YOUR SIGHT FOR A SECOND!)
☐	☐	7. Get locker room key from/to home team's coach
☐	☐	8. Collect warmups

*Check off items to be taken before leaving gym either way.

PLAYER EVALUATION FORM—PRESEASON TRYOUTS

Name _____ | Age | Birthday | Class

_____ ( ) | _____ ( ) | _____ ( ) | _____ ( ) | _____ ( )
Height | Weight | Stand. Reach | Wingspan | Vert. Jump

_____ ( ) | _____ ( ) | _____ ( ) | _____ ( ) | _____ ( )
Shuttle Run | Leg Press | Bench Press | 20-sec. FTs | Drib. Suicide

_____ ( ) | _____ ( ) | _____ ( ) | _____ ( ) | _____ ( )

_____ ( ) | _____ ( ) | _____ ( ) | _____ ( ) | _____ ( )

Strengths _____

_____

_____

_____

_____

_____

_____

Weaknesses _____

_____

_____

_____

_____

_____

Recommendation _____

_____

_____

_____

_____

_____

_____

_____

© 1992 by Parker Publishing Company

DAILY PRACTICE SCHEDULE

THOUGHT FOR TODAY:

DAILY
PRACTICE
PLAN
FOR: _____
(Date)

TIME	ACTIVITY	POINTS TO STRESS

WEEKLY PRACTICE SCHEDULE

Skill/Activity _____   Drills _____   Drills _____

_____   _____   _____
_____   _____   _____
_____   _____   _____
_____   _____   _____
_____   _____   _____
_____   _____   _____
_____   _____   _____
_____   _____   _____
_____   _____   _____
_____   _____   _____
_____   _____   _____
_____   _____   _____
_____   _____   _____
_____   _____   _____
_____   _____   _____
_____   _____   _____
_____   _____   _____
_____   _____   _____
_____   _____   _____
_____   _____   _____
_____   _____   _____
_____   _____   _____
_____   _____   _____
_____   _____   _____

PREGAME SCOUTING FORM

Teams (circle scouted team) _____   Location _____   Date _____

I. GYM CONDITIONS

    A. Lighting _____

_____

    B. Unusual court dimensions/features (e.g., short or long court, wide or narrow court, sideline/baseline space floor surface, baskets/backboards, special ground rules, etc.)

_____

_____

_____

_____

_____

II. INDIVIDUAL PLAYERS (e.g., shooting form, jumping ability, left-handedness, injuries, etc.)

    # _____ - _____

_____

_____

_____

_____

    # _____ - _____

_____

_____

_____

_____

    # _____ - _____

_____

_____

_____

_____

Pregame Scouting Form, continued

_____ - _____

_____

_____

_____

_____

_____ - _____

_____

_____

_____

_____

_____ - _____

_____

_____

_____

_____

_____ - _____

_____

_____

_____

_____

_____ - _____

_____

_____

_____

_____

_____ - _____

_____

_____

_____

_____ - _____

_____

SCOUTING CHECKLIST—INDIVIDUAL SKILLS

I. SHOOTING/SCORING

☐ Who are their best (and worst) perimeter and inside shooters? Who are their best scorers?

☐ Where do their best shooters like to shoot from? What is their effective shooting range?

☐ How do their scorers likes to set up their shots? (Off the dribble, or do they shoot coming off screens?) Do they use shot-fakes against tight one-on-one coverage?

☐ Who are their best (and worst) free-throw shooters?

☐ In last-second game situations, who do we want to keep the ball away from?

II. REBOUNDING

☐ Who are their best rebounders/offensive rebounders? How big are they? (Approximate height/weight)

☐ Do they block out aggressively, or do they rely on vertical jumping ability? How do they compare to our best rebounders?

☐ Can they be trapped after defensive rebounds? Where do they look for the outlet pass receiver in fast-breaking after rebounds? Which big men fill the lanes in fast-break situations?

III. BALLHANDLING

☐ Who are their best ballhandlers? To what extent does the team's success depend on their ballhandling ability? Do they become flustered if denied the ball constantly?

☐ How effective are they at high-speed dribbling, and dribbling and passing under pressure? Do they protect the ball well? (Can they be trapped or do they consistently find the open man?)

☐ How well do they penetrate? (Do they favor one side over the other or can they go either way?) Can we neutralize their driving ability without resorting to double-teaming?

☐ Who do we want to keep the ball away from when the game is on the line?

☐ Can we press them effectively?

IV. SPEED AND QUICKNESS

☐ Whom are their fastest players? How does their quickness compare to that of our players?

☐ Do they play effectively at full speed or do they tend to play out of control offensively or defensively?

☐ Can we neutralize their speed advantage, if any? How?

© 1992 by Parker Publishing Company

V. DEFENSE

☐ Who are their best inside defenders? How tall/mobile are they? (Approximate height/weight) Can we get them in foul trouble by isolating them one-on-one? Are they susceptible to shot-fakes to get them airborne to block shots? Do they work hard? Are they in good shape physically?

☐ Can we drive, penetrate, or force double-teams against their guards?

☐ Who are their weakest defenders? How can we take advantage of them?

VI. GENERAL

☐ Who are their key players? (Do they rely heavily on one or two players offensively?) How can we neutralize those players offensively and/or defensively?

☐ Who are their most effective subs off the bench? How, if at all, does the team's performance diminish when they're in? Why?

☐ Which players are most likely to get rattled in pressure situations?

☐ Of the players who receive the most playing time, which ones are the youngest or most inexperienced?

☐ Are any players sick, injured, suspended, or otherwise not in uniform? Will they be back in the lineup when we play them?

SCOUTING CHECKLIST—TEAM DEFENSE

I. PRESSING DEFENSES

☐ What kind of presses do they use? (Full-, three-quarter-, or halfcourt? Zone or man-to-man?) When do they use them? How effective are they?

☐ Do they trap or run-and-jump? (Where do they like to set up the traps and confrontations?)

☐ Do they guard the inbounds passer? (Do they double-team the best ballhandler?) Are they susceptible to court-length passes for layups?

☐ How can we beat their press—by dribbling or by passing through or around it?

☐ Do they recover quickly when their press is broken? (How susceptible are they to fast-breaking?)

II. ZONE DEFENSES

☐ What alignments do they use? How do they guard the point and high post? Who covers the passes to the wings?

☐ Do they trap? (If so, where?) Match up? Help-and-recover?

☐ With the ball at the wing, do they use three or four defenders on ball side? (If three, can we attack at high post or the corner? If four, are they vulnerable to rapid ball rotation and weak-side mismatches?)

☐ Are they basically aggressive, passive, or lazy in their coverage and movement? What are their most obvious weaknesses, and how can we take advantage of these?

☐ How effective is their inside coverage? Do they ever double-team at low post? Do they tend to overlook the middle during ball and player rotation from one side of the court to the other?

☐ Why are they using zone defense rather than man-to-man?

III. MAN-TO-MAN DEFENSES

☐ How much pressure do they apply to the ball? Do they try to influence the dribbler by overplaying toward the sideline or toward the dribbler's weak hand? Are they susceptible to backdoor cuts?

☐ Do they fight through screens, or switch? (If the latter, are the switches called or automatic?)

☐ How do they guard the posts—by fronting or by overplaying? How effectively do their big men deny the inside passes?

☐ Can we drive on them? How effective is their inside help?

☐ Does their coverage have any weaknesses that we can exploit? How?

IV. COMBINATION DEFENSES

☐ Do they use a standard combination defense (i.e., box-and-one, diamond-and-one, or triangle-and-two)? If so, which player of ours will they put the chaser on?

☐ Do they match up with their other players or simply shift with the movement of the ball along the perimeter?

☐ Where is their coverage weakest? At high post? In the corners? On weak side?

☐ Do they use man-to-man principles from a zone alignment or use zone principles in man-to-man coverage?

V. OTHER CONSIDERATIONS

☐ Do they zone inbounds passes on baseline bring-ins in their defensive half-court?

☐ How often (and when) do they change defenses? Are their changes called verbally? (If not, how do they signal their changes?)

SCOUTING CHECKLIST—TEAM OFFENSE

I. ZONE OFFENSES

☐ Are their zone offenses basically perimeter oriented, inside oriented, or do they attack both ways? (If we have to give up something, where are they least likely to hurt us?)

☐ How effective is their perimeter shooting/passing? Do they try to pass over the zone or around it? Can the ball be trapped in the corners?

☐ How effective is their inside game? Do they use one post player or a high–low arrangement? Will their post player require double-teaming?

☐ Do they attack the defense by dribble-penetrating from a balanced alignment and forcing double-teams to free teammates for shots? Or do they use cutter patterns or overloads to create numerical superiority or mismatches on weak side or ball side? (If they operate from overload alignments, do they overload with three or four players on ball side? And will overplaying the rotation passes to weak side upset the timing of their offense?)

☐ How can we reduce whatever advantages their zone offenses afford them? (How successful were their opponents in this regard, and why?)

II. SET PLAYS/CONTINUITY OFFENSES

☐ Are they patient in their shot selection, or do they take the first open shot they get?

☐ Will their play execution cause us trouble defensively? (Can we fight through their screens and overplay passing lanes to disrupt their offense? Or will we be better off using passive sinking and switching techniques to combat screens and protect the lane and post areas?)

☐ Do their automatics permit them to continue attacking the defense, or do automatics merely serve to reestablish the basic pattern?

☐ Do all of their players handle the ball in their plays or patterns, or do they rely on one or two players to run the offense? (Can we match up to reduce those players' offensive effectiveness?)

☐ What are the weakest aspects of their offense? How can we best exploit those areas?

III. UNSTRUCTURED MAN-TO-MAN OFFENSES

☐ How do they initiate their offense? (Do they begin their attack from the middle of the court? If not, which side do they seem to prefer, and why?) Will pressure defense force them farther outside than they prefer to begin their patterns? (Can we match up in such a manner as to create problems for them in the initial stages of their offense?) Do they use backdoor cuts effectively against pressure man-to-man?

☐ How do they key their movement (e.g. air pass, bounce pass, entry pass to high post)?

☐ Is their offense basically oriented toward guard, forward, or post? (What do they like to do in their half-court offense? Isolate their best scorer for one-on-one matchups inside or along the perimeter? Drive and shoot or pass to an open teammate? Use inside screens or movement away from the ball to free their big men inside for open shots or one-on-one matchups around the paint? Isolate two-on-two for pick-and-roll, give-and-go, etc.?) How can we play our man-to-man to disrupt their offense and take away their favorite moves and tactics?

☐ Are all five players actively involved in trying to score, or just two or three at a time, with the others setting screens to alter the matchups or simply clearing out and watching the action from weak side? How active are their weak-side players? (Can we take advantage of their inactivity to offer help on ball side?)

☐ Do their big men play better facing the basket or with their backs to it? Do they favor one side over the other in cutting to the ball or establishing position? Do they attack from high post?

IV. FAST BREAKING

☐ How committed to fast-breaking are they? Do they fast-break (1) after turnovers or transitions, (2) after missed shots, (3) after scores, (4) against pressure defense, (5) all of the above, or (6) none of the above? How many players will we need to get back on defense to stop their fast-break?

☐ If their initial offensive thrust is denied, do they tend to press their attack and go for the first open shot or to settle into their half-court offense?

☐ How many ballhandlers can lead the fast-break? How effective is their court vision and ballhandling at high speed? Do they prefer to force the ball upcourt on the dribble or to pass the ball ahead to a teammate?

☐ Do they consistently get as many as three players involved in the break? (If so, who?) Do they use a sideline fast break or bring the ball up the middle of the court? Can we deny the pass to their outlet pass receiver, or pressure the passer into turnovers? (Can we trap him effectively?) Are there other ways we can slow down or stop their fast-break?

V. SLOWDOWNS AND DELAY PATTERNS

☐ Do they generally use the middle of the court or the corners in their spread formation? (Can we trap them in the corners?)

☐ How many players do they feature in their delay patterns? Are all of them good ballhandlers? Are they basically dribble oriented or pass oriented in their delay game?

☐ Who are their best (and worst) free-throw shooters? (Can our matchups force the ball away from their best ballhandlers and/or free-throw shooters? Whom do we want to put on the line if we have to foul to catch up?)

© 1992 by Parker Publishing Company

VI. BEATING THE PRESSES

☐ Is their inbounds passer's arm good enough to make the full-court pass accurately and consistently?

☐ Can we dictate where they receive the inbounds pass? Which ballhandlers should we try to keep the ball away from or attack? Should we double-team their best dribbler on the inbounds pass?

☐ Do they prefer to beat the press by dribbling through or around it, or to move the ball downcourt by passing?

☐ Do they fast-break when they beat the press? (At what point should we call off the press and retreat to our half-court coverage?)

☐ How well do they react to unexpected pressure in the backcourt? Which players are most likely to respond poorly and commit turnovers?

VII. SPECIAL SITUATIONS

☐ On baseline bring-in plays at their offensive end, which do they try to set up—inside scoring opportunities or shots from the perimeter? Or both? (Or do they just try to inbound the ball safely?) Do they throw lob passes to the big man inside? Where do they set their screens?

☐ Where do they prefer to inbound the ball to on sideline bring-ins? Do they use any trick plays such as rear screens and alley-oop passes for slam dunks, or back door cuts by the inbounds passer?

☐ What plays do they run in last-second-shot situations? Who is their most likely preferred shooter (1) from the perimeter and (2) near the basket? How do they set up his shot?

VIII. OTHER CONSIDERATIONS

☐ How many players do they send to the offensive boards? How effective is their offensive rebounding? Are they susceptible to fast-breaking?

☐ What are the offensive signals they use during the game?

SCOUTING FORM

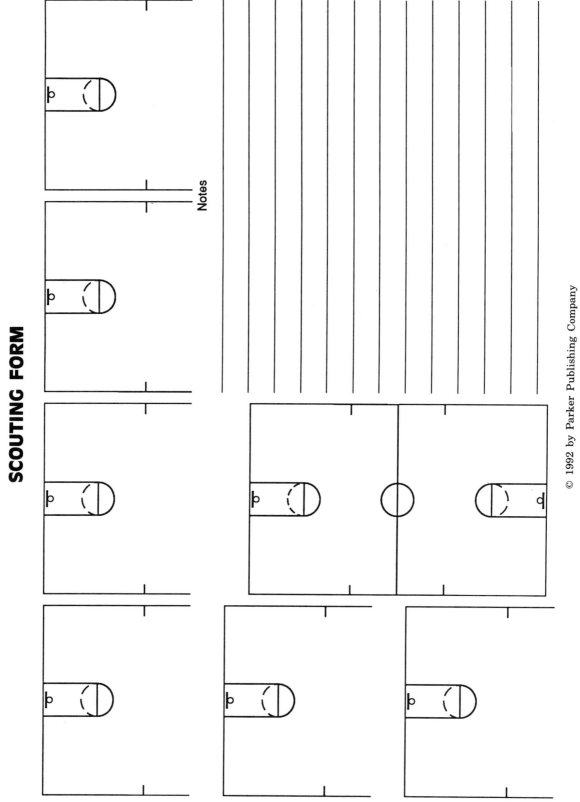

Notes

SCOUTING REPORT

_____ vs. _____ at _____
Scouted Team   Opponent

I. STARTERS _____   Date _____

II. SCORE BY QTRS.

Team	1st	2nd	3rd	4th	Final

III. OVERALL EVALUATION

_____

_____

_____

_____

_____

_____

_____

_____

_____

_____

_____

_____

_____

_____

_____

_____

_____

_____

Scouting Report, continued

IV. INDIVIDUAL PLAYERS

_____ - _____

_____

_____

_____

_____

_____ - _____

_____

_____

_____

_____

_____ - _____

_____

_____

_____

_____

_____ - _____

_____

_____

_____

_____

_____ - _____

_____

_____

_____

_____

V. BEATING THE PRESS

_____

_____

_____

_____

_____

_____

_____

_____

_____

_____

VI. PRESSING DEFENSES

_____

_____

_____

_____

_____

_____

_____

_____

_____

_____

_____

_____

_____

_____

_____

_____

_____

VII. SPECIAL SITUATIONS

_____

_____

_____

_____

_____

_____

_____

_____

_____

VIII. TEAM OFFENSE

_____

_____

_____

_____

_____

_____

_____

_____

_____

_____

_____

_____

_____

_____

_____

_____

_____

_____

IX. HALF-COURT DEFENSE

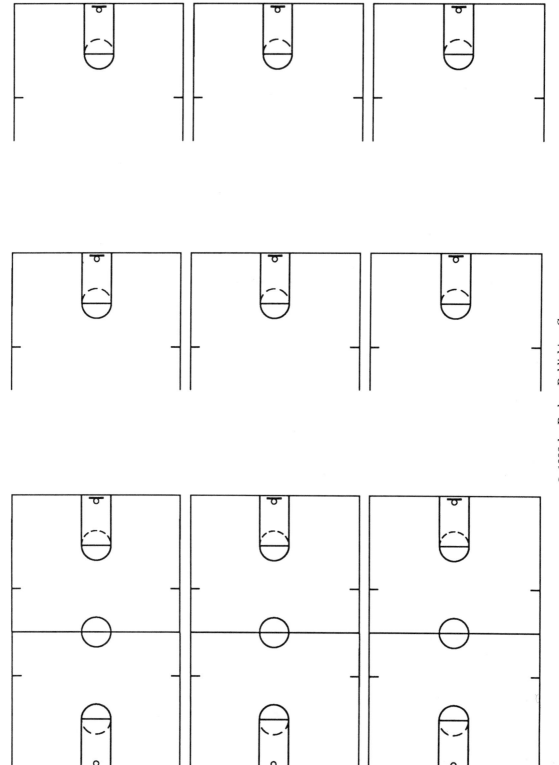

SCOUTING SCHEDULE

Date	Teams (circle team being scouted)	Location	Game Time	Scout
———	—————————————————	———	———	———
———	—————————————————	———	———	———
———	—————————————————	———	———	———
———	—————————————————	———	———	———
———	—————————————————	———	———	———
———	—————————————————	———	———	———
———	—————————————————	———	———	———
———	—————————————————	———	———	———
———	—————————————————	———	———	———
———	—————————————————	———	———	———
———	—————————————————	———	———	———
———	—————————————————	———	———	———
———	—————————————————	———	———	———
———	—————————————————	———	———	———
———	—————————————————	———	———	———
———	—————————————————	———	———	———
———	—————————————————	———	———	———
———	—————————————————	———	———	———
———	—————————————————	———	———	———
———	—————————————————	———	———	———
———	—————————————————	———	———	———
———	—————————————————	———	———	———
———	—————————————————	———	———	———
———	—————————————————	———	———	———

SHOT CHART

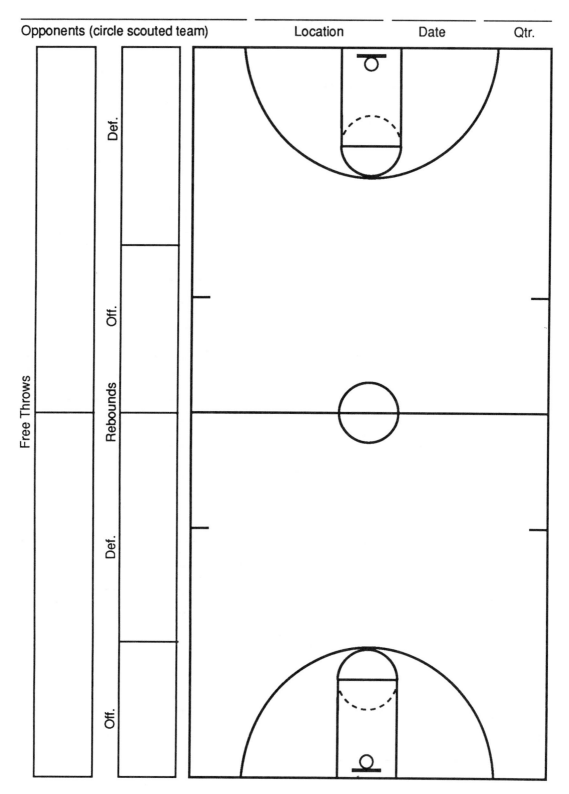

Opponents (circle scouted team)   Location   Date   Qtr.

Free Throws

Def.   Off.   Rebounds   Def.   Off.

© 1992 by Parker Publishing Company

GAME PLAN

Opponent _____   Location _____   Date _____

I. OVERALL APPROACH _____

_____

_____

_____

_____

_____

_____

_____

_____

_____

_____

II. INDIVIDUAL PLAYERS

_____(_____)_____

_____

_____

_____

_____(_____)_____

_____

_____

_____(_____)_____

_____

_____

_____

_____

Game Plan, continued

———(   )——————————————————

——————————————————————————

——————————————————————————

——————————————————————————

———(   )——————————————————

——————————————————————————

——————————————————————————

——————————————————————————

III. TEAM OFFENSE ————————————————————

——————————————————————————

——————————————————————————

——————————————————————————

——————————————————————————

——————————————————————————

——————————————————————————

——————————————————————————

——————————————————————————

——————————————————————————

——————————————————————————

——————————————————————————

——————————————————————————

——————————————————————————

——————————————————————————

——————————————————————————

——————————————————————————

——————————————————————————

——————————————————————————

——————————————————————————

IV. TEAM DEFENSE _____

Game Plan, continued

_____

_____

_____

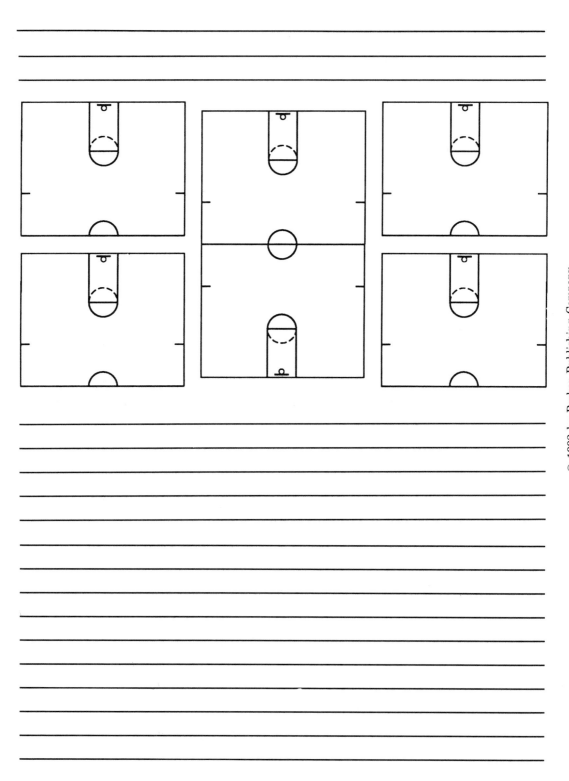

_____
_____
_____
_____
_____
_____
_____
_____
_____
_____
_____
_____
_____
_____
_____
_____

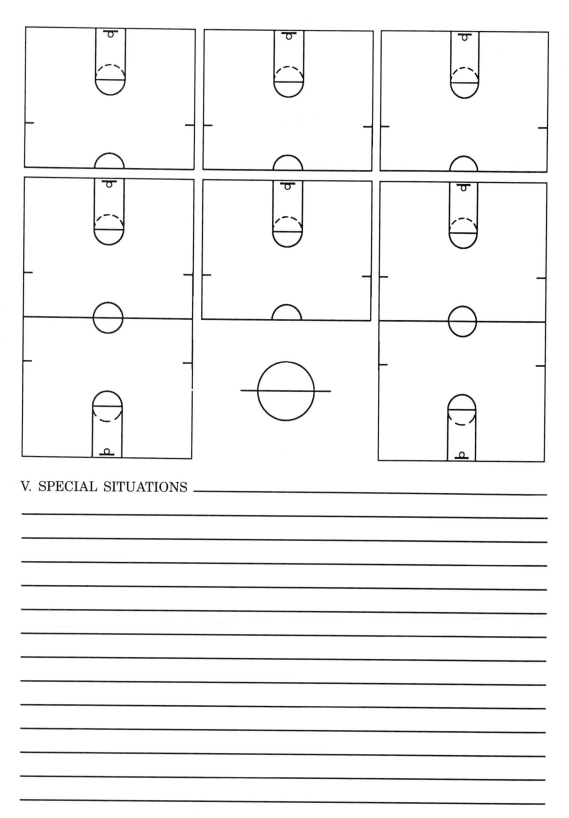

V. SPECIAL SITUATIONS _____

GAME PLAN EVALUATION

Opponent _____ Location _____ Date _____

1. What Worked Best for Us. _____

_____

_____

_____

_____

_____

2. What They Did That We Didn't Expect—and How We Reacted to It. _____

_____

_____

_____

_____

_____

_____

_____

3. What Didn't Work for Us and Why. _____

_____

_____

_____

_____

_____

_____

_____

_____

_____

_____

4. Possible Changes Next Time. _____

_____

_____

_____

_____

_____

_____

DEFENSIVE STAT SHEET

_____ vs. _____

_____ _____

Location   Date

Name	Offensive Rebounds	Defensive Rebounds	Charging Fouls	Forced Turnovers	Steals

GAME PATTERN CHART

Off. Pattern/ Def. Style	Possessions	Shots Taken	Shots Made	Pct.

Totals

LINEUP EFFICIENCY CHART

Lineup	Possessions	Shots Taken	Shots Made	Pct.

Totals

OFFENSIVE STAT SHEET

_____ vs. _____

_____   _____
Location   Date

Name	Assists	Offensive Violations	Turnovers/ Held Ball	Minutes Played	

STAT SUMMARY SHEET

Opponent ————

Date ————

Name	Fouls		Field Goals Made (3/2)	Field Goals Attempted (3/2)	Fg Pct. (3/2)	Free Throws Made	Free Throws Attempted	Fg Pct.	Total Points	Assists	Violations	Turnovers/ Held Balls	Min. Played	Off. Rebounds	Def. Rebounds	Total Rebounds	Charging Fouls	Forced Turnovers	Steals
Totals																			

INDEX